Reviews and Readers' Comments

An exciting rollercoaster ride through the world of theatre and publishing.
Philip Fisher, *British Theatre Guide*

What transforms In Search of Gielgud are Croall's startling illuminations of the great actor. The man, innocent and lyrical, lives in these pages.
Simon Callow, *The Guardian*

Deceptively short and light, the book is packed with insights not only into Gielgud himself, but also into the theatre of the twentieth century. Croall comes across as a man of humour and humanity, often self-deprecatingly honest about his own mistakes and shortcomings. Highly recommended.
Harriet Devine, *Shiny New Books*

A fascinating and chastening account of the dark art of biography. It is a testament to Croall's tenacity and hard work that the book ever got published.
Nick Smurthwaite *The Stage*

I enjoyed your latest Gielgud book very much, though necessarily very sad. So much lost.
David Hare, playwright

I loved the book, an absolute page-turner with all the anecdotes about theatre people. It was fascinating to follow the whole process, from research to writing to publication.
Megan Jones, theatre historian

I enjoy so much your method of work, and hearing all the lovely nuggets from people I used to know or have seen; so many now gone. **Julian Glover**, actor

I am so glad you kept the diary. What a brilliant idea. This will definitely be my Book of the Year.
Frances Hughes, theatre scholar

The Author

Jonathan Croall comes from an acting background: his father John Stuart was a star of the early British cinema, his mother was an actress, drama-school teacher and voice coach. He has been successively editor of *Arts Express* magazine, the National Theatre's magazine *StageWrite*, and the programmes at the Old Vic theatre.

He is the author of over twenty books, including the biographies *John Gielgud: Matinee Idol to Movie Star* and *Sybil Thorndike: A Star of Life*; the collection of interviews *Buzz Buzz! Playwrights, Actors and Directors at the National Theatre*; *The Coming of Godot: A Short History of a Masterpiece* (nominated for the 2005 Theatre Book Prize); and, in the series The National Theatre at Work, *Hamlet Observed*, *Inside the Molly House* and *Peter Hall's 'Bacchai'*.

His other books include the biography *Neill of Summerhill: The Permament Rebel*; the oral history *Don't You Know There's a War On? Voices from the Home Front*; and the children's novel *Sent Away*. His most recent books are *Forgotten Stars: My Father and the British Silent Film World* and *Closely Observed Theatre: From the National to the Old Vic*.

Further details can be found at www.jonathancroall.com

In Search of Gielgud

A Biographer's Tale

JONATHAN CROALL

Herbert Adler

Herbert Adler
PUBLISHING
3 Brynland Avenue, Bristol BS7 9DR
www.herbertadler.co.uk

First published in 2014 by Herbert Adler
Reissued November 2014

ISBN 978-1-84289-022-6

– Contents –

– Introduction –

When John Gielgud agreed to let me write his biography, I could hardly believe my good fortune. Here was a chance to explore the life and work of arguably the greatest classical actor of the twentieth century, a man who had made an indelible mark on the theatre of his time, and gone on to become, in the words of *Time* magazine, 'a major movie star'. It seemed like the dream project, but gradually it turned into a nightmare, becoming a desperate struggle to keep the book afloat in the face of a series of totally unexpected and potentially disastrous setbacks.

Not long after I started work I found myself under sustained attack from a rival biographer. Having delayed his own work for several years, Sheridan Morley did everything he could to prevent mine from seeing the light of day. Then, after I had spent nearly a year researching his life, Gielgud himself suddenly turned against the idea, declaring to my astonishment that he had been wrong to encourage me to write the biography. To make matters worse, I had to cope with an elusive and inefficient editor at Methuen, who failed to respond to my draft chapters for weeks on end, then suddenly vanished at a critical stage in the book's creation. At these moments of crisis I feared the whole project would collapse.

During the four years I spent researching and writing the book I kept a detailed diary. I used it to set down my doubts and fears about the quality of my writing, my ability to meet various deadlines, and not least my struggle to keep afloat financially. But I also described the emotional turmoil I experienced during what proved to be an extremely hazardous journey. Along the way I tried desperately to prevent Gielgud withdrawing his permission, while at the same time struggling to deal with my wayward editor.

Morley's increasingly desperate efforts to kill off my book inevitably loom large in the diary. They took up an inordinate amount of my time and energy that could have been better spent on research. But I persisted in the fight, not only because I felt I had justice on my side, but because I refused to be beaten by such an arrogant, self-important and spectacularly lazy hack writer. The Epilogue tells the story of the final stages of what came to be labelled by the press 'The Battle of the Biographers'.

Throughout this time I talked to many actors, directors, playwrights and friends who knew or worked with Gielgud. Inevitably, I was only able to include in the biography a fraction of the rich material that resulted from these interviews.

So alongside my diary, these pages record the vivid observations and memories of over a hundred friends and colleagues of Gielgud, as well of my impressions of them. They include stars such as John Mills, Alec Guinness, Sarah Miles, Richard Briers, Dirk Bogarde, Anna Carteret, Peter Ustinov, Rosemary Harris, Ian McKellen, Helen Mirren, Simon Russell Beale and Dorothy Tutin; playwrights such as Edward Albee, Christopher Fry, David Storey, Charles Wood and Hugh Whitemore; and directors such as John Schlesinger, Peter Brook and Bill Gaskill. I also had a valuable correspondence with Judi Dench and Paul Scofield.

I believe this material offers a valuable addition to theatre history, a wealth of previously unpublished opinions, stories and recollections. But I hope the diary has another use. My aim throughout has been to paint an honest picture of a writer's life, of the struggle I had to create a worthwhile book, of the trials and tribulations as well as the many joys and delights of authorship. All of these I experienced in abundance while trying to make sense of and do justice to the life of a complex personality and a great man of the theatre.

– PROLOGUE –

The Green Light

5 December 1996

Dear Sir John,

I am writing to ask whether you would allow me to write a new biography of you, one that would I hope provide a rich and comprehensive record of your life and work in the theatre.

Before I go any further perhaps I could introduce myself. I am an experienced biographer, social historian and editor, with a special interest in theatre and theatre history. For the last five years I have been editor of the National Theatre's magazine *StageWrite,* in which role I have interviewed and written about many leading actors and playwrights.

My life-long love of the theatre derives from my parents, who were both actors. My father John Stuart, whose name you perhaps know, was a star of the 1920s and 1930s, mainly in films (he was in two early Hitchcock productions) but also in the theatre. My mother, Barbara Francis, began as an actress with Barry Jackson's company, and later taught for many years at Central School. In such an environment it was perhaps inevitable that I became in my youth, and have remained ever since, an ardent theatregoer and film fan.

I'm sure you will wonder, as others might, why a new biography should be needed, when you yourself have written so extensively and entertainingly about your theatrical life in your autobiographical volumes, and so many others have put down their thoughts about you and your work in numerous essays, memoirs, reviews and autobiographies.

Can I suggest three reasons why a detailed, up-to-date biography would be of value? First, I am sure a great many people would welcome a work which told your story simultaneously through your eyes and those of your contemporaries, bringing together in one volume the wonderful range of perceptions, insights and memories of your life in the theatre provided both by yourself and your fellow-actors, playwrights, critics and friends.

Second, a quarter of a century has elapsed since Ronald Hayman's biography appeared, during which time you have of course played a huge range of roles on stage, film and television. I would of course want to document this period, and if possible interview many of those who have worked with you during this time, such as Peter Hall and Harold Pinter.

Third, I would want to weave into the narrative a good deal of British theatre history, since your career has at once greatly influenced it and been affected by it. For instance, in writing about JB Fagan's pioneering 1924 production of *The Cherry Orchard* in Oxford, which marked such a significant moment for you as a young actor, I would want to show why Chekhov was at that stage so unfamiliar a playwright in Britain, to actors and audiences alike. To do this, I would draw on contemporary accounts (Shaw, Granville Barker, etc), as indeed I would aim to do throughout the book.

I hope this brief outline will give you a fair notion of the kind of book aimed at the general reader that I have in mind. I think it would probably take two years to write and research in the necessary depth. When I recently floated the idea tentatively with a publisher, I got an extremely enthusiastic response.

I realise you may feel unable to help me actively, though of course if you were able to talk to me at some point that would be terrifically helpful. Either way, I do hope you will give your approval to a project that would be both an enormous pleasure and a great privilege for me to undertake.

If you would like further details of my background or my published books, or would like to meet to discuss this idea, I would be happy to oblige in any way that would be helpful.

Yours sincerely,

Jonathan Croall

PS I hope the enclosed two items, because of their Terry connection, might be of some interest to you. One is a copy of a letter from your great-uncle Fred Terry to my mother, when she was a stage struck girl of nineteen. The other is a copy of a still from the 1923 production of Maugham's *Our Betters*, in which my father was a very young member of the company, which of course included your great-aunt Marion Terry.

11 December 1996

Dear Mr Croall,

I am not very keen about your kind proposal. Sheridan Morley was given a contract to write a life by Hodder & Stoughton several years ago, and I believe he has been working on it ever since. I imagine he is waiting to finish it until I am dead, by which time of course I shall be unable to read it, for better or for worse!

I have been approached by various other people to contribute details and forewords to their books, and I must say I dread ransacking my memories beyond what has already been in print about my life and career.

In the time I have left I try to look forward rather than backward. The past begins to make me rather morbid, and I miss so many of my favourite friends and colleagues.

Sincerely yours,

John Gielgud
PS I well remember seeing your father in the Maugham play.

* * *

18 December 1996

Dear Sir John,

Thank you very much for your letter of 11 December, and for kindly explaining your feelings about my proposed biography. I quite understand and sympathise with your not wanting yet again to ransack the past for memories.

My own feeling is that your personal involvement would not actually be essential for such a book, since as you say so much is already in print. Most of the work would involve bringing together existing material, from your books and those of others, into a single narrative. Otherwise it would be a matter of interviewing some of the theatre and film people who have worked with you since the Hayman book was published, and going back to primary sources for the earlier years of your career, notably the 1920s and 1930s.

I wonder, therefore, if such a work could be researched and written without you yourself having to expend any time and energy whatsoever on it, whether you might then agree to my undertaking it? It's a book I would dearly love to work on, and I would be in a position to start straight away on what would probably be a two-year assignment, if you felt able to give it your blessing. Needless to say I would be more than happy to show you a draft at the appropriate moment – but only if that were your wish.

I note what you say about the Sheridan Morley book, but feel quite sure that – as has been the case with both Ralph Richardson and Laurence Olivier – there is room for more than one biography.

I do hope you might be sympathetic to this arrangement, and look forward to hearing from you in due course.

Yours sincerely,
Jonathan Croall

* * *

6 January 1997

Dear Mr Croall,

Many thanks for your previous letter. It's nice of you to write about another biography, and of course I cannot refuse my consent. Very probably I shall not be here if you take two years to put it together, and I wish you well with the project.

Sincerely,
John Gielgud

– ONE –

Early Skirmishes

Thursday 9 January 1997

I've read his postcard twenty times. To my astonishment Gielgud, in his minute, spidery, but still just legible handwriting, has given me the green light.

I've been musing on possible explanations for this wondrous decision. A true generosity of spirit? A desire not to be pestered further? A conviction he won't be around to read the result? Pleasure at the idea of there being two new biographies instead of one? I don't suppose I'll ever know which was the key one.

Midnight. I'm sitting with a large whisky, as the enormity of the task begins to sink in. Just two years in which to excavate Gielgud's rich and astonishing career, to investigate, question, sift, probe, ponder, weigh up, then write it all down. Am I up to it? Do I *want* to be up to it? Of course I do. Meanwhile I've resolved to keep a diary for the next two years.

Saturday 11 January

After waking up to reality I wrote again to Gielgud, asking for a formal note confirming he's happy for me to quote from his books, letters, etc, as 'publishers like having these things spelt out'. I feared this might scare him off, but back comes a postcard today, giving me what I ask for. Surprisingly, he has not responded to my suggestion that I show him the text when I have a draft. So now we're off.

Thursday 16 January

First task completed, to read Ronald Hayman's 1971 biography properly. I find it deeply unsatisfactory, an uninspired, and uninspiring, re-hash of Gielgud's career. He has an irritating near-obsession with costume and scenery, and clearly suffers from having Gielgud metaphorically looking over his shoulder. There's little sign of any interview-based research, so there's virtually no other voices. It's simplistic, dry and humourless, and dreadfully lacking in any analysis or interpretation, or objectivity (summed up in the use of 'John' throughout). Clearly I need to avoid these traps. But first I need the contract, which means a detailed outline, which means a reading blitz.

Monday 20 January
I've now read Gielgud's two autobiographical volumes, *Early Stages*, written in his mid-30s, and *An Actor and His Time*, produced forty years later. Both are delightful. I'm impressed by his astonishing memory, his eye for detail, his humour, his love of stories. They are rich sources, which I can't wait to plunder.

Thursday 23 January
A bombshell. Yesterday in a second-hand bookshop I found a biography of 'Binkie' Beaumont, Gielgud's friend and a celebrated West End manager. In it there's a detailed account of Gielgud being arrested in 1953 for 'importuning', and the ensuing scandal. Clearly this was a key episode of his life, but a desperately humiliating one. So how can I possibly cover it while he's alive? My gut feeling is that I shouldn't do so, never mind The Search for the Truth. I note that Hayman made no reference to it. But how will a publisher in these warts-and-all days feel about omitting such an event? This could be very tricky indeed.

Tuesday 28 January
I've found two further books on Gielgud, both heavily illustrated. Robert Tanitch's survey of his career is an extensive collection of photographs, with plot summaries and review quotes, which will obviously be an invaluable sourcebook. It has a quirky, irreverent tone that I like.

The other is a celebratory book by Gyles Brandreth, published for Gielgud's eightieth birthday. Confusingly, he refers to him sometimes as John, at others as Gielgud, as if unsure of the nature of the book. In fact it's a very clear account of his career, though based entirely, as far as I can see, on existing sources.

There's only one reference to the arrest, and even then it's an oblique one: 'This was a difficult time for Gielgud personally.' This discretion is to be expected, since Gielgud actively helped both him and Hayman. My position is different, and paradoxically freer. But how should I handle that whole episode? Happily it's not an immediate problem

Thursday 30 January
The outline is done. It's hard to encapsulate the essence of someone you hardly know, and give an authentic shape to his life and career. At this stage it's very much a conventional chronological approach, covering the major productions, with a sketch of his character, based on my reading so far, which is minimal. I hope to God it does the trick for a contract: it would be unbearable to have to drop the book having got so enthused about the project.

Friday 7 February

A setback. My agent, Derek Johns at AP Watt, rings to say that Constable have made an offer, but only a paltry advance of £5000. This he rightly rejected without even consulting me. The offer apparently might be better if I could get official access to Gielgud's papers – which I've already explained I won't be asking for – and could find out where the official biography has got to. Derek agrees we have to try other publishers. Meanwhile I must try to find out what progress Sheridan Morley has made.

Tuesday 11 February

I'm working my way through some key source books. Olivier's *Confessions of an Actor* must be one of the most unpleasant, self-centred and unconsciously revealing theatrical memoirs ever written. He comes over as mean-minded, crude, boorish, and a male chauvinist of the worst order. His style is dreadful, embarrassingly self-referential, and full of the 'Well, squire' brand of louche remarks.

I can't help comparing his book with Gielgud's graceful, witty, generous-spirited autobiography. Both of them write about Gielgud's production of *Romeo and Juliet* (1935), in which they alternated Romeo and Mercutio. Gielgud weighs up the strengths and weaknesses of them both; Olivier just talks about his own performances. I can see their rivalry and difficult relationship is going to be a key theme.

Thursday 13 February

I'm depressed by the loss of my original publisher, but determined not to give up. I spoke last night to Tony Lacey, a friend at Penguin and Alec Guinness' editor. He's interested, says he's 'in the mood to buy big books'. Derek suggests putting it out to auction with half a dozen publishers, including Penguin.

Tuesday 18 February

I have finished Geoffrey Wansell's excellent biography of Terence Rattigan, a key figure in Gielgud's life. It's an impressive defence of his virtues as a writer, and a shrewd account of his flaws as a man: his vanity, insecurity, his readiness to compromise his writing in order to make money. I like the way Wansell makes spare and judicious use of psychological interpretation. He handles the homosexuality issue head on, but sensitively, showing how Rattigan's need to conceal it shaped his life, mostly negatively.

Being given access to all the Rattigan papers was a great boon, but also I feel a drawback. Wansell overdoses on information about the subject's daily movements, to the detriment of analysis, context and interpretation. The early chapters are the best – they so often are in biographies – as Rattigan struggles to make his mark, and come to terms with his philandering father's errant ways. I'm fascinated to read that the central incident in the second half of *Separate Tables* was prompted in part by Gielgud's court appearance. And I enjoy the laughable absurdity of the Lord Chamberlain's requests for cutting totally innocuous lines.

Thursday 1 May
Endless negotiations over the last few weeks, but at last I have a publisher. The choice could hardly be better: Methuen are very strong on theatre and drama. My editor, Michael Earley, seems a civilised character with a wide knowledge of theatre, so I'm lucky there too. He tells me he signed me up because he liked my biography of AS Neill, so he is also clearly a man of judgement.

The advance, £28,000, is very reasonable, but the way it's staggered will make life hard over the next two years. I get £10,000 on signature, £5000 on delivery of the first 25,000 words, £5000 on delivery of the complete text, £5000 on publication, and the final £3000 only when the paperback appears. Annoyingly, this means I'm going to have to keep other work going meanwhile. I want anyway to carry on as editor of the National Theatre's magazine *Stage Write*, since it might provide me with a useful short cut to an actor or director. I had hoped not to take on any journalism during these two years, but I can see I'll have to do so.

Friday 2 May
New Labour, new book. After yesterday's general election putting Tony Blair in power, it feels like a new beginning, a good moment to start my research. I'm exhilarated at the thought of being able to devote two years to investigating a subject in depth, reading widely about the theatre, coaxing material out of actors and directors, delving into libraries and archives. A dream project – except I'll then have to write the book, and that's always the hardest part.

Monday 5 May
I have compiled a hit-list of key people to approach for an interview. Oldies first, in case the curtain's about to ring down on them. Targets include the designer Margaret Harris of Motley (93), Christopher Fry (89), Jean Anderson (89), Frith Banbury (85), Phyllis Calvert (82), Wendy Hiller (85), Rachel Kempson (87), Jocelyn Herbert (80) and Alec Guinness (83). I'm already worried some of them might leave the stage before I can get to them.

Tuesday 6 May
For the benefit of those people I approach I've composed a one-page summary, plus a short biographical note on myself, stressing the parental acting background, and underlining Gielgud's blessing for the project. I hope this will show that I'm not merely out to collect Gielgud bricks and gaffes (though I'm sure plenty of these will be offered), but am putting together a full-blown life, and painting in the backcloth of his theatrical times – which, my God, is virtually the whole of the twentieth century.

Friday 9 May
I've just read Simon Callow's biography of that troubled genius Charles Laughton. Callow's style is like no other biographer's: conversational yet learned, and wonderfully exuberant. He's slightly protective of Laughton, but very good on his tortured sexuality. I agree with Gielgud's quote on the blurb, that his book is 'extraordinarily well written, perceptive and rivetingly sympathetic'. I'll be pleased if I can inject some of Callow's dash and vigour into mine.

Wednesday 14 May
Lunch with agent Derek in an upmarket cafe in Camberwell. I express my nervousness at not yet having received a contract. Methuen is part of Reed, which has just been taken over by Random House, and I wonder if this swallowing of one giant by another could cause a last-minute hitch? Derek reassures me that a verbal agreement between agent and publisher is binding, since otherwise neither side could operate properly. I'm amazed to hear of this vestige of gentlemanly conduct in publishing. Derek also generously offers to advance me a couple of thousand to tide me over. Slightly embarrassed, I decline at first, but then accept. It feels like a vote of confidence.

Thursday 22 May
No luck with my oldest potential source, the writer Naomi Mitchison. A friend of Gielgud's brother Lewis at Oxford and afterwards, she'll be a hundred later this year. But her grand-daughter Amanda says her papers are in a state of chaos in Scotland, and her memory not good enough for her to be able to help. I suppose I'll meet this quite often. At least there's material to be found in her books.

Another person I want to contact is Gemma Fagan, the daughter of the director JB Fagan, with whom Gielgud worked at the Oxford Playhouse in the mid-1920s. I knew the family in my youth, and have been trying to track her down through her son Stephen, a playwright. But no one, including the Writers' Guild, has any record of him. Gemma could be a valuable first-hand early source, so I'll keep on her trail.

Friday 23 May

I've finished *Upper Circle*, the memoirs of Kitty Black, who worked for the theatrical management HM Tennent and Binkie Beaumont, and was briefly Gielgud's secretary. Chatty, lively and humorous, if somewhat gushing, her book is full of solid information about Gielgud's productions, while the complete chronology of Tennent productions is a real bonus. She's also good on detail about the theatre in wartime. When I meet her next week I suspect the problem will be to get beyond her adoration for Gielgud.

Saturday 24 May

A major embarrassment. I wrote to the composer Michael Tippett about Gielgud's production of his opera *A Midsummer Night's Dream* - which of course was written by Benjamin Britten, Tippett's being *A Midsummer Marriage*. Puzzled how I could have been so stupid, then realise I had unthinkingly repeated an error in a published Gielgud chronology. I should have stopped to think. In the circumstances the note from Tippett's assistant is the epitome of courtesy.

Tuesday 27 May

My first interview. It's with the surviving member of Motley, the three women designers whom Gielgud discovered in the early 1930s. On the way to her house I pass the old Barnes theatre (now a recording studio) where Gielgud first made his name in Chekhov.

Aged 93, Margaret Harris – for some reason everyone calls her Percy – is a delight. In exchange for the friesias I have brought her she offers me vodka ('I'm not quite virtuous yet', she explains). Dressed in snappy jeans, she's full of laughter, strong of voice, warm of heart, and palpably modest. We sit in her studio/sitting room, where she still works. She's doing another book, on designing Shakespeare's plays, and still teaches three days a week on the Motley design course in Covent Garden. A truly remarkable woman.

She talks with undimmed enthusiasm – about being discovered by Gielgud, about working with him in the 1930s on *Romeo and Juliet*, *Richard of Bordeaux* and *Three Sisters*. I get a strong sense of the theatrical family he surrounded himself with at that time, with its base in the Motley studio: George Devine (who married her Motley sister Sophie), Peggy Ashcroft, Harry Andrews, Gwen Ffrancon-Davies and all. She remembers Gielgud's father coming to the studio and playing

Chopin very elegantly.

She's acute about the Gielgud/Ashcroft working rapport, and a passionate defender of Gielgud in relation to Olivier. 'Larry wouldn't have had anyone in the company he thought would steal his thunder, and he never offered John any stage work,' she says vehemently (not sure if the latter is true). I reflect that, as Austen has Janeites, so Gielgud may have Johnites. Margaret H is definitely one of them, though she sees his faults too. 'Once he said to us, "I thought I'd ask Roger Furse to do the sets, because after all you're only women." We were quite angry about that.'

She recalls his kindness to the third Motley member, Elizabeth Montgomery. When she was ill and hard up, Gielgud bought her painting of Edith Evans as Millament, paying a lot more money than was necessary, then giving it to the Theatre Museum. She also remembers her own eightieth birthday party, given at the Royal Court. 'John made one of his slightly tactless speeches, nearly all about Elizabeth. But it didn't matter, everyone was so pleased to see him.'

A delightful hour of recollection, yielding much hard information. If all interviews are this rich, I shall need three volumes.

Thursday 29 May

A brief phone call from Nora Swinburne, who admits to 95. She has one blitz memory from the war-time run of *Dear Brutus*, and a recollection of Gielgud's kindness when her husband Esmond Knight lost an eye during a sea battle. But otherwise, despite my probing, I get only routine remarks about 'Dear kind John that everybody loves.' Suspect I may get rather a lot of this, especially on the phone; face to face it's easier to press people to go beyond the banalities.

Monday 2 June

A good session in his exquisite village home in Sussex with Christopher Fry, the man dubbed England's most promising playwright during the postwar period. I have to confess (though not to him) that I thought he was dead. On the contrary. Slight, modest and kindly, sporting a natty woollen tie, he's impressively fit in his ninetieth year. His memory is good too – what is it with these octogenarians? Only occasionally is a name forgotten, a lapse which causes him to smile broadly, and which soon becomes a recurrent joke between us.

He tells me how Gielgud's early performances were a catalyst for his own writing. We talk of the famous production of *The Lady's Not for Burning* (1949), and the contrast between Gielgud's interpretation and that of Alec Clunes, who originally commissioned the play. He recalls Richard Burton's wretched initial audition, and his near hijacking of his scenes with Gielgud, which he puts down to Burton's 'extraordinary stillness'.

We discuss the phenomenon of verse drama, why it rose and fell. He says he's puzzled that no one thinks it's odd to have both prose and poetry in literature, but when it comes to theatre it's somehow different.

At lunchtime we wander across the village green to the pub, where 'Mr Fry' is treated with great deference. Is this because of his age, his fame, or his unassuming personality? I suspect all three. During lunch he tells me an anecdote about Edith Evans and his play *The Dark is Light Enough*. Asked if she would be happy for Wilfrid Lawson to be given a role in the production, she replied: 'I can't remember whether I like him or not, but I do know he named his bicycle after me.' His loud, Lady Bracknellesque delivery of this eccentric remark echoes round the room, and temporarily silences all conversation.

Afterwards he searches for some Gielgud letters in his well-ordered study. I'm tingling with anticipation at the prospect of my first Primary Document. Alas, the bunch of letters in tiny handwriting signed John prove on closer inspection to be from another John. He sees my disappointment, and promises to get the Gielgud ones back from the Theatre Museum, where they're being copied.

I remark on the ancient Corona typewriter that sits on his desk. He tells me he still uses it to write poems for his friends, most recently an obituary poem for Laurie Lee. I ask if anything is being done to mark his ninetieth birthday in December, and he says four of his plays are being performed in this part of the country. So much for the forgotten master of verse drama.

At the end he takes me round his beautiful garden, which includes a revolving gazebo that allegedly once belonged to the writer Jerome K. Jerome. He gives me a quick turn in this obviously prized possession.

Four hours have passed in a flash: it can't go on being this delightful, can it?

Wednesday 4 June

To Kitty Black's house in Kensington, for what proves to be my first difficult interview. Austere and aloof in her elegant sitting-room, his former secretary sits me down opposite her and, before agreeing to be interviewed, grills me for half an hour about the book: why am I doing it, who have I seen, and so on. As it goes on I feel like Jack Worthing in *The Importance of Being Earnest*, being questioned by Lady Bracknell about his suitability as a husband. Getting her drift, I emphasise my desire to write a theatrical biography, rather than one that explores Gielgud's private life in minute detail.

Finally she asks me to pour the tea, so it seems I've passed the test. She then gives me some good inside stuff on the Tennent years, on her employer Binkie Beaumont, whom she calls a genius, and on the much-hated director Basil Dean ('a fiend in human form'). When I ask about Gielgud's close friend John Perry, who also worked for the Tennnet management, she rather melodramatically asks me to switch off my tape recorder, and then reveals the nature of his relationship with Gielgud, which I had already guessed at. Useful though to have it confirmed from a reliable source.

Unfortunately this triggers a diatribe against gay people. I try the 'Some of my best friends are gay' line, but she ignores it. She then moves on to the topic of illegitimate children. Rather than stand up for bastards – I'm one myself – I manage to shift the conversation back to Gielgud. Once it's there, she talks animatedly of Hamlets old and new. Evidently a fervent Johnite, she compares the royal qualities of his performances to those of later actors, whom she says 'come over like barrow boys'. This turns out to be a reference to Richard Burton and Peter O'Toole.

By the end the atmosphere has thawed, and I'm allowed to inspect her extensive collection of theatre posters on the stairs and landing. But it's still a relief to step out into the warm London air.

Thursday 5 June

Red face time again. Having written to the conductor Rafael Kubelik, who worked with Gielgud on the Berlioz opera *The Trojans* at Covent Garden in 1957, I get a brief note today from his widow, explaining that he died last year. Must remember that *Who's Who* is not always bang up to date.

Friday 6 June

Several hours today in the windowless, dingy study room in the heart of the Theatre Museum in Covent Garden. There are only two red Gielgud box files, fewer than I expected. I sit down at random at one of the dozen seats, and looking up find myself face to face with a striking oil painting of my subject. He clearly intends to keep a close watch on my labours.

The boxes have a lot of cuttings, programmes, a cluster of photographs. Most intriguing, though not very useful for the book, is a collection of cards sent to Gielgud on his eightieth birthday. They range from doggerel rhymes from complete strangers, to Evelyn Laye drinking a long-distance glass of champagne in his honour. There's one from a John Harcourt Williams, with an address on it. Maybe he's the son of Harcourt Williams, Gielgud's mentor at the Old Vic – a possible lead? Another is inscribed 'To Kate Terry's grandson from Kate Bateman's grand-daughter' (I think this is Fay Compton).

There's a fulsome one from an adoring fan: 'Twenty years ago your voice first entered my soul. If the bomb drops tomorrow and there is no God, the time has not been in vain, because you have moved and spoken.' Also one from the tailor Hayward's in Mount Street 'to our favourite customer', and another from the photographer Angus McBean, featuring a crazy picture of himself in pyjamas. Saddest is one from actor George Howe, a stalwart member of many a Gielgud company: 'Wish I'd been asked to your party, but I'm almost forgotten by everyone.'

Thursday 12 June

A jolly morning with the theatrical partnership of Michael Denison and Dulcie Gray. Amazingly, they live in the very house in Buckinghamshire where I was born, a huge mansion turned into an emergency maternity hospital during the war. So Michael D insists on giving me the full guided tour of their part of this grand building, with its gorgeous high Adam ceilings and spacious windows, offering captivating views of the surrounding countryside.

I'm a little intimidated by the grandeur of the surroundings, but soon warm to the two of them. He is exactly like his public persona: urbane, witty, very much the ex-Harrovian. He enjoys telling stories in exhaustive detail, the resonant voice echoing through the room. He reads out with relish a letter Gielgud wrote to him in the 1930s, politely advising him not to become an actor.

Dulcie G is more down to earth, incisive, and very mischievous. She confesses in passing that she was among those doing the rounds of the pubs with Cyril Cusack just before his notorious sacking from a West End production of *The Doctor's Dilemma* (Gielgud later stepped into the breach for a week).

They're both perceptive on Gielgud's skills as an actor, and his limitations as a director. Good too on his character, while admitting they are not amongst his intimates. Apparently he comes here twice a year to lunch: Michael D recalls him standing dreamily in the drawing room looking out across the rolling landscape. Odd to think he should be doing so in the very place where I first mewled, and no doubt puked, in a nurse's arms.

After an unexpected but welcome offer of lunch, and with too much claret inside me, I drive on to Chipping Norton, to see the director Peter Cotes. The elder brother of the Boulting Brothers, he used to run little experimental London theatres such as The Boltons and the New Lindsay in the postwar years.

It's a sobering and sad encounter: he's seriously ill in bed, his hands paralysed, his mind befuddled by morphine. I wonder aloud that he didn't put me off, but he seems determined to help, and digs with extreme difficulty into his memory. He has total recall of casts of long-forgotten productions, but under the influence of the morphine tends to get bogged down in recalling them, and needs constant coaxing back to Gielgud. This makes me feel hard-hearted, but I persevere.

His early recollections of Gielgud are those of a boy actor seventy years ago ('I was an Italia Conti chick'), so they need treating with caution. He was a good friend of Gielgud's brother Val from his radio days, and is helpful on the contrast between the two of them. He says there's a view that Gielgud's bricks are his homosexuality coming out, having to be nice to everybody, and then the guard slipping. Food for thought.

He makes no secret of his dislike of Binkie Beaumont. 'He'd put the dagger in anyone who crossed him, he was a real tyrant.' On Gielgud's court appearance, he says Binkie was horrid: 'Instead of showing solidarity, he said, "Why didn't he come to me? I could have pulled strings and got him off." Not a single moment of regret, and all the people around him took their tone from him.' He says that Val never forgave HM Tennent, that he felt they had ruined his brother as a person, that he was in their grasp and didn't want to be. 'He didn't realise they were as dependent on him as he was on them.'

He gets muddled on certain matters, including a gay play written by Hallam Tennyson, which he says Gielgud badly wanted to do. Realise I shall need to send him a transcript of our talk when (or rather if) he gets better. At the end he says sadly: 'I expect you'll be my last contact with the theatre.' But he says he's glad I've come, which is a relief, as I was beginning to feel pretty bad about doing so.

Monday 16 June
Better late than never, my contract finally arrives. I'm horrified to find that I'm being asked to pay all the photo permission fees. Derek says this is normal these days, and suggests I sign now and try and negotiate sharing the costs when the time comes. 'Pass as much as we can on to the poor bloody author' seems to be the attitude. It could cost me anything up to £3000.

Wednesday 18 June
I'm deep in Alec Guinness' hugely enjoyable memoirs *Blessings in Disguise*, as idiosyncratic as their author. There are delightful descriptions of the sufferings he endured as a young actor at Gielgud's hands, but also generous acknowledgment of the debt he owed him for giving him his first break. The book includes sharp, invaluable portraits of key people in Gielgud's life, such as Edith Evans, Ralph Richardson, Martita Hunt, Tyrone Guthrie, and the director Komisarjevsky,

about whom I know little.

I know Guinness is a very private, not to say secretive man, but I shall pull out all the stops to get an interview with him.

Friday 20 June

I've been frustrated over the last few days in my efforts to contact Georg Solti, who's in London briefly to conduct at Covent Garden (and did so when Gielgud directed Britten's *A Midsummer Night's Dream* there in 1961). His secretary held out some hope of a few minutes with him this week, but it proved impossible. Probably not a significant loss, but I need some first-hand memories of Gielgud's opera productions.

Monday 23 June

A brief and slightly tetchy phone conversation with Wendy Hiller. Originally she wrote suggesting I come and see her, but forgot to give a phone number, and she's ex directory. I finally got it through her agent, who checked, and reported back to say she'd rather talk on the phone. All very frustrating.

Her memory seems rather hazy. She can't remember *From Chekhov with Love* (1968), a television programme she did with Gielgud. When I mention his beautiful voice she says rather sharply: 'Everyone has a voice!' But she does have a clear picture of his work as a director, creating mayhem among the cast of a forgotten wartime play by constantly changing his mind. And she's good on his generosity as an actor. But I know I'd have got more if I'd been able to see her.

Thursday 26 June

'You're lucky to catch me, I nearly died a few weeks ago,' says actor turned director Frith Banbury quite casually. We're sitting in his plush penthouse flat overlooking Regent's Park. Apparently he recently collapsed while directing a play at Chichester. Happily for both of us, but especially him, he's fully recovered, his mind razor-sharp, his recall of names and incidents almost total.

Initially he complains mildly – and I'm sure he won't be the last – at having to go over ground he's already covered with Sheridan Morley. (In the same way that Scrooge was plagued by Marley's Ghost, I am clearly to be haunted by Morley's Ghost.) He tells me the critic Hilary Spurling was very keen to do a Life of Gielgud, but that 'Sheri' got in first.

Now aged 85, he saw John Barrymore play Hamlet when he was twelve. 'I thought he was a wonderful actor, but now on recordings he sounds ludicrous.' He talks amusingly about the trials of being under Gielgud's mercurial direction in the 1934

Hamlet (he played a courier): he was so unhappy he opted out of the subsequent tour.

Of Gielgud's performances, he rates his Joseph Surface in *The School for Scandal* one of the best. He was less impressed by his Lear: 'The best Lears haven't been the sexy, beautiful romantic leading actors, but people like Randle Ayrton and Eric Porter.' He thinks Gielgud was never at home in straight parts in contemporary plays. He recalls his mischievousness, and his irritation with a young actress in *Crime and Punishment* (1946). 'I came on from the other side, just to annoy her.' Of Gielgud's gossipy side he says: 'When he's doing his social chitter-chatter you wonder how he could be the wonderful artist that he is.'

I have some difficulty in persuading him of the value of his memories of other characters in the Gielgud story, such as Beaumont, Richardson, Edith Evans. Binkie he describes as an unacknowledged genius, then proceeds to tell me about his thoroughly dirty dealings. He recalls saying to Tennent's casting director Daphne Rye, 'I can't stand being lied to', to which she replied, 'Then don't work for HM Tennent Ltd.'

We talk about directing actors. He's worked with Edith Evans ('the greatest talent I've ever seen'), Ralph Richardson ('the penalty was he always made his own tune'), Sybil Thorndike, but unfortunately not Gielgud. He thinks male actors are more difficult to handle than women. 'They seem to feel being directed is a reflection on their manhood.' I don't think Gielgud ever suffered on that score.

Friday 27 June

A phone chat with Helen Cherry. She's very amusing about the 1955 *King Lear*, known as the 'Noguchi Lear' because of the weird costumes created by its Japanese designer. Says she turned down the part of Goneril, but George Devine persuaded her to change her mind, saying there would be 'plenty of jewels and a lot of sitting around on sofas' (in *King Lear*?). Instead, she says, 'we had to walk around in tents in all that Japanese stuff.'

She recalls how Gielgud and her husband Trevor Howard got on famously during the filming of *The Charge of the Light Brigade* (1968). Also the jolly time they had in Ireland making the television adaptation of Molly Keane's novel *Time After Time*. Says they were all dining one night with the Bishop of Kerry, and Gielgud went to the loo at the same time as the bishop. On their return he said: 'I always wanted to see a bishopric,' to which the B of K replied. 'Here we call it a diocese.' It's in character, but surely apochryphal?

June Progress Report

So far, so positive. Everyone seems very willing and pleased to cooperate.

Christopher Fry and Margaret Harris provided unexpected riches, as did Frith Banbury, eventually.

Two rejections to my letters, both for valid reasons. Wendy Toye was only twelve when she played one of the fairies in *A Midsummer Night's Dream* at the Old Vic in 1929, so reckons she'd be unable to provide reliable memories of Gielgud's Oberon. George Rylands, who coincidentally directed him in the 1944 *Dream*, would love to be able to help but, according to the bursar at King's College, Cambridge, he's not well enough to talk. A great pity: I would like to have got his thoughts on the production, but also on directing Gielgud's last Hamlet in the same season at the Haymarket.

Wednesday 2 July
A phone call from Joan Hickson's son Nicholas Butler. He says her memory is now very hazy, and all she can recall from filming with Gielgud in the re-make of *The Wicked Lady* is his frustration at the inordinate amount of time director Michael Winner spent lighting Faye Dunaway from the right angle.

Nicholas B is writing a biography of the famous actor-manager John Martin Harvey. Ah, the transience of fame: no publisher is interested, so he's publishing it himself. I promise to copy for him Gielgud's remarks about Harvey. It feels good to be able for once to do a favour for someone else, when so many people are doing them for me.

Friday 4 July
Nothing beats a contemporary document. Gyles Isham was at the Old Vic with Gielgud in the late 1920s. A chance sighting of the name Isham in *Who's Who* has led me via two branches of the family to the Northamptonshire Record Office. Today copies of two Gielgud letters arrive, written to Gyles' sister Virginia when he was eighteen and nineteen. Riches indeed: they're wonderfully fresh and skittish.

A postcard from Alec Guinness, who says he will be 'happy to help (briefly)'. This is terrific news. He can't make a date yet because of a forthcoming eye operation, but says he will be in touch shortly. This would be invaluable, since face to face he might expand not only on Gielgud but also Komisarjevsky, Saint-Denis, Guthrie, Martita Hunt and others I have little detail on so far.

It's been an encouraging day.

Monday 7 July
Preparing to meet Guinness, I've moved on to his wonderfully titled diary *My Name Escapes Me*. Less revealing than his memoirs, it makes for touching reading,

with his laconic, sometimes waspish view of the daily life of a 'retiring actor'.

There's little on Gielgud, apart from a reference to him looking like a cucumber in the TV *Gulliver's Travels*. This I must see. But he has useful fragments on bit players in the Gielgud story: Robert Flemyng, Peter Glenville, Stephen Haggard. I'm intrigued to read that when Guinness is reading a novel he acts the dialogue out loud, significant pauses and all. I wonder how many other actors do the same?

Wednesday 9 July

An interview with Gielgud's 1934 Fortinbras, aka Geoffrey Toone. Sitting in his small but perfectly formed garden in west London, I enjoy an hour of lager and chat in the sunshine.

He knew Gielgud socially in the early 1930s, and was part of the crowd that went down to his Essex farmhouse at weekends. A noble, still handsome man at 87 (he was once understudied by Errol Flynn), he says Gielgud didn't want to direct the 1934 *Hamlet*, but couldn't think of anybody else to do it! Can this be right?

As Tybalt in the 1935 Gielgud/Olivier *Romeo and Juliet*, he has some tales to tell. On the verse-speaking comparison, he remembers how after one exit some of the actors had to stay hidden on the set until the interval. 'When John was Romeo you kept absolutely quiet and listened; when it was Larry's turn we used to play cards.'

Interesting how some memories are more visual than others: he recalls every costume detail on Gielgud's production of *Lady Windermere's Fan* (1945). I marvel at the lavish spending on Cecil Beaton's sets and costumes in a time of such austerity, but he reminds me that 'no one had seen anything beautiful for a long time.'

I ask about Gielgud's flaws: 'His sex life was a bit bizarre, but he was not alone in that.' He says his best friends bullied him and sent him up, but that he rather enjoyed that kind of treatment.

As I leave, the actor Frank Middlemass turns up. He's just been filming *A Dance to the Music of Time*. He says Gielgud had a fall and hurt his head, and was looking frail. 'And the silly bugger still refuses to use the autocue.' Good for him.

Thursday 10 July

There's a message on my answer machine from Alec Guinness, suggesting a lunch date. I'm thrilled – until I hear a further message saying he's now got to see his eye specialist on that day, so will have to postpone our meeting. Damn.

Friday 11 July

A letter from the Canadian actor Hume Cronyn, directed in America by Gielgud in *Big Fish, Little Fish* (1963). Says he kept a diary of rehearsals, but has just moved house, and doesn't know where to find it. He kindly encloses a copy of his autobiography, which I see has a few extracts from the diary in it.

Another letter, this from John Allen, once principal of Central School. He was in the Old Vic company in 1932 when Gielgud directed *The Merchant of Venice*, his first stab at directing. He remembers his Antony from 1929, and the erotic charge of Dorothy Green as his Cleopatra: 'What's stuck in my mind is that physical plainness does not deter an actress from convincing an audience of her beauty and sexual attractiveness'. He remembers a student at Central who never came to fight classes, but on stage succeeded because he could 'act fighting'. Gielgud also skipped those classes at RADA, but with him it showed.

Monday 14 July

To Sussex to see Marius Goring, Gielgud's Ariel in *The Tempest* (1940). I sit with him and his wife Prudence in the garden of their lovely old house. Charming setting, delicious lunch, but all else is sadness. Despite her gallant efforts to prompt his recollections, at 85 Marius G's mind is beginning to wander, and it's impossible to make sense of anything he says. There are moments of lucidity: 'Who? Gielgud? He was a bloody good actor, the best!' Otherwise his memories of the Old Vic days, of Lilian Baylis, Harcourt Williams and Gielgud himself, get hopelessly tangled up.

When we move on to the 1939 *Hamlet* at Elsinore, he asks me if I was there. If only! I mention *The Tempest*, which prompts him, in his dapper blue linen suit and white moccasin shoes, to execute a nimble little dance on the gravel. 'I was Ariel, and I danced like this in all the performances,' he says gaily. It's a very poignant moment. His wife astonishes me with her determination to cajole memories out of him, and to laugh simultaneously at the absurdity of the results.

She says there may be some letters, but shows me the chaos of his study to illustrate the problem of finding them. She then takes me into a darkened room, where a huge pile of folders and documents fills a large table. They're the papers of Michel Saint-Denis, that guru of 1930s theatre, unsorted and uncatalogued. So near and yet so far....I half-wonder whether to offer to sort the material for her. But even if she agreed, would it be worth it?

As I leave she tells me her husband had been fine until recently: when Simon Callow came to talk about Laughton for his biography he got a lot of material from him. Oh well.

Thursday 17 July
I've just read Irving Wardle's *The Theatres of George Devine*. It's sympathetic but critical, and a real goldmine for me. I can see that Devine was a crucial member of the Gielgud circle in the 1930s, as much for his Motley connection (he managed the firm for a while) as for his acting, which was never brilliant. Contains some terrific material on Saint-Denis, and the inside story, or one of them, on the notorious 'Noguchi *Lear*', when Gielgud, as someone put it, had so many holes in his costume he looked like a gruyère cheese.

Wednesday 23 July
A helpful letter from Corin Redgrave, who says his mother Rachel Kempson would be pleased to see me. He warns me that her short-term memory is poor, but long-term very good. He advises me to see Charles Wood, who he says created a brilliant portrait of Gielgud in *Veterans*. Says his niece Natasha Richardson may have correspondence between Gielgud and her father Tony, who directed him in *The Loved One* (1965) and *The Charge of the Light Brigade* (1968). He also says that he himself (and possibly Vanessa) would be glad to talk about working with Gielgud. All these pretty Redgraves at one fell swoop!

Thursday 24 July
I'm reading Rachel Kempson's memoirs *A Family and Its Fortunes* in tandem with Michael Redgrave's autobiography *In My Mind's Eye*. Hers is a beguiling mixture of vividly remembered detail from her childhood, and a rare honesty about her supposed failings: her lack of confidence, her feeling of always being an outsider in any group. In contrast, his book is all opinions and events, carefully hiding the man himself. But it has good material on his work in the 1930s with Gielgud, who clearly had a powerful effect on his acting.

Monday 28 July
A useful talk with Rachel Kempson in her attractive Chelsea flat. Still immensely handsome at 87, elegantly and simply dressed, she acted with Gielgud in *The School for Scandal* (1937) and *The Return of the Prodigal* (1948), and admits to being a fervent admirer. 'I was always falling in love with somebody, and it was usually one's director. I was almost in love with John at one point, which was pretty silly. But his voice had a hypnotic effect on me.'

She talks about his influence on Redgrave, and also of their failure to hit it off. 'I don't think jealousy came into it. But later in his life Michael said to John how sorry he was, that he admired him so much, and that it was a lack on his part that they weren't friends.'

I ask about Guthrie, and she remembers Stratford in 1933, and her first stage appearances as Juliet, Ophelia and Hero. 'The Old Bensonians were horrible to all the new ones, they couldn't bear us, they said we couldn't act. Tony used to say after rehearsals, "You're having a rotten time, so let's do something jolly", and we'd do improvisations and very inventive things. He was fun, and utterly original.'

Anecdotes too about the dreaded Basil Dean (Redgrave once sacked him from his own production of *The Aspern Papers*) and her friend Peggy Ashcroft ('When we toured *Hedda Gabler* I remember the King of Norway told her he thought Ibsen a bit of a nutcase'). We get on to Glen Byam Shaw, and here there's a surprise. 'A lovely man, the exact opposite of Basil Dean. I suppose I can say it now, but we were madly in love with each other for many years, and it was wonderful.' How well-deserved, I reflect, in the light of her difficult marriage to the bi-sexual Redgrave.

She recalls her disappointment at having to turn down Ophelia in Olivier's Old Vic *Hamlet* because she was pregnant with Vanessa. 'Still, it was quite a special baby,' she says with a merry laugh. You can say that again.

Tuesday 29 July
Today I interview my third Ariel in a row: after Marius Goring and Rachel Kempson (she played the part at Stratford) I talk to Leslie French, class of 1930 at the Old Vic.

We chat for an hour in the sitting-room of his south London house. I can see why he cornered the market in Pucks and Ariels in the 1930s, notably in the Open Air Theatre in Regent's Park. At 93 he's irrepressibly impish, full of chuckles, and sharp in his recall of the Old Vic period, especially his rapport with Gielgud in their Prospero/Ariel and Oberon/Puck partnerships.

Inevitably there are Lilian Baylis anecdotes. I like especially the one about Queen Mary visiting the Vic, and asking her about a photograph of a woman hanging in a prominent position. 'That dear, I mean Your Majesty, is my aunt Emma Cons,' she supposedly replied. 'We do have one of your dear husband, but Emma has done more for the Vic than he ever has.'

He has clear memories of Harcourt Williams, who directed so many of Gielgud's youthful performances; of the stunningly eccentric Martita Hunt; and of the megolomaniac Donald Wolfit: 'A dreadful actor, a joke,' he says.

I ask if it was true that he himself was the inspiration for Eric Gill's statue of Ariel, set above the entrance of the BBC's Broadcasting House. 'Turn round,' he says. I do so, and find myself looking at a fine sketch of a naked Ariel, the original given to him by Gill. 'He came to the Vic and then asked me to pose. It was winter, so it was a bit cold.' Not obviously so.

Wednesday 30 July
Charlton Heston is in Britain for a short tour. He was Mark Antony in Gielgud's second filmed *Julius Caesar* (1970) and directed him in *A Man for All Seasons* (1988) for American television. I've been scattering letters to various theatres he's visiting, in the hope of an interview. Today his assistant rings: Sorry, Mr Heston just has no time, but refers you to his book. Never mind: it was a crazy long shot. I check in his book, but find only bland worship: 'I'm proud to have acted with him, even prouder to have directed him. Like all the great actors I've seen, he is infinitely directable.' Thank you, Moses, for handing down those tablets of wisdom.

July Progress Report
I feel I'm at last on the case. The Redgrave/Kempson axis is bearing fruit; Leslie French is an unexpected and wonderful find; Geoffrey Toone an excellent source; Isham letters little gems.

Disappointments: Guinness' eye op, Marius Goring's loss of memory. All part of the chase, I suppose.

Wednesday 13 August
To the Mander and Mitchenson Theatre Collection, which is housed in a dilapidated country house in the middle of a golf course in Beckenham. So different from the Theatre Museum: no red tape, atmosphere friendly and informal. They've even got a microwave oven.

It's a magnificent collection, covering every branch of theatre. Richard Mangan, the very friendly and helpful administrator, shows me the Gielgud material: three boxes containing a dozen press cuttings books, three more full of programmes, cuttings, letters etc. Then there's his collection of programmes from his youth, donated by his mother. A treasure trove, no less.

Before I begin Richard removes a file from one of the boxes, 'as Sir John has requested'. I assume it's correspondence to do with his arrest. But why is it here if it's such sensitive material?

Thursday 14 August
I drop in briefly on journalist Joy Melville in her charming little house in Battersea.

She's just put together an hour-long radio documentary on Lilian Baylis, and kindly lends me a tape of Gielgud talking about her. Among her other biographies she's written about Ellen Terry and Edith Craig, I ask her what her next one will be. 'All the big ones have been done,' she sighs. I'm reminded how lucky I am to have landed one of the very biggest.

On to an excellent session in Wandsworth with Sam Beazley, a survivor of both the 1934 *Hamlet* and the 1935 *Romeo and Juliet*, who boasts a white beard of Tolstoyan proportions (he grew it recently for the Almeida *Ivanov*).

We have a long and fruitful lunch in his tiny garden. A shrewd and intelligent man beneath an amiable exterior, he recalls the hierarchical nature of theatre in the 1930s: 'In those days it was Miss Evans or Mr Gielgud, it was rather like royalty. You didn't casually chat to the stars, you waited for them to chat with you. You had to dress very carefully, with flannel trousers, pressed if possible, and a hat. No one came with an open neck to rehearsals.'

He recalls watching from the wings as Gielgud mesmerised the audience with the great Hamlet soliloquies ('He didn't vary his performance, but it was never stale'). But he suffered, like Guinness and Banbury, under his scattergun, sometimes cruel direction. He prefers not to talk in detail. 'I don't want to upset John,' he says, rather sweetly.

I bring out the *Hamlet* programme as a memory jogger, and he recalls the cast down to the last waiting woman. Says the soldiers were played by real guardsmen, who were given tea during matinees in Gertrude's dressing-room. (I wonder what the fledgeling Equity thought of that?) Among the walk-ons is one Jean Winstanley, 'as beautiful as her daughter Anna Ford,' he says. Another potential source?

Thursday 21 August

I've been reading a fine biography of Gielgud's arch-enemy, Donald Wolfit, who left Ronald Harwood £50 in his will to write his official Life. Considering Harwood was both a friend and Wolfit's dresser for some years, it's an impeccably balanced piece of work: a surprisingly touching portrait, but also very well informed, detailed, amusing and intelligent. It tells a good story of the Unfashionable Actor battling for recognition. I'll be delighted if I can match his standard.

I envy Harwood the fact that he has an angle: the need to rescue Wolfit's forgotten acting abilities. These tend to have been lost beneath the huge, overwhelming, monster personality, an image reinforced by Harwood's own powerful play *The Dresser*. But Harwood brings out those abilities triumphantly. He certainly alters my perception of Wolfit's place in the theatrical pantheon, which has been much influenced by the dismissive remarks of other actors.

Thursday 28 August

A useful phone conversation with a chirpy Juliet Mills, whose first professional part at the age of sixteen was under Gielgud's direction, in *Five Finger Exercise* (1958), Peter Shaffer's first play. She remembers how sweet he was to her but, more importantly, his method of directing her. She came straight from drama school into the part, and played it for two years, including a stint on Broadway. Gielgud told her: 'Think of it as your national service in the theatre.' She recalls his child-like excitement when they took the production to America, and his delight in showing her, Michael Bryant and Brian Bedford the famous New York landmarks.

August Progress Report

A thin month, the Beazley interview apart, though I've done some solid reading. Cheered to hear from an apparently reliable source that Sheridan Morley is saying he has only got as far as the 1930s. Hope this refers to the research, not the writing: if the latter, were Gielgud to die tomorrow, he's bound to be first past the post.

Monday 1 September

To Kensington, and a session in her small elegant flat with small elegant Muriel Pavlow. Like everyone else, she's still stunned by the news of Princess Diana's death yesterday. She's been round the corner to Kensington Palace and put a rose outside the gates. 'I just felt I had to,' she says. Apparently many others are making the same kind of gesture.

As a child actress before the war she made her name in Dodie Smith's *Dear Octopus* (1938). She recalls how Gielgud turned on real tears at precisely the same moment in every performance. She has memories of Marie Tempest nailing another actress' chair to the floor to stop her upstaging her; and of Martita Hunt, who in one scene had to eat bread: 'This wouldn't do for Martita: wherever we were on tour, she had little sponge cakes sent up from Fortnum & Mason.'

As the young girl in *Dear Brutus* (1941) she had a 20-minute duologue with Gielgud, who also directed. 'It was very exciting, he just sat at his easel while I flitted around the stage. But I don't remember any guidance on my character: he was more interested in the technical side.' She recalls his kindness in helping her break out of child parts: 'I thought I'd be playing them until I was 40,' she says. Nowadays, still looking youthful at 76, she has problems getting grandmother parts.

I remember her as a 1950s screen actress, being winsome with Dirk Bogarde in *Doctor in the House* and similar films. So I'm surprised when she shows me a

Stratford programme for 1954, with pictures of her as Titania, Cressida, and two Biancas. This leads her to offer me valuable thoughts on Stratford directors who worked with Gielgud: Devine, Byam Shaw, Quayle.

Afterwards I walk round to Kensington Palace, where hundreds of people are streaming across the grass to the railings. It's eerily quiet, no one seems sure what to say. Flowers for Diana lie there in abundance, together with hundreds of messages, many of them pathetic. One of the more restrained is from 'All the staff at Boots in Kensington High Street'. Several people are in tears. I feel like a voyeur, and move away.

Tuesday 2 September
At the Theatre Museum I hear from someone in the study room that Sheridan Morley's researcher was here last week. Nice to be able to afford such a luxury, but I'm not sure I would hire one, even if I had the money. Half the fun of working on a theatrical biography is the digging around in old newspapers, stumbling across an unexpected letter, finding a long-forgotten review.

The museum's filing system is from the dark ages. To find details of a book you have to search through trays of grubby, well-thumbed index cards in truly gloomy light. I wouldn't have much eyesight left if I spent very long in here. On reflection, a researcher might have their uses.

Wednesday 3 September
To Holland Park, and designer Jocelyn Herbert's house. Slim, casually dressed, still bearing those striking cheekbones, she's just back from a three-month documentary tour of Europe with poet Tony Harrison. They're doing a modern version of the Promethean myth as a film for Channel 4. Not bad going at eighty.

At sixteen she saw Gielgud in *Richard of Bordeaux* (1933): 'It's stayed in my mind as one of the most beautiful productions in the theatre.' She has vivid recollections of rehearsals for David Storey's *Home*, one of Gielgud's later triumphs, for which she designed the sets and costumes. Problem: Could the two theatrical knights be persuaded out of their usual smart clothes? She remembers how Lindsay Anderson skilfully brought down the over-the-top playing of Gielgud and Richardson. 'He was brilliant at communicating the meaning of the play to actors; he was unique in that way.'

I'd hoped to get some specific thoughts about George Devine, with whom she lived for many years, and who played in some of Gielgud's finest productions in the 1930s. But somehow we end up talking about others she knew well: Anderson, Beckett, Peggy Ashcroft, Peter Hall. She remembers Edith Evans being disconcerted on first looking at her bare set for *Richard III*, nothing but a wooden floor and a huge tower, and complaining: 'There's nowhere to sit down.'

Saint-Denis clearly influenced her greatly: she was a student at his London Theatre Studio ('the best drama school in the world') and thought his lectures on text and style invaluable. They made her realise, she says, that the text is the lifeblood of the theatre, that you're there to serve it, not use it to do your own thing. Unlike some of the newer breed of directors, is the implication.

We get on to Greek drama, her favourite form of theatre. She recalls a battle with Peter Hall over *The Oresteia*, especially over masks ('He didn't know how to use them') and the use of a choreographer ('He gave the chorus what he thought were female movements, but they just looked like tarts'). Apparently she sent Hall a stiff memo on the subject – which he framed.

She thought Garry O'Connor's recent life of Peggy Ashcroft scandalous, and wrote an angry letter of protest to *The Times*. Clearly I should read it as soon as possible. I mention my admiration for Irving Wardle's biography of Devine. She agrees it paints a fair portrait, but remembers having to persuade him to balance up the gloomy sections about the Court era with some of the good times. 'Journalists do love the darker side,' she says. It's true. I'm about to feel persecuted, but then she generously offers to look out photographs and any relevant Devine letters on her next visit to her country farmhouse.

Friday 5 September

To Notting Hill, to see actor Alan MacNaughtan. Here I get the first inside dope on Gielgud's 1940 *King Lear*, which Granville Barker came over from Paris to direct. MacNaughtan saw Barker as 'a real martinet of the old school', and recounts in exuberant detail the story of The Young Man Who Dared to Say No to Granville Barker – himself.

He remembers Gielgud's effect on other actors, notably Cathleen Nesbitt: 'She would start off a scene playing all the Goneril stuff, then just stand there and look in wonder at Gielgud, then suddenly realise it was her cue.' Gielgud's comment was: 'Dear Cathleen, such a nice girl, but not quite with us.'

He tells a wonderful story of Gielgud being stopped in full vibrato by a RADA student walk-on (Laurence Payne), and how he got his revenge. Also of the night when, playing Lear, he declared: 'Nothing, I have sworn, I am firm', and on the last word an eyebrow fell into his hand, and he was convulsed. 'He was a great giggler, which was one of the nice things.'

He remembers Gielgud and Ralph Richardson going for a canteen lunch at the National during *No Man's Land*: Richardson went to the front of the queue,

Gielgud to the back. I'm obviously in for a wealth of such stories. Apparently trivial, yet they often, as here, illuminate character.

On the tube it seems every third person is clutching flowers on their way to Kensington Palace. Quite amazing.

Monday 8 September
One mystery solved. In my pursuit of a well-known, somewhat androgynous actor of the 1930s and 1940s, I've been passed from agent to agent. They've all seemed evasive, and now I know why: the man in question has had a sex-change. At this point I tactfully withdraw.

Tuesday 9 September
Another day at Mander and Mitchenson. The collection includes Gielgud's youthful play reviews, scribbled on his programmes. To my dismay I find they're not in one place, but scattered among scores of boxes devoted to individual theatres. Fortunately many are printed in *Notes from the Gods*, a book of them which Richard Mangan has compiled. Reason says they should be enough, but my horror of missing something precious wins out, and I decide to copy them all. It probably means two days' extra work, but I can't bear to leave any stone unturned.

Wednesday 10 September
A pleasant, rambling but very worthwhile hour in his Thames-side house with Stuart Burge, who directed Gielgud in his second film version of *Julius Caesar* (1970). I have yet to see it, but know it was panned by the critics.

He gives an amusing account of casting battles with the American production company, which wanted a star in almost every role, including Napoleon Solo (Robert Vaughn) as Casca. They even insisted Raquel Welch read for Calpurnia: 'She was all right, but totally unsuitable,' he remembers with a smile. 'I had to explain there was no evidence that Caesar had a child wife.' And what did Gielgud think of this crazy notion? 'I didn't even dare tell him about it!'

He says actors of status are reluctant to play the relatively small role of Caesar, so it's usually played rather crudely. But Gielgud, he recalls, turned in a fine performance. 'His whole being was one of civilised authority.' I get an inside take on how American stars such as Charlton Heston, Jason Robards and Richard Chamberlain all idolised him.

Stuart B taught at the London Theatre Studio ('the only innovative drama school we've ever had'), and provides a useful thumbnail sketch of Saint-Denis, whom he remembers as a good interpreter of Stanislavsky's ideas. 'Women felt persecuted by him, but on the whole he was much admired,' he recalls.

Before the war he was an actor, and appeared in Olivier's 1937 *Hamlet* as the Player Queen. 'He was very athletic, but not a good Hamlet,' he says. Gielgud apart, he most admired Guinness' Hamlet, 'brilliantly conceived by Guthrie'.

Wednesday 17 September
An interesting letter from film historian Kevin Brownlow, with two promising leads. He offers to send me the transcript of an interview he did with Gielgud about the silent-film era. Also to put me in touch with his sister-in-law, who's writing a biography of the writer Molly Keane, a good friend of Gielgud. She's also his god-daughter, so she could be a fruitful contact.

Thursday 18 September
A couple of hours in her Kensington studio home with Tanya Moiseiwitsch, Tony Guthrie's chief designer both in England and at Stratford, Ontario. She's 83 but thoroughly on the ball, despite her suggestion that 'there's a little box at the back of my head with a leaky fuse that drops out'. Charming, modest and self-deprecating, she admits to being besotted when young with Gielgud the matinee idol.

On Guthrie, she says: 'His admiration for John G was enormous, but he never seemed to be happy directing him. Perhaps the method of working didn't suit: they were both notorious for changing their minds.' I discover her step-father was the playwright John Drinkwater, whose work is now pretty much forgotten. In 1924 Gielgud was in his play *Robert E Lee*. I scent new material, but my excitement is brief; she says there are no papers, and no mention of Gielgud in Drinkwater's third, unpublished volume of autobiography. Bother.

Friday 19 September
Another day among the faded cuttings and ancient reviews at Mander and Mitchenson. Over lunch with Richard Mangan I get the lowdown on Peter Brook's famous/infamous *Oedipus* at the National, on which he was assistant stage manager. He remembers the violent conflict between Olivier and Brook over the giant golden phallus that appeared at the end: 'A screaming row you could hear all round the building. "Sir" in full throat was not to be missed.'

He recalls Gielgud's attitude to Brook's experimental production. 'John was not at all grand, but very deferential, and wanting Peter to like it. He was finding it difficult doing new things, but there was no animosity, he was always very committed. I stole a look at his script once: it was extraordinary how much detail he had gone into to shape his part.'

One of Richard's jobs was to guide the blinded Oedipus on to the stage. Gielgud wore black eye patches; later he inscribed for him a copy of his memoirs, 'The Eyes Have It'. Richard offers an alternative version of a famous Gielgud witticism during rehearsal, which he claims was made by another actor. I clearly need a third opinion.

Gielgud was friends with Raymond Mander and Joe Mitchenson (both now dead), who dedicated their book *The Theatres of London* to him. The connection apparently continues: he's always happy to identify photographs of Edwardian actors that everyone else has long forgotten. 'He's wonderfully generous with his time, and scrupulous about replying,' Richard says. 'Little notes come straight back with the information.'

Monday 22 September
A phone call from Derek Granger, former theatre critic, television producer (notably of *Brideshead Revisited*), and friend of Gielgud. Says he'd be glad to meet and talk, but not quite yet. He's doing a new biography of Olivier, the first since his death. I wonder aloud about Donald Spoto's book, which he dismisses roundly, not least for its muck-raking speculations about an affair between Danny Kaye and Olivier. 'No evidence, no evidence!' he cries in horror. He drops a few tantalising anecdotes about Olivier and Gielgud. I feel he could be a very good source. He suggests we exchange lists of contacts. Why not?

Wednesday 24 September
Lunch with my friend Tony Lacey from Penguin, who tells me Alec Guinness' eye operation has been a success. He promises to put a word in when Guinness has recovered. Apparently he's now doing another book, a journal of 1997, so a meeting looks possible again.

Friday 26 September
Another Mander and Mitchenson day, searching for material from Gielgud's own productions. Some exciting discoveries, including many letters he sent to his mother while touring or abroad. Mostly accounts of rehearsals, which are invaluable, but also evidence of their warm relationship: she's forever sending him little presents, of pots of honey, handkerchiefs, flowers. I also find letters to her from other actresses in his companies, and effusive ones about 'Jack's wonderful performance etc' from family friends. Without official access to his papers, such finds are like gold dust.

Monday 29 September
A difficult, tragi-comic half hour with Ninette de Valois, still going strong in her Barnes riverside flat at 99, although she now has to be helped to walk by a carer. Her short-term memory is poor, so at first she's forgotten why I've come. She's partially deaf, so I have to bellow somewhat. But she seems mentally very tough. Over a cup of tea she remembers a little about Gielgud: 'He was one of Miss Baylis' boys. I used to give them deportment lessons, or something dotty. It was the fashion to have a choreographer help the producer, and we did all the entrances and exits with the actors. Some of them resented this, they didn't think it was our business.' Lilian Baylis she recalls as 'a very shrewd old lady, but bats'.

After ten minutes I realise I'll get little more than this. Rather than rush rudely away I put a simplistic question or two to her about ballet, about which I know little. I ask if she worked with Robert Helpmann, to which she replies sternly: 'Worked with him? I made him! He was just a unknown dancer from Australia when he came to me.' Whoops. I make a mental note to do more thorough homework on my interviewees.

We get on to her childhood in Ireland, and also her memories of her Vic-Wells ballet company being cut off in occupied France during the war. Her hearing seems to improve when we focus on her own life. Seeing my empty teacup she suggests I find 'something more exciting to drink'. She points to a screen, behind which I discover several bottles, and pour myself a whiskey. Her poor short-term memory leads her to repeat the offer twice more. It seems impolite to refuse. Three whiskies later I stagger out, musing sadly on the fact that someone who once danced with Diaghilev's company is now only just able to walk.

September Progress Report
A really excellent month. Six very substantial interviews, and a lot of solid material from Mander and Mitchenson and the Theatre Museum. I feel greatly encouraged.

Reading: Only time for one book, an illuminating biography by James Harding of Gerald du Maurier, whose suave skills Gielgud admired so much in his youth. A model of its kind: witty, informative, astute, carefully researched and stylishly written, and critical of its subject.

Disappointments: Angela Lansbury can find nothing in the family scrapbooks relating to her mother Moyna MacGill, a star of the 1920s, who acted with Gielgud in Eugene O'Neill's *The Great God Brown* (1927). A pity: but I find actors' sons and daughters are often a good source, and always worth a shot.

Thursday 2 October

To Winchester, to hear authorised biographer John Miller talk about Ralph Richardson, Gielgud's greatest professional friend. His book is packed with interesting material, with a characteristically generous foreword by Gielgud. This is full of his special brand of self-deprecation, including an interesting comment about his friendship with Richardson: 'There are many things about me that he must have found deeply unsympathetic.' I take this to be a coded reference to his homosexuality, perhaps the nearest he got in print to 'coming out'. Afterwards I meet John, who also helped put together Gielgud's memoirs *An Actor and His Time*, and is clearly someone I should talk to. He helpfully promises some contact addresses.

Saturday 4 October

A message on my machine from Irene Worth, a close friend of Gielgud, and a frequent co-star, most famously in the Peter Brook *Oedipus* (1968). She's returning to America tomorrow, sorry to have missed me, back in six months. Should I ring back for a phone interview, or wait and catch her in person later? Though she's 81 she sounds in rude health, and very friendly, so I opt for delayed gratification.

Monday 6 October

I drive down to Hove to see Edward Thompson, who published several of Gielgud's books while he was an editor at Heinemann. We talk in his vast sitting room, stuffed to the ceiling with books and dotted with portraits of the famous, including one of Gielgud prominently displayed on the mantelpiece.

Now eighty, he can just remember Gielgud's first 1930 Hamlet. As a publisher he found him the perfect author: 'When you're talking to him, however poor or remote you may be, he listens as if he really wants to know. I was a youngster, but he treated me as an equal. He was easy as pie as an author, so fluent a writer that no editing was ever needed.' He recalls the time when, at Gielgud's suggestion, he went to France to see Edward Gordon Craig about publishing his autobiography. The night before, Gielgud asked him if he would take money to Craig, his second cousin, who was often hard up. 'You weren't allowed to take currency abroad then, and I've never been so terrified in all my life. Imagine, smuggling contraband money from John Gielgud to Edward Gordon Craig.'

He brings out a rare typescript: notes made by Hallam Fordham of Barker rehearsing the 1940 production of *King Lear*, with Gielgud's thoughts interspersed between each scene. Impossible to find a publisher, he says in some bewilderment.

Gielgud lent him his mother's notebooks, which eventually became her book *A Victorian Playgoer*, which I've already seen. It's a fascinating volume: each night when she got back from the theatre Kate Gielgud wrote an account of the play for a friend who was unable to go. She's an incisive, knowledgeable critic; I feel sure it was her example that prompted Gielgud to embark on his own reviews in his youth.

Edward T also published the Hayman biography of Gielgud. He remembers that when approached about it Gielgud 'was neither reluctant nor enthusiastic, he just gave his consent'. I'm uncertain whether to come clean about my critical view of the result, but happily he beats me to it. 'When it came in, my heart sank,' he says. 'It didn't catch John at all.'

On the way back to London I call in on Olive Markham, in her cottage in the Ashdown Forest. A sweet woman, mother of Kika, Petra and Jehane, she's the widow of actor David Markham, who acted in Gielgud's 1954 production of *The Cherry Orchard*. She recalls that the actor playing Firs was driven to resign by Gielgud's butterfly directing methods. This was not long after the arrest, and she remembers a view of it then current. According to this version, the police had been told never to bother Gielgud if he was seen 'cruising'. Unfortunately one new young policeman was unaware of this edict. I suppose I better look further into the scandal, but I don't enjoy this part of the research. It feels too intrusive, at least while Gielgud is still alive.

Thursday 9 October
To Chelsea, to catch two birds with one stone; the actress Judy Campbell and her daughter Jane Birkin. The latter is still in bed, so I have a useful hour first with her mother. Tall, slim and elegant, she recalls at sixteen 'going weak at the knees' seeing Gielgud four times in *Richard of Bordeaux* (1933). She was directed by him during the war, in the supremely forgettable comedy *Ducks and Drakes* (1941). I ask about his consciousness of life outside the theatre, and she says, 'I think it was more a question of, Has a bomb damaged the theatre?'

She's very sharp on Binkie Beaumont, who now and then took her out to shows and to the famous Ivy restaurant. Then they quarrelled: 'He said actresses should lie in hot baths and wait for him to telephone them, not go off and live in the country and have three children.' She reckons the story was true about there being a Tennent spy in every West End theatre.

As we finish Jane Birkin dashes in, crumpled hair, jeans and sweater, yet exuding chic. She tells me admiringly of Gielgud's chivalry on the film *Leave*

All Fair (1985), when he stayed on late as she struggled with a scene. 'He really wanted to help, he stood behind the camera, refusing to sit, and helped me with his tears.' My shortest interview yet: in two minutes she's off to lunch – at the Ivy of course. The tradition continues.

In the afternoon I knock on Phyllis Calvert's door in Putney. 'You *are* like your father,' are her first words. She shows me some stills of the two of them in the wartime film *Madonna of the Seven Moons*. She talks very warmly of him, and I wonder if...no, better not ask. On with the other John.

She's a delightful woman, modest and natural. There's a Terry link: her first stage appearance, aged ten, was in a play that marked Ellen Terry's last. Sadly the great actress' mind had gone, and she spent all her time off stage in the wings, muttering Shakespeare to herself.

Phyllis C 'fell in love with John' after seeing him in the film *The Good Companions* (1933). 'I love him for his fun, his wit, which is almost unconscious, and his kindness,' she says. 'He wrote me a beautiful letter when my husband died. The last time I saw him he said, "The thing I hate about getting old is that it takes me half an hour to get my trousers on every morning."'

The subject of Binkie Beaumont comes up again: she was one of his protegees, so got work all the time from Tennent. She hated the Richard Huggett biography: 'So many untruths in it, it made me sick!'

In the evening I watch *A Dance to the Music of Time*, the television adaptation of the Anthony Powell books. Superficial, ridiculously fragmented, all frocks and dinner jackets and no substance. Gielgud twinkles briefly as an ageing novelist. He still gives magnificent shape and sense to a lengthy sentence, but he's looking old. Could this be his last television appearance?

Sunday 12 October
An all-day marathon at the National Film Theatre, watching *Brideshead Revisited* (1981) in its entirety. This is real dedication. I flag in mid-afternoon, but manage to make it through the fatigue barrier and stay on. By the end I don't want it to stop. I saw the original broadcast, but it's still a spell-binding piece of work. Seeing it straight through in this way highlights the brilliance of the story-telling. Such a relief, especially after the Anthony Powell nonsense, to have sustained scenes lasting several minutes, in which the actors have room to breathe, bring out the subtleties, and show their characters developing.

Gielgud is in five of the episodes. It's a witty and at times clinically vicious portrait of Charles Ryder's father. This time round I watch every gesture. He keeps his mannerisms under control: even his trademark sniff suits the haughty demeanour of the character. It's delicious stuff.

Monday 13 October
A friendly phone chat with Robert Tanitch, whose lively pictorial biography of Gielgud is already proving of great use to me. He says Gielgud was very cooperative, lent him his cuttings books, then dropped a typical brick when Robert presented him with a finished copy. After looking through it he said: 'Such witty remarks. Did you really write them all yourself?'

Tuesday 14 October
A lively session with a spritely, 80-year-old Paul Rogers in his north London house. A charming man, with the most uproarious laugh I have ever heard. He has made a little list, and takes me steadily through his encounters with Gielgud. As a teenager he saw his 1934 Hamlet: 'It was an experience I've never got over, and never shall. It was absolutely breathtaking.' He saw his 1944 Hamlet very differently: 'Amateurish in comparison, flat where the other one was fluid.'

He's not too strong on detail, as he confesses, but good at capturing the emotion of acting with Gielgud. He was in Julian Mitchell's *Half-Life* (1977) at the National, as the butler who turned out to be the Gielgud character's lover. 'I'm about as straight as can be, but I felt this wonderful rapport with John.' Disarmingly, he confesses he 'glows with foolish pride' when Gielgud addresses him as 'Dear Paul'.

He recalls with particular vividness Gielgud's recording of *Hamlet* in the mid-1950s, in which he himself played Claudius. 'John introduced the director, and said he proposed to say nothing himself. So we started: "Who's there?" – "Stop!" John said. He then took the play to pieces with great authority. It was everything: how to speak the text, the motivation of the characters; it was a most wonderful education for an actor.' He admits this experience 'fed my one and only Hamlet', which he played in Australia.

I liked his comparison of Gielgud and Olivier. 'The secret of John's greatness was his imagination. Larry had it too, but you could see the wheels go round. With John, and also Ralph, the ideas were absorbed into their beings.'

Wednesday 15 October
Suddenly one of the two red Gielgud boxes which I have been consulting regularly at the Theatre Museum has filled up with envelopes full of cuttings I've never seen before. Where on earth have they come from? My first paranoid thought is that the Other Biographer has been allowed to borrow them so he can copy them at leisure. But if him, why not me? I shall ask.

Thursday 16 October

Back yet again to Kensington: how many of the profession does it boast per square mile? Curiously Mavis Walker, Gielgud's travelling companion for ten years during the 1980s, lives in the same building as Tanya Moiseiwitsch. Both she and, I learn, Sam Beazley have passed me as a fit person to talk to.

She starts by pointing to a typescript of her own book on her travels with Gielgud, now being considered by Penguin. She says, very reasonably, that she wants to have first use of the material. I look at the folder wanly, and say I take her point. Apparently Gielgud's companion Martin Hensler thought the book was a betrayal, 'because it gave too much away'. Since then there's been no word from Gielgud, though she's written often.

She mentions Sheridan Morley, though she's not seen him yet; and another biographer, a woman whose name she can't recall – she wrote a biography of Frederick Ashton – and who appears now also to be on the Gielgud trail. I have a moment of alarm. But surely I would have heard of her if she was a serious contender? I suddenly have a vision of Gielgud enthroned in his country seat, merrily dispensing his approval to every biographer who comes to the door. This I will have to investigate.

Mavis W turns out to be an excellent witness: shrewd, intelligent, and pleasingly articulate about life on the road with Gielgud. 'He once said to me, "The thing to do with Shakespeare is to breast the waves, have the courage to let them take you, and don't think too much."' She remembers his thrill at being offered Edward Ryder in *Brideshead Revisited*: 'I know exactly how I'm going to play it,' he said. 'It's my father.' She also talks movingly of how he coped on their visit to Buchenwald during the filming of *War and Remembrance* (1987).

As an actress she had a small part in *The Chalk Garden* (1956), and recalls Gielgud's one note to her. 'One day he said, "Wouldn't it be fun if she had a laugh like the sound of a teaspoon tinkling in a medicine glass." I think this was a reference to a Katherine Mansfield story. But my part gave me no chance to laugh, and that was his sole contribution to it.'

Over a glass of sherry she tells me a charming story of Edith Evans, and her longing to find the common touch. Mavis once introduced her to a bevy of heavy-drinking artists at her Kensington studio. They sat around drinking, then played a mild practical joke on her. 'She fell about laughing, and came dancing back through the dustbins, crying out: "It's the *Quartier Latin*! The *Quartier Latin*!"' A wonderfully unexpected image.

Friday 17 October

A brief, chastening encounter with Dirk Bogarde, in his flat 'a short walk from Harrods'. Paralysed down his left side after a stroke, he's nevertheless generously agreed to talk to me about Gielgud. I've been told by my go-between, his editor Tony Lacey, to stay no longer than half an hour, as he tires quickly.

Despite his condition he reminiscences clearly about 'this dear, brave and very noble man'. He wonders if the universal adoration is giving me a problem. 'Everybody adored him, and there's nothing you can do about it.' He knew Gielgud first socially. 'I never found him remotely intimidating, just very matter of fact and friendly. I liked his modesty and enthusiasm. He's totally disarming, very self-critical, and blindingly honest . That's the trouble sometimes. He's got all the old-fashioned manners, and he's always meticulous with his thank-you letters, which look like a tadpole's tail, starting out broad and ending up narrow.'

Curiously, he thinks Gielgud isn't really a film actor: 'His limitations aren't obvious to the public: he just does what he's told, and does it very well.' Bogarde played his son in Alain Resnais' *Providence* (1977), probably Gielgud's best film. 'When Resnais told me he was bringing John in I thought, Oh! it's not my film any more, I've lost it. You couldn't win against John, he's an overpowering personality. He's very good in the film, but I don't think he knew what he was doing.' He recalls in moving detail how Gielgud played the final scene of the film; in his description I hear Bogarde the writer.

We talk about the different ways actors create a character, and I ask him about his immersion in Von Aschenbach in *Death in Venice*. He says he's an instinctive actor, but thinks Gielgud a very cerebral one. I'm not sure that's right, but I let it pass.

He mentions the cottaging incident, and Gielgud's reaction to it: 'He thought it was all rubbish, and he was quite right. Poor John.' We talk of Gielgud's friends, notably Vivien Leigh, a close friend also of Bogarde. ('She used to call Larry's new wife Miss Blow Right.') I ask him about Olivier: 'I found him rather double faced,' he says. He admits to preferring Gielgud's acting, 'but then if you prefer someone as a person this colours your view'.

As we talk his careworn face occasionally breaks into a smile, and I see a flash of the younger Bogarde that sent all a-quiver the girls of my generation (and maybe some of the boys too). We talk about his next book, a collection of his book reviews. He tells me, with frustration in his voice and face, that he can no longer write a postcard or cheque, that he now has to dictate his reviews to a typist.

My half-hour is up, and I sense he's had enough.

Monday 20 October

I've just read Sheridan Morley's book on Sybil Thorndike. It's competent, easy to read, but sycophantic and severely lacking in depth, and 'theatrical' in the pejorative sense. Most useful to me for Gielgud's warm preface, and in particular the reprinting of his address at her memorial service, in which he ranks Sybil Thorndike alongside Ellen Terry.

Tuesday 21 October

I'm startled to be suddenly faced with Gielgud on television, giving a puff to the BBC on its 75th birthday. He's filmed in a stately home, talking about his early radio days ('We called it the wireless then'), admitting he's still rather sentimental and romantic minded ('I like plays in which ladies wave handkerchiefs'). The soft focus and fast editing almost disguise the weakness of his voice and his general fragility. Why does this depress me? Probably because I see the chance of meeting him slipping away.

Wednesday 22 October

After Bogarde, another trip back through my teenage cinema-going years, this time in the company of John Mills, in his beautiful house in the Buckinghamshire village of Denham. We sit close together, as he is partially blind. This apart, he seems as chirpy and Mr Pollyish as ever.

I've caught him preparing for his one-man show at the Haymarket, when he'll be 90. Says he loves talking about Gielgud 'because he's just about the only actor who's older than I am'. Gielgud directed him in *Charley's Aunt* (1954), 'a very well-manicured production, so very John'. He's on the side of those who liked his quick-fire directing methods, last-minute changes and all. 'He was a superb director, great fun to work with, and he gave you plenty of freedom.'

He acted with him only once, in Charles Wood's *Veterans* (1972), and laughs in remembering the reaction to its violent language when the play opened in Brighton. 'I'd been given the bird before, but it was something new for John.' Despite being a great buddy of Olivier, he reckons Gielgud was the greater classical actor. He admires him especially for his generous casting of Olivier as Romeo.

As I leave he winks, and promises to 'ring Sir John and tell him I ripped him apart!' Quite a lad.

Friday 24 October

An agreeable lunch at the Barbican with Diana Devlin, a friend from university days, grand-daughter of Sybil Thorndike and Lewis Casson, now teaching at the

Guildhall School of Music and Drama. I've just read her excellent biography of her grandfather, full of good detail on theatre history, an inside account but rigorous and critical, not cosy as they often are.

Her father was William Devlin, who married Lewis and Sybil's daughter Mary Casson, and acted in Gielgud's OUDS production of *Romeo and Juliet* (1932). She very helpfully brings along his scrapbook, which has yellowing cuttings of the production. He's forgotten now, but in his youth he was considered a shining talent. An old face for his age, he played Lear at 22 and soon after, almost equally unbelievably, the Ghost of Hamlet's father in Gielgud's 1934 *Hamlet*. He too, Diana recalls, suffered under Gielgud's sometimes insensitive direction. 'They were rehearsing *Twelfth Night* at Stratford, and John suddenly said to my father, "Billy, can't you do something a little more *interesting*." My father, thinking what the hell can you do with a part like Antonio, was fuming. Fortunately Olivier, who was playing Malvolio, broke the atmosphere by calling out, "Lunch!"'

I ask her about Sybil's support for Gielgud after his arrest. She's convinced the famous story, of her saying to Gielgud 'What a silly bugger you've been' at rehearsals next day, is apochryphal. 'I'm sure she made the atmosphere all right again, but that phrase doesn't sound like her.' I can see it will be tricky deciding between this view and the published versions.

Sunday 26 October
To the tiny, ramshackle King's Head pub theatre in Islington, for a one-man show about the critic James Agate. A peculiar audience: only about 15 of us, mainly elderly men of slightly downtrodden appearance. I suspect most of them are actors who remember Agate, the Tynan of his day, from their distant youth. It's a thin monologue affair, though actor Rowland Davies has the right bulk, and catches well Agate's eccentricity, outrageous wit and sharp critical mind. I decide that Tynan in all his acerbic nastiness might have made an even better subject.

Tuesday 28 October
A helpful note from Nigel Hawthorne, a contact in my search for the papers of Gwen Ffrangcon-Davies, one of Gielgud's leading ladies. He can't resist adding a Gielgud anecdote as a postcript. Gielgud is in his dressing room when there's a knock at the door. 'Yes, who's there?' 'John dear, it's Yehudi.' 'Yehudi who?'

October Progress Report
A wonderfully full month: the interview with Mavis Walker is an especial gem, but those with Judy Campbell and Phyllis Calvert are also valuable. Sad though to

be confronted with Bogarde's illness and John Mills' near blindness.

Disappointments: Missing Irene Worth. No reply from Meriel Forbes, Ralph Richardson's widow.

Story of the month, probably apocryphal: Gielgud rang his agent on Boxing Day last year to ask him if there was any work in the offing.

Monday 3 November

A light lunch with Jean Anderson in her Kensington flat. She worked with Gielgud in film and television, but also in the theatre in Rattigan's *Variation on a Theme* (1958). 'The surprise was how wonderfully easy he was, how interested in people, and utterly unstarry, never doing the big act. He loved gossip, even if you were talking about a maiden aunt.'

She says a lot of people, though she was not one of them, became desperate about his directing. She recalls during the Rattigan rehearsals his clash with one young actor. 'John once spent an hour teaching him to be flamboyant, how to don an opera cloak and make an exit. When he asked him the next day if he had practised overnight, the young man said he'd preferred to go out and forget all about it.' – 'You know, Jean, he thinks we're so old fashioned,' Gielgud complained. The actor was sacked, but the play was a flop.

She was also with him in *The Barretts of Wimpole Street* (1957), in which he played the heavy father of Elizabeth ('I was awful,' was Gielgud's verdict, shared by several critics), and in one of the last episodes of *Inspector Morse* (1993), in which 'I was cast in the slightly improbable role of his wife'. She says someone ought to write a play for them as brother and sister: 'We have the same kind of nose, the same frown lines, and the same straight back!'

Tuesday 4 November

An interview for the NT magazine *StageWrite* with Ian McKellen, about his playing of Captain Hook in the National's *Peter Pan*. Afterwards he readily offers me his thoughts on Gielgud.

As an actor who enjoys impersonation he puts himself in the Olivier camp, but Gielgud has still been a strong influence. 'I was aware when I was doing Hamlet that he could get through it twice as quickly as I could, and the play would be the better for it. He was very much in the back of my mind.'

He was enthralled by his *Ages of Man* recital. 'On stage it was a miracle, and the record is a wonderful lesson for actors on how to speak Shakespeare quickly without losing anything. His Hamlet and Richard and Benedick were not to do with being or sounding different, but with making you understand the verse. That's probably been his greatest influence on me, and I suspect many others of my generation.'

I'm uncertain whether to mention the gay issue, but he does so himself, touching on Gielgud's reluctance to come out publicly. 'His arrest was a fascinating bit of social history, but it still seems to be a painful memory. As he so triumphantly came through, it could be a wonderful thing for the world to know about. But it's something he just won't talk about, which is a pity. The irony is that when he does die, people will talk about that side of him, but not on his own terms.'

Thursday 6 November
The Theatre Museum won't let me borrow the Gielgud cuttings for a weekend and photocopy them myself. It seems an absurdly bureaucratic decision given they're so under-staffed: the story is that they have 10,000 items still uncatalogued. There's no answer to my query about their earlier removal.

Friday 7 November
I've finished Garry O'Connor's life of Ralph Richardson. A wayward and eccentric book, which somehow still captures him vividly. There's a lot of useful stories and information on the many productions he did with Gielgud. I like O'Connor's device of interweaving the chapters with episodes from his enjoyable pursuit of the constantly elusive Richardson.

Monday 10 November
I'm enjoying Bryan Forbes' lively, very personal biography of Edith Evans. It's sympathetic and shrewd, quite rambling but immensely readable, and he really knows his theatre history. His subject worked with Gielgud on eight productions, and there's some excellent material on several of them, including *The Importance of Being Earnest* (1939). It was Gielgud who asked her to play Lady Bracknell, a part she eventually grew to detest, because people were obsessed with the famous 'A handbag!' line.

Forbes knew her well during her last years, and this holds him back from being too critical. Indeed he goes so far as to call his relationship with her 'a love affair' – in the metaphysical rather than the physical sense, I assume. He argues that 'there is no such thing as an impartial opinion'. Perhaps that's especially true if you become too friendly with your subject.

Tuesday 11 November

A phone conversation with Clive Robbins, who handled all the affairs of Gwen Ffrangcon-Davies'. He says that her niece handed the writer David Spenser all her papers, with lots of photographs, cuttings etc, and that he's written three chapters. The trail is hotting up.

Wednesday 12 November

An unexpected gem among the press cuttings. In a 1972 interview Gielgud admits to having been to Disneyland, not just once, but *six* times! 'You have to queue for hours, but you really get a lot for your money,' he says. 'They've got a new Haunted House. Absolutely divine. Much better than their Pirates of the Caribbean.' What was that about actors being like children?

Thursday 13 November

I've been brooding on Bryan Forbes' remark about impartiality, and my changing attitude to Gielgud. I started off being in awe of his achievement and reputation. But after six months I think I've developed a more balanced stance. His greatness as an actor isn't in question, though I'm fascinated to discover that he had some resounding failures. As a man he seems to have many fine, even loveable qualities, and I'm intrigued to find how cultured he is compared with most actors. But the veil is gradually being lifted on his flaws: his impetuosity, his indecisiveness, his frequent insensitivity. Whatever Dirk Bogarde says, I know I'll have no difficulty in painting both light and shade.

Saturday 15 November

A wonderfully rich and entertaining letter from Australia from actor John McCallum, now in his eightieth year. Among other memories he has a recollection of Barker directing *King Lear* in 1940: 'He was a very hands-on director, always on the stage among the actors, not only giving them the sense and interpretation of the verse, but speaking it himself. He was the most authoritative director I've ever known, and John obviously thought so too.'

Sunday 16 November

An instructive evening at the Orange Tree theatre in Richmond, where the *Guardian* critic Michael Billington talks about writing *The Life and Work of Harold Pinter*. I read the book last week: it's very intelligent and shrewd, though rather too admiring. But it will be very useful to me when I get to the 1970s and *No Man's Land*.

Billington says one of the pleasures of writing about a living author is access, and that he was relieved to know that Pinter would look at his text before publication. He admits he was biased in writing about him as a man because he admires him as a playwright. Says his aim was not to write an independent biography, but to discuss Pinter's work in the context of his life. Pinter, he says, speaks like his own dialogue. He suggests this is a hallmark of a good playwright, and cites Shaffer and Ayckbourn as other examples. I wonder if that's really so?

In passing he tells the story of another Pinter biographer – let's call him James – who had talked to Billington and many others, but was not making much headway with the book. After Billington had been commissioned by Faber (and implicitly Pinter), James phoned him again: *Billington*: I'm afraid I've got some bad news. *James*: You can't help me any further with the book? *Billington*: Worse than that: I'm writing the same book myself.

Friday 21 November
I've spent a nerve-wracking few days dealing with Sheridan Morley. On Monday, in the William Hickey gossip column in the *Daily Express*, a 'giggling' Gielgud was quoted as saying mischievously of his biography: 'I gave Sheridan permission to do it and that was the last I heard. Apparently he's now reached my forties, but hasn't asked me a single question. I rather like that kind of biographer.'

Earlier this month, I now discover, Morley wrote to Michael Earley at Methuen, saying he is worried about my biography. He claims that Michael told him it was to be more of a history of a century's theatre than a history of Gielgud, and that Gielgud has said several times that he never authorised me to do a biography. Finally he writes that several of the people I have interviewed say I am telling them the book *is* authorised, and that it will be out next year.

Clearly all this is desperation on Morley's part. Evidently he's trying his best to scupper my book. What's all this about a history of the century's theatre? We all know the book is a biography. Why should Gielgud pretend he didn't give it his blessing? And who says it's coming out next year, when I don't plan to finish it until 1999?

At Michael's suggestion, but with great reluctance, I talk to Morley on the phone. He's clearly rattled by the *Daily Express* item, and says he's writing to people to explain that he is the official biographer. He claims he has done some two hundred interviews, and that 'elderly actresses like Connie Cummings [whom I have never approached] and Judy Campbell are getting confused about the situation'. I tell him I'm certainly not describing myself as the official biographer, and remind him that Gielgud gave me his blessing to do the book.

I offer to show him the letter I send to potential interviewees, but after putting the phone down think better of it. Why should I have to defend my conduct when I've done nothing wrong? Michael says Sheridan is obviously feeling the heat, and that given his proprietary nature he's sure his unease over my book will never go away. He suggests I write to Gielgud, and apologise for any misunderstandings that might have arisen. I decide to sleep on this idea.

Saturday 22 November
I'm much cheered by a charming letter from Paul Scofield. He says he'd be delighted to help, but that 'being more articulate on paper than I seem to be in assembling my thoughts in conversation,' he would rather answer written questions. This doesn't surprise me: everyone says he's an exceptionally private man (apparently he's twice turned down a knighthood), and in all the biographies I've read his help is always by letter. I decide to wait until I see Peter Brook before compiling the questions, so I can get some thoughts on *Venice Preserv'd* (1953), in which Scofield and Gielgud were directed by Brook.

Monday 24 November
Michael faxes me a copy of a letter he's sent to Morley, in which he puts it on the record a) that I am writing a biography, not a theatre history, b) that I have Gielgud's permission to do the book, and c) that I would be happy to meet him if necessary. The last suggestion isn't true: I wouldn't trust myself to keep the necessary cool. But I have to remember that Michael is also Morley's publisher for various Coward volumes, so I can't afford a bust-up with him. It's a complication I could do without.

Tuesday 25 November
A promising response from Kevin Brownlow's sister-in-law Sally Phipps, who's about to start her Molly Keane biography, and agrees we could be of mutual help. What I didn't know when I wrote to her, which is now embarrassing, is that Molly Keane was her mother. She's about to sort her papers, 'now reposing in plastic bags, boxes, small suitcases' etc. Tantalisingly, she says she knows they contain letters from Gielgud, as well as from his lover John Perry, a close friend of Molly Keane.

Wednesday 26 November
A letter from Morley to Earley, saying that he is reassured by Michael's recent letter, which surprises me. He suggests if Michael puts me in touch with him, he'd be happy to compare notes and progress, since he believes things would be

much better if there was some liaison between us. What does he take me for, a fool? Perhaps he's calmed down for the moment, but I don't trust him one inch. Meanwhile, after talking to Derek, I decide not to write to Gielgud, since I see no advantage in doing so. If Morley is telling the truth, then Gielgud's behaviour is very odd. But it's a very big If.

Thursday 27 November
Further uplift after a merry hour with Peter Sallis, this time in my house in Barnes. He adores Gielgud unashamedly: 'It's the combination of his wickedness and his almost saint-like kindness. In all four productions I've been in with him he's never lost his temper. A lovely man.'

We focus on the season at the Lyric Hammersmith in 1952/3. He offers me the definitive version of a famous Gielgud gaffe during the casting of *Richard II*, definitive because he himself was the victim. Also a sample of Gielgud's perfectionism. 'He'd come into your dressing-room and suggest different emphases to a certain line. He just couldn't leave it alone, his mind was so inventive.'

He gives a poignant description of being sacked by Coward during the pre-London tour of *Nude with Violin* (1956), and Gielgud's sweet and sympathetic reaction to it. Also a vivid on-the-spot account of audience reaction to his arrival on stage the evening after his knighthood was announced, during the run of *Venice Preserv'd* (1953).

He tells me an amusing but surely apocryphal story highlighting Binkie Beaumont's stranglehold on the West End during the 1950s. He supposedly slipped in unnoticed to watch a long-running play at the Queen's, and found the actors fooling round. Furious, he went backstage and asked the director to assemble the company, then tore them off a strip for their unprofessional behaviour. Finally the director piped up: 'I hope you don't mind my saying so, Mr Beaumont, but this isn't actually one of your productions.'

Later I meet Moira Lister in her smart, expensively furnished Belgravia flat, to talk about the 1955 Stratford season and its tour. A glamorous seventy-something, she's much more intelligent and perceptive than her rather fluffy autobiography suggests. She recalls the notorious 1955 Noguchi *King Lear* (she was Regan), and George Devine's attempt to explain the symbolism of the strange costumes to the actors. Also Gielgud's habit of playing a scene and then coming off to fill in a clue in the *Times* crossword.

She's good on the chemistry between him and Peggy Ashcroft in *Much Ado about Nothing* (1955), which she watched from the wings every night during a long European tour. 'Their integrity and truth and depth of concentration was quite staggering. He was an amazing actor, there was a tremendous aura about him.'

She's heard from someone who lives near Gielgud that he's lonely. Sad if true, but it makes me consider again whether I should find a reason to visit. It's so bloody hard to gauge what's the best thing to do.

Friday 28 November
To the King's Head theatre in Islington again, this time to see Barrie's *Dear Brutus*, in which Gielgud played the failed artist Dearth in his own 1941 wartime production. A weird play, rather over-egged with whimsy, but based on an intriguing idea: What would we do with our lives if we had a second chance?

The long central scene between Dearth and his young daughter, the one Muriel Pavlow spoke about, is undoubtedly the most compelling. It's easy to imagine Gielgud pulling out all the stops in this moving duologue. His 1997 successor stands out amidst a mediocre cast, as does the girl, who suggests a wonderful mixture of innocence and sensitivity.

November Progress Report
Good, detailed material culled from McCallum, Lister, Anderson and Sallis. Also a good reading month, with five juicy volumes consumed.

1. Billington on Pinter.

2. Hugo Vickers on Vivien Leigh, well-researched and reliable, but a bit overwhelmed with detail in parts.

3 and 4. Two volumes of Donald Sinden memoirs, good source books, and a fruity read: you can hear the mellifluous voice as the stories come pouring out.

5. Paul Eddington's memoirs, especially good on *Forty Years On* (1968), and Gielgud's vulnerability during rehearsals.

Hopes: Scofield's agreement is excellent news. Alicia Markova has agreed to talk, but not yet.

Disappointments: Gillian Cadell writes from France to say letters to her mother Jean, a good friend who acted with Gielgud in *The Importance of Being Earnest* on stage, radio and record, have been lost. Designer John Bury says he's not well enough to help. Still no reply from Meriel Forbes or Patrick Woodcock, Gielgud's doctor, to whom Judy Campbell had suggested I write.

Gossip I'm told by someone who worked with Gielgud that he said of Morley's biography: 'I expect it will be very respectful and dull.'

Wednesday 3 December

To the Art Workers' Guild in Bloomsbury, to hear actor Richard Bebb address the Society for Theatre Research on 'The Hamlets of John Gielgud', with extracts from the 1931 and 1948 recordings. It's instructive to hear the differences in speed, thought and meaning of the same speech spoken so many years apart. Bebb is slightly pompous, but shrewd, knowledgeable, and obviously passionate about his subject: he saw the 1944 Haymarket production seven times. 'Gielgud *was* Hamlet for my generation.' Afterwards, over wine and mince pies, he invites us to drink a solemn toast to 'Sir John'. He's obviously considered theatrical royalty, but it's all a bit too reverential for me.

Monday 8 December

A lively two hours with Nancy Nevinson in St John's Wood. An energetic actress and teacher, she's still bursting with life in old age, and insists I come soon to *Truths and Trifles*, her one-woman show about the last fifty years of theatre, in which several Gielgud stories apparently feature. She has some delicious first-hand recollections of his postwar tour of India and the Far East, varying in significance from the day he left his jockstrap in Bangalore, to the powerful effect of his Hamlet on the troops in Singapore.

She offers an interesting explanation for the cottaging incident: 'I think it was loneliness, meeting somebody who didn't know who he was. He just longed for people to like him for himself, he had too many hangers-on, who adored him, but not so he could be himself.'

She looks for some letters in a desk full of theatre files, which she'd meant to sort out before my visit. On the phone she'd mentioned a diary she kept on the tour, but she's forgotten to read it before we meet. So we strike a deal: she'll read extracts into a tape, and I'll come back and sort out her theatre files. She's fun to be with, so I don't mind a second visit, especially if it means getting to look at her diary.

Tuesday 9 December

An hour with Peter Brook, in an appropriately austere and almost empty space, a bare dressing-room at Riverside Studios in Hammersmith. I'm unusually nervous about this interview, partly because of Brook's reputation for unflinching seriousness, partly because of Morley's Ghost hovering in the air. Brook saw him only last week, and is I suspect not terribly thrilled to be going over the same ground again so soon. Nevertheless, here he is.

We get off to a disconcerting start when, fixing me with a flinty gaze, he says he really has no interest in the past, and that 'John is a subtle and complex man, but when it comes to his work there isn't much to tell that isn't self-evident'. However, he listens attentively to my questions, and soon belies his opening words by talking eloquently of the four plays in which he directed Gielgud: *Measure for Measure* (1950) at Stratford, *The Winter's Tale* (1951), *Venice Preserv'd* (1953) and *Oedipus* (1968). I ask him why he thinks he and Gielgud got on so well. 'We wanted to listen to one another,' he says. 'I liked and admired him, and knew I could be direct and frank. He's a man of exceptional purity and loyalty, and eternally open and enthusiastic. He's a very intuitive actor, and delighted to have someone he trusted, someone who could say, "That isn't as good as that", "That doesn't follow on as clearly", "That is losing its thread".'

He has a different view from most people on Gielgud's whirlwind directing style. 'What makes him such a good director, when he interrupts someone, is that he recognises that people are doing something cheap, and that they could do something of a better quality. People say he doesn't know what he wants. The truth of it is that more than anyone else he knows what he wants, but he can't express it in a conventional way, only by a refusal of anything that isn't of the best quality. That's deep in his nature.'

Gielgud, he feels, embodies the good side of the British aristocratic tradition. 'His basic nature is tender and humble, and his upbringing has given him all the positive values: he is noble, honest, modest, unassuming and plainly generous.' He contrasts his openness and honesty with very different qualities in Olivier, whom he directed at Stratford in a famous *Titus Andronicus*: 'Olivier was a man with a powerful talent, but very closed, suspicious and malicious. He had a burning need to make an effect.'

I try to get him to talk about his mentor Barry Jackson, who first introduced him to Stratford, and gave Gielgud his first shot at Shakespeare in London in 1924. He gives me a rare smile, and says: 'My autobiography is coming out in May.' Nevertheless it's been a fruitful interview.

Wednesday 10 December
A lovely session with the friendly, amusing Geoffrey Bayldon. It's said a theatrical biographer should gather the memories of the spear-carrier as well as the leading player. This is he *par excellence*, an actor with a good memory and a track record of small supporting roles, including several at Stratford in 1950.

He remembers Gielgud on the first night of the Brook *Measure for Measure*.

'He was very nervous, he was standing beside me, and Leon Quartermaine dried, and he said, "Oh my God." He was frightened to bits.' This didn't stop him giving one of the most ferocious and surprising performances of his career. He recalls Gielgud's dislike of that year's *Julius Caesar*, with its cramped set, which meant the actors often couldn't be seen by the audience. They soon started to misbehave. 'Even Robert Hardy misbehaved. He would come on in a hat from *Henry VIII*, with a bar of soap to hand out to anyone he came across.'

Geoffrey B was also in the season at the Lyric, Hammersmith when Gielgud directed Scofield as Richard II, and present at a memorable dress-rehearsal at the Winter Garden when Gielgud briefly took over the part. 'He saw the company in front of him and thought we must be bored, so he started to send up the part. We began to giggle, but then he went into it properly. And he was sublime. Tears were streaming down my face, and when I looked to my left there were five other actors weeping.'

He reproduces Gielgud's changing instructions to him at a rehearsal of *The Way of the World*. 'He said to me: "Go to the left of him. Come in again. Go to the right of him. He's a comic character: think of something funny. (By now the company was massing in the wings.) Go round him. No not round his *body*, round *him*. (I never knew what that meant.) Oh, let's stop there." I walked off boss-eyed into the wings, and there was Pamela Brown with a large double-brandy. He just didn't know he was doing it.'

He casts doubts on Gielgud's famous ability to complete the *Times* crossword. 'He came into our dressing-room at the Lyric: Peter Sallis and Brewster Mason were the crossword experts. *John*: Anyone done the crossword? I can't get the bottom right-hand corner. *Brewster*: I can't get the top left. *John*: No trouble with that. It's Didymans. *Peter*: It isn't, it's Dustbins. *John*: Oh, I got Didymans. He said it without turning a hair. You wonder what the rest was like.'

Friday 12 December
To Muswell Hill, for a valuable session with Hallam Tennyson. As assistant head of radio drama at the BBC he worked often with Gielgud. 'My boss Martin Esslin thought I would be suitable because I was upper-middle-class,' he recalls. He did readings and poetry with him rather than the big productions.

'John did the whole of *In Memoriam* for me. He'd never read it before, and he looked up in the middle and said, "This is splendid stuff, isn't it." We had to do a re-take.' He's shrewd on Gielgud's skills as a radio actor, but recalls also his uncertainties. 'He felt he would fall back on his beautiful voice and lose the character very quickly. He used to say, "All I am is a voice, I'm not really an actor,

I can't change roles." I liked this modesty, this total lack of side.'

He overlapped briefly with Val Gielgud at the BBC, and is amusing about his conservative taste in drama. 'Val had a great quality of choosing people to work with him who would fill in for his deficiencies. He thought Pinter was a dreadful playwright, but his number two was Donald McWhinnie, who was *the* avant-garde commissioner, and if Donald said that's what the intelligentsia wanted, that's what they would get.'

He says Val was 'very polite and courteous, but less easy-going than John, much more buttoned up. He wanted to be the English gentleman, and was always giving house parties with whichever wife he was then with. None of them was his intellectual equal, but four of them came to his funeral: one did the drinks, one the food, one arranged the garden, and one greeted the guests. It was charming.' He claims Val worshipped John: 'He couldn't read a bad notice about him.'

I bring up the gay play mentioned by Peter Cotes, and he confirms Gielgud's enthusiasm for it. 'He was very interested in producing it, and cast it, with Alan Bates in the lead. But his agent was terribly against it, didn't want him to be associated with a gay play, and talked him out of it. This seemed extraordinary to me, because anyone who took the theatre at all seriously knew he was gay. He was very disappointed.'

Over tea it emerges that he's the grandson of 'The Poet', as he calls him. He tells me he now lectures on the photographer Julia Margaret Cameron, a friend of Tennyson. Later I look at my book of her photographs: his likeness to his grandfather is remarkable.

Tuesday 16 December
I ring David Spenser, Gwen Ffrangcon-Davies' biographer, but get through to someone else in the same Essex village, who puts me on to a woman who's lived there longer, who puts me on to a man who sometimes does work for David S, who says he's away now for quite a while. After this exhausting trail I'm very tempted to give in, but Gwen FD was one of Gielgud's first leading ladies, and if Spenser has her papers, then it's worth my persevering.

Friday 19 December
Lunch today with a neighbour, Perry Walker, who tells me that twenty years ago he and some friends founded a society called SPASM - the Society for the Prevention of Authorship by Sheridan Morley. He says they started it because they thought his prose style so dreadful. They even had some headed notepaper printed, and sent him a sample. Clearly it's time for this organisation to be revived; I'd willingly

become a life member.

Later I get a phone call beginning 'Donald Sinden here', surely the most superfluous announcement in theatrical circles. He's happy to talk, but is moving house, so we fix to meet in a couple of months. Good: in addition to the fact that he worked with Gielgud on *The Heiress* (1949), he's a real expert on theatre history.

Saturday 20 December

A puzzling and disturbing letter from Richard Attenborough, in response to my standard request for an interview. 'It may be that Sir John has been discussing a number of undertakings recently and, therefore, has many projects to keep in mind. However, I am afraid that when I mentioned your biography to him, it was not something that immediately came to mind.'

Am I in a dream? Can Gielgud have actually *forgotten* about the book? Is this the onset of Alzheimer's? This news is worrying in itself, but even more so is Attenborough's next point: 'I fear that I have made it an absolute rule never to collaborate with a biographer unless I have the subject's permission. In the light of this, I do hope you will understand why I feel I must pass.'

I fear there may be others, especially friends of Gielgud, who will adopt the same stance. Which means I could lose some of my most important witnesses. This is truly bad news.

Sunday 21 December

Watching a South Bank Show devoted to Zeffirelli, I waited to see how it dealt with his disastrous 1961 production of *Othello*, with Gielgud as the Moor. I waited in vain. This notorious debacle is skipped over with nothing more than a two-second shot of some critical headlines ('The pity of it, Zeffirelli' – Ned Sherrin). No hint of why, after his vibrant *Romeo and Juliet*, his second attempt at Shakespeare went so dreadfully wrong. It was a very disappointing programme, mainly taken up with Melvyn Bragg massaging Zeffirelli's ego. I realise now that Zeffirelli will not answer my letter, in which I disingenuously asked him if he'd like to put the case for the defence of his production. There obviously isn't one.

Tuesday 23 December

To the National Film Theatre, to see Gielgud in *The Picture of Dorian Gray* (1976). Originally made for television, Wilde's play sits oddly on the big screen, with the actors seeming larger than usual, and the action startlingly slow and static. As Henry Wootton, bedecked in a striking red wig, Gielgud delivers the Wildean epigrams with wit and evident relish. He and the other actors – Jeremy Brett is especially good here – underplay 'the love that dare not speak its name', which makes it infinitely more effective. At first Gielgud tends to simper somewhat, and the epigrams become tiresome since, as so often with Wilde, they arrive not as single spies but in battalions. But in the last scene he gives Wootton considerable depth and subtlety.

Monday 29 December

The Attenborough letter is still haunting me, but I'm cheered this morning by a very friendly one from Bryan Forbes. Sadly he no longer has a transcript of Gielgud's memories of Edith Evans, which he elicited from him while researching her biography. He also thinks the correspondence between them has gone to the American Academy with his other papers. But he generously offers to search for them and other items that might help, including Gielgud's obituary of Edith E.

He was present earlier this year at the unveiling of a plaque on her house in Ebury Street, at which Gielgud spoke very warmly of her. 'But I felt he was very frail, very unsteady on his pins.' That sounds ominous.

Later I have a phone conversation with Olga Edwardes, who played in Gielgud's production of *Landslide* (1943). She reminiscences about the dancing skills of Val Gielgud, who courted her once: 'I was fortunately level headed enough not to be danced away by him.' Later, unsolicited by me, she calls back to say she's discovered that Rita Vale, one of Val's wives, died last year, but that Belle Chrystal, one of his mistresses, is alive, but in a nursing home, and not up to talking. Disappointing: I could use an inside view of the brothers' relationship, but I think all Val's wives are dead.

Tuesday 30 December

After writing recently to Robert Hardy, I've discovered he's Morley's uncle. Oh well. Of course there could be a family feud....

Year 1: Progress Report

After eight months' work I'm a third of the way through my allotted time. I've made plenty of progress, but when I consider the people I need to interview, the books I need to read, the films and television plays I must see, I realise I'm still only at base camp.

On the positive side, only two potential interviewees (Rosalie Crutchley and Isabel Jeans) have died on me, and I've just about covered the 75+ target group. I'm getting a little scratchy about the Guinness interview, though I think this will still come off. Otherwise, Attenborough apart, everyone has been amazingly cooperative.

I make some New Year resolutions for 1998:

* To be more selective about the people I approach for interview. I must concentrate on plugging gaps, getting more directors and writers, and fewer actors.

* To be more ruthless in my reading, to plunder books swiftly for relevant Gielgud material rather than read them right through. Exceptions are the very best biographies, e.g. Wansell on Rattigan, Callow on Laughton.

* To avoid spending time travelling down obscure by-ways to find snippets of information. Keep to the main road.

 * To think about getting some words down, not least in order to get the next instalment of the advance. I think I can probably stick solely to research until Easter. Getting the starting time right will not be easy.

* To decide soon whether or not to contact Gielgud with some questions. I feel I know him intimately, yet not at all. It seems crazy not to meet him while his mind's still alert. But I don't want to risk a rebuff or, after Attenborough, a 'What biography?' response.

– TWO –

Battle is Joined

Monday 5 January 1998

A fascinating letter from the writer John Bowen. A couple of years ago he suggested doing a biography of Gielgud to Methuen. They were enthusiastic, but he did nothing about it. 'I began to wonder whether I had the stamina for such a long life, whether I should be allowed to explore his emotional and sexual life – not just the arrest, but the whole complicated social and emotional mess, and the gay underground that existed, especially in the theatre, during the days when homosexual congress was illegal.'

I can empathise with that concern. I feel I have to tread very warily, and be selective as to whom I raise the issue with. Most of the gay actors I've interviewed bring it up without prompting, which makes me feel sheepish about my caution. But the tricky bit will be the writing of it, knowing that Gielgud might decide to take up my offer to send him the text.

Wednesday 7 January

A visit from Terence Longdon, still noble of feature at 75. It turns out he was one of the few actors to be actually contracted to Tennent; Richard Burton was another. He offers further evidence of Gielgud's directorial insensitivity, during *Treasure Hunt* (1949): 'He didn't like one of the girls, and she got the sack. He used to say to her, "You point too much, you have such big fingers." Those sharp, spiky remarks just slipped out. I don't think he meant to be unkind.' He also acted with Gielgud in Euripides' *Medea* (1948), which opened the second-ever Edinburgh Festival. Bizarrely, the organisers sent a Greek interpreter to Waverley Station to meet Gielgud's very British company.

Thursday 8 January

I've forced myself to read Morley's biography of Coward, *A Talent to Amuse*. It's the social diary school of biography, without critical edge or any analysis of his subject's talent. He crams a lot in, but quite fails to illuminate, for instance, Coward's darker, more unpleasant side. Obviously he's hampered by writing during Coward's lifetime; there's no mention of his homosexuality. Even so it's not much more than an autobiography 'as told to': 'Noel was appalled', 'Noel was delighted' etc. He's interviewed scores of people, but used his material very little. The final section is characteristically self-promoting: Morley watching Coward watching *Star!*, the film about his life.

A good talk with director Michael Langham, who took over from his mentor Tyrone Guthrie as the mainstay of the theatre at Stratford, Ontario, and now works in Canada. A weird experience for me following my trip to my birthplace in Amersham: his London flat overlooking Battersea Park is next door to the one in which I spent most of my childhood.

He's keen to set the record straight about the 1950 *Julius Caesar* which he co-directed at Stratford with Tony Quayle. In his memoirs Quayle says Langham left the production because Gielgud was not happy with him. Never trust an actor's memoirs: the truth, as ever, is more complicated. Michael L is disarmingly honest about Gielgud's criticisms of his directing, and admits the wound went deep, that he took about two years to recover.

We talk about the changing styles of acting Shakespeare. 'John was from another age. He didn't exactly sing the verse, but he let the verse ride, and he did it beautifully. I came in very much on the new wave of more realism and less romance, but I always found him very compelling. As an appreciator of poetry he was difficult to beat.'

Later his small and merry actress wife Helen Burns joins us. She recalls Gielgud directing her in *Cradle Song* (1944) and being continually moved to tears by the play. She has an interesting take on his character: 'I think he's more melancholy than he lets on. He has a great deal of courage, of not giving in, of rising above. There's a simplicity about him, he's very secure in his roots and his antecedents. He doesn't need to have exterior signs of status, because it's innate.'

Monday 12 January
I phoned Mavis Walker, ostensibly to check the phone number of a contact she gave me, but actually to check on the situation with her 'Travels with Gielgud' book. It seems Penguin has rejected it as too light, and she now feels it will have to wait until after Gielgud's death before there's a chance of publication. Bother. She tells me in passing that Frederick Ashton's biographer Julie Kavanagh is not after all doing one of Gielgud, but merely a lengthy feature for the *New Yorker*, of which she is the London editor. So that's a relief.

Tuesday 13 January

To Gloucestershire, to meet the celebrated Edwardian actor Henry Ainley's daughter Patsy. She takes me to see Gielgud's sister Eleanor in her large house near Tetbury. She will surely have consulted her brother about our meeting, so I assume he knows that I'm still at work, and is not going to interfere, which if true is good news.

Dressed in fetching beige trousers and a reefer jacket, small and rather stooped, with the Gielgud cheekbones, Eleanor seems utterly different from her brother: direct, well organised, down to earth, not a trace of shyness or self-consciousness. I'm intrigued by the contrast: the Voice Beautiful against the Voice Gravelly (she chain-smokes throughout), the patrician vowels compared to a classless accent, his formal mode of speech and her earthy colloquialisms. But they share a merry sense of humour.

She recalls her thwarted ambition. 'I was taken to the theatre when I was knee high to a duck. My grandmother, Kate Terry, had the stage box, and I was always stuck in the corner, so I couldn't see very much. Like John I wanted to go on the stage, but oh dear me no, father wouldn't play. So I became a book-keeper and secretary.'

She takes me into her den, and proudly shows me the family pictures, including a fine portrait of her father. She's delightfully blunt and humorous about her family, and mildly indiscreet about Lewis' love life ('I got him out of a lot of marital complications'). She's forgotten how many wives Val had, but remembers saying to him: 'Now we are seven, isn't it time to stop?' He also had what she calls 'permanent girl-friends', which he was 'usually quite good at hiding, but if the news got abroad, he had to make an honest woman of them. Once he put a ring on their finger it was hopeless. I used to say, "For God's sake don't marry them, just live with them." But he wouldn't listen.'

My carefully prepared list of questions goes by the board as we jump from topic to topic across the years. She has a great memory for detail, and a fascination with the dynamics of family relationships. 'We're a funny mixture, half Polish Lithuanian, a quarter Welsh and a quarter Scots. We're mongrels, and we can be jolly awkward, all of us. People have to know us to take some of our major eccentricities. John's is that he can't say No. If anyone is in trouble, whether he knows them or not, out comes the chequebook. When he's asked out to lunch half the time they give him the bill, and he pays.' She says he's frightened of London now, but gets frustrated when he's housebound. 'He still loves walking, he's still very upright, though he has to use a stick. He hates the phone, but he'll ring three or four times a week, and if he thinks I'm not fit he gets into a tizzy. My friend says he looks upon me as the next best thing to Mother, but I never feel I can live up to it.'

It's a rich hour with a unique source. My fear had been that Patsy A, who seemed initially quite managing, might take charge of the interview. In fact she sits quietly in the corner, and only prompts Eleanor with the occasional name. I realise that she's appointed herself as unofficial chaperone to her friend, which is fair enough. She and I go for a pub lunch, where she fills me in on the chaotic Ainley family history. I take to her, but my hopes of an interview recede as we are joined by two of her relatives, and we get slightly tight on Special Brew. But then out of the blue she hands me a unique document: the diary of her weeks in the USA with Gielgud on the *Ages of Man* tour. This is a real excitement. We agree to meet again after I've read it.

Thursday 15 January
Back to the Art Workers' Guild in Bloomsbury, for a session on 'Fifty Years of British Theatre Criticism'. It's under the watchful eyes of portraits of the guild's founders: William Morris, Walter Crane, etc. For artists they look curiously respectable.

Ian Herbert, who edits the magazine *British Theatre Record*, is sharp and witty, and steeped in theatre. He takes a stimulating gallop through the Agate/Darlington and Tynan/Hobson eras. In passing he refers to the species *Criticus Rotundus Oxoniensis*. Am I the only one to steal a glance at the girth of tonight's chairman, Michael Billington? I enjoy Herbert's side-swipe at Morley: 'At least once a year Sheridan nominates a musical as the musical of the decade.' Billington is good on the pressures on today's critics. He says arts editors tend to be more interested in restaurants and money than in theatre. Then there's the proprietors: last week David Montgomery, owner of the *Independent on Sunday*, suggested theatre could be covered by a general reporter. My God!

Friday 16 January
A visit to Chiswick to see Ann Playfair, daughter-in-law of Nigel Playfair, who started the Lyric Hammersmith, and gave Gielgud his break while he was still at RADA. An American, once an actress herself, she has the programme for one of Gielgud's first amateur performances, and a couple of his letters to Playfair's wife. One, written on Playfair's death, is wonderfully eloquent; the other includes a plea in 1940 for her to allow him to stage *The Beggar's Opera*. More gold dust. I'm able to sit and skim through the family copy of her husband Giles Playfair's book *My Father's Son*, which has some useful material. She also lets me copy an unpublished

essay of his, on the theatre of his youth. I marvel again at the helpfulness of so many of the people I approach.

Monday 19 January

Back to Nancy Nevinson's house. As promised I sort out her theatrical papers. This time she has her 1945 diary of the India and Far East tour ready, and reads extracts into my tape recorder. Nothing sensational, but some invaluable authentic background stuff, and a few entries that reflect vividly a young actress' perception of Gielgud in his prime.

Wednesday 21 January

A further session with Margaret Harris of Motley. She seems younger than when I saw her eight months ago. This time I supply the vodka, and we work through a list of designers, about whom she's kindly agreed to enlighten me. We also cover the Gielgud/Motley productions which, in my then ignorance (and first interview), I had omitted to ask her about. What an excellent source of information (and gossip) she is.

Thursday 22 January

Another bolt from the blue. Last week I wrote to the headmaster of Westminster School, asking if they had any relevant material in their records of their former pupil, and if so whether I might have access to it. This morning I received an astonishing reply from the head's secretary.

'I wrote immediately to Sir John requesting his authorisation for providing the information. Sir John rang me in some distress this morning to tell me that he has *not* authorised such a biography, and that he does not wish us to give you any of the information you request. He tells me further that Mr Sheridan Morley has been under contract for the past two years to write an authorised biography of him; Sir John will be most grateful if you will refrain from contacting any more of his friends about your proposed book, which does not in any way have his blessing.'

I am devastated, and appalled. How can he tell such a flagrant lie? Who will talk to me now? Is this the end of the road? After the first shock I try to think rationally about possible explanations:

1. A genuine loss of memory, confirming the drift of the Attenborough letter.

2. The hidden hand of Morley, or his agent, or his publisher, or all three.

3. A sudden impulse, prompted by a stream of people asking him if it's OK to talk to me.

4. A combination of 2 and 3.

I need to think long and hard about my next move. My gut instinct is not to give up after getting this far. I'll sleep on it – if I can.

Friday 23 January

I decide to write to Gielgud and remind him gently but firmly of our agreement. I talk to Michael Earley, who sympathises, and agrees. He suggests some useful amendments to my draft letter. In great trepidation I send it.

'Dear Sir John,

You may recall that just over a year ago you very kindly gave me permission to put together an account of your life in the theatre, and to talk to colleagues and friends in the profession who have worked with you over the years. Since then I have been working on the book virtually full time, and have received a wonderfully warm and positive response to my requests for help. However, I gather from a letter I received this week from Westminster School that you may have forgotten about your agreement to my proposal. I thought it might be helpful therefore if I enclosed copies of our correspondence.

Of course I fully understand that this is not the official biography, which is being written by Sheridan Morley. But I'm sure you will appreciate that, having got halfway through my proposed interview schedule (covering roughly the years 1930-1955), I would be very keen to complete the book with your continuing approval. This would, I hope, enable me to fulfil one of my fundamental aims, which is to do justice to the richness of your theatrical career.

Yours sincerely,
Jonathan Croall'

I found it hard to be polite writing this letter. I'm determined to carry on, but am furious that I will probably never get to key witnesses such as Guinness and Irene Worth. My fear is that, now Gielgud has 'forgotten' he gave the book his blessing, he may withdraw his permission to use his copyright material. That would kill the book stone dead. I feel extremely bitter towards him, which is not going to help at all. All my enthusiasm for going on with the book has evaporated.

Wednesday 28 January

My worst fears are confirmed by Gielgud's reply.

'Dear Mr Croall

I must thank you for your last courteous letter and for sending me the copies of our correspondence last year. I do feel guilty of encouraging your efforts to undertake the book. Knowing of several mentions of the Morley 'authoritative' [sic] biography I had hoped you would not embark on your own project, and was dismayed to gather from various friends of mine from whom you had requested interviews and reminiscences that you had begun the work already. I am afraid I cannot offer my definite consent, and I do sincerely apologise for wasting your valuable time. I really do feel that quite enough has been written and published about my life by now.

Most sincerely yours,
John Gielgud'

What an astonishing letter! Has he lost all touch with reality? Oh sorry, when you said go ahead, I assumed you meant it. How stupid of me. No of course I don't mind wasting a year of my life, just as I'm sure you wouldn't mind rehearsing *King Lear* for a year, only to be told that the production is off. I'm very angry, and fax the letter to Michael, who is helpfully calm. He says he's just had an angry call from Morley's agent, complaining that I'm posing as The Official Biographer. For God's sake!

We agree that Gielgud's letter is best left unanswered, and that meanwhile I should soldier on. Michael suggests I should now describe the book as 'a study of JG's acting career' when approaching people. I'm not happy about this, but agree to avoid the obviously provocative word 'biography' where possible. As it happens, he's seeing Morley on Friday: perhaps after all there are advantages in sharing the same publisher. We'll see what happens.

January Progress Report
In the light of Gielgud's letter I've decided to start writing sooner than planned, and to lie low on the interviewing front for a while. In some ways this setback might just be a blessing in disguise: with only 15 months to the delivery date, and not a word written, it's probably time to stop enjoying myself and get down to the more difficult task of writing. Perhaps also my attitude to my subject needed toughening up. It certainly has been now.

(Other) Disappointments: A polite letter from Paul Daneman, who says he can't

help because Gielgud has sanctioned Morley. The shape of things to come, I suspect. I also fear that the Westminster letter means I can't now follow-up the one I sent to RADA only days before, requesting similar information.

Hopes: Cordelia Monsey, Yvonne Mitchell's daughter, has agreed to see me. So has John Schlesinger. Excellent; I need more directors.

Wednesday 4 February
I finally read Garry O'Connor's now infamous life of Peggy Ashcroft, *The Secret Woman*, in which he trawls pruriently through her private life. The sexual shenanigans aside, it's full of cod psychology, especially about her dependence on her father; spurious speculation about her thoughts ('Probably she cast her mind back' etc); and irrelevant quotations designed to show the width of the author's learning. It's also disappointingly skimpy on her childhood. In places it's ungrammatical, rambling, and dotted with non-sequiturs. It beats me how it got past any half-decent editor at Weidenfeld.

It's also full of cheap comments: he seems only marginally interested in her theatrical work compared with her private life. The unattributed quotes are irritating, as is the absence of source details. Given Peggy Ashcroft's passion for cricket, he commits the ultimate sin, referring to Len Hutton's England opening partner as Chris rather than Cyril Washbrook. Such a man is not to be trusted.

Friday 6 February
This week's surprise, revealed in a 1980 interview: Gielgud once went to a Rolling Stones concert. 'Ian Richardson took me; he was a great friend of Mick Jagger. It was deafening. The Stones are half my age, but I'm sure they'll go deaf before long.'

Monday 16 February
Two more actor memoirs plundered, one fruitful, one not. Jack Hawkins' *Anything for a Quiet Life* proves very disappointing. Trivial and tedious, it only comes alive, ironically, as he faces death from throat cancer. Considering how often he worked with Gielgud in the 1930s, it's astonishing that he says nothing significant about him, either as an actor or a director.

Anthony Quayle's *A Time to Speak* is altogether different. I began reading it as a duty, but it quickly became a pleasure. It's beautifully written, one of the most sensitive evocations of childhood I've ever read. He conveys graphically his life as an apprentice actor, there's an astute analysis of Gielgud's art, and he provides other invaluable material. His account of his years running Stratford, written when he knew he had only months to live, is especially rich.

Wednesday 18 February
Tony Lacey rings to tell me Alec Guinness would rather be sent a list of questions than meet face to face. This is disappointing news, but at least it seems he's not been nobbled by Gielgud or Morley. Apparently he was recently confused by a letter from Morley's researcher, requesting an interview about Gielgud, to be done by the researcher rather than Morley himself. Understandably, Guinness found this extraordinarily offensive. What a gaffe.

Monday 23 February
I'm trying to begin writing, but can't decide where to start. I don't feel I have enough on Gielgud's early years to begin at the beginning. I'm tempted to begin with the Oxford Playhouse period 1924/25, when his career really started. I decide to prevaricate a little longer.

I've been skimming through Roland Culver's unbelievably dire autobiography, hoping for useful observations on *Five Finger Exercise* (1958) and *Ivanov* (1965). Not a bit of it. Banal, trivial, misspelt, a catalogue of seductions, gambling sessions and days at the races, it's written in the most dreadful nudge-nudge, wink-wink style. It could almost be a clever pastiche of the theatrical memoir. The author was clearly a self-obsessed ass: I can quite understand why his father threw him out of the family home. There are useful titbits on RADA in the 1920s (he was there just after Gielgud), but nothing else.

Wednesday 25 February
Eight months after my first contact with him I finally get to talk to Alec Guinness, though sadly only on the phone. Nevertheless it's well worth the wait. My questions prompt a good mixture of opinion, anecdote, and memories of specific performances, all given in that careful, measured voice.

On Gielgud in the 1930s: 'He was the light of the theatre then. To be in a production by him was the cat's whiskers. Everything he touched seemed to have a freshness to it.'

On acting with Gielgud: 'When I was young it was difficult doing a scene with him, because he knew the plays so well, and couldn't resist saying your lines at the same time as you did. He seemed to be worrying more about your performance than his own.'

On the Gielgud voice: 'It was a beautiful instrument, but I'm afraid there were times when he was listening to himself, and being moved by the beauty, when really he should have disguised that.'

On being directed by Gielgud: 'He was very precise about language, and could reduce you to tears of despair, sometimes spending a whole morning on one speech. Although he could be appreciative, he could also be unintentionally cruel, and damage you for years with things you can't quite forget. It took me a long time to throw off the self-consciousness he instilled in me.'

On Gielgud the film actor: 'At first he was just glamorous, but later he became a frightfully good one. His confidence has grown, and in the last twenty years he's given some gloriously witty performances.'

Finally I ask tentatively if his wife Merula Salaman, who also worked with Gielgud, might be willing to answer a few questions. 'Oh no,' he says firmly. But then he adds a couple of stories about Gielgud which she had passed on to him.

Thursday 26 February

A heavy cold, but I struggle down to the Epsom Playhouse for another small-scale theatre evening, to see Nancy Nevinson doing her one-woman show on theatre history, centring on Edith Evans (Nancy was Charmiane to her Cleopatra in a 1946 production of the Shakespeare play). There's only a couple of dozen elderly folk in the tiny studio space. It's a touching show, a mixture of gentle reminiscence and re-creation of speeches from Edith Evans' major parts, done very effectively by Nancy. Can she really be 80? Clifford Allen does the necessary male parts, including a poor impersonation of Gielgud in *The Lady with the Lamp* (1929).

There's a reference in her show to the day when Gielgud sought Edith Evans' advice about whether he should accept an offer from the Old Vic. I suddenly realise this is the moment, a turning point in his career, where I could start writing some chapters, since I have a wealth of material on his two seasons on the Waterloo Road.

February Progress Report

Guinness is finally in the bag, but after Gielgud's letter I've resisted sending out any new requests for interviews. Instead I've done plenty of reading, though the books have not yielded as much as previous ones. I have also buried myself again in the fabulous Mander and Mitchenson collection, working doggedly through the boxes and trying desperately to forget the project is in jeopardy. At least, having agonised for a month, I've decided on my starting-point.

Disappointments: Silence from Edward Craig (son of), Eileen Herlie, Joan

Littlewood, Anthony Quinn, David Lynch. Also from John Neville who, I've discovered since I wrote to him, hates being compared to Gielgud. In my ignorance I had asked him what influence Gielgud had on his work, so that's that one scuppered.

Hopes: A note from Pauline Rumbold, daughter of Hermione Baddeley, who's sent my request for information from the Baddeley family on to George Byam Shaw, the son of Angela Baddeley and Glen Byam Shaw. He could be a rare if second-hand source for the 1930s.

Thursday 5 March
I've just finished James Forsyth's biography of Tyrone Guthrie. It's profoundly irritating, written with an awful fey archness. As official biographer he had unique access to Guthrie's papers. Result: everything is seen from his subject's perspective, with few comments of worth from others. What a waste, with such a fine subject. But the book has fragments of useful theatrical background, and material about his dealings with Gielgud's family. Guthrie's drive and energy emerge, but mainly from the extracts from his own book *A Life in the Theatre*, which I now put to the top of my reading list.

Wednesday 11 March
After several attempts I finally get to talk properly on the phone to Alicia Markova. I'm getting used to these evasive octogenarians, invariably away lecturing, teaching, running seminars, as she still amazingly does at 87. She says she was Gielgud's 'greatest fan' in his Old Vic days, and that his 1935 production of *Romeo and Juliet*, which she saw many times, inspired her when she later came to dance Juliet. She tells me that he sent her a beautiful bunch of flowers for her eightieth birthday, and that I should come and see her in May. Here's hoping.

Friday 13 March
I rang James Forsyth about some material he'd promised to send to me, notably a letter Gielgud wrote to Guthrie about Alec Guinness' Hamlet. He says he's now writing his autobiography, so will look it out. (Why do I think this will never happen?) He recalls a message he got from Gielgud via Guinness on the day war broke out: 'Tell Forsyth to take to the hills!'

Monday 16 March
I begin my research into Gielgud's film career, which I have deliberately ignored

up to now. First up is *The Prime Minister* (1941). Only his fourth film if you exclude his silent ones, which I don't imagine I'll find, even if they still exist. As Disraeli he gives an awkward, often embarrassing performance, with a lot of grimaces and lip-pursing. It's good to see the lovely Diana Wynyard for the first time: she seems much more at ease on film than he does. Fay Compton plays Queen Victoria like a suburban matron. A cutting tells me there were problems over the title. At one stage it was *An Empire Was Built*; Gielgud wittily suggested *The Cabinet of Dr Disraeli*.

I see the film courtesy of friend, neighbour and film buff David Gillespie, a man who lives and breathes cinema. He's also got a copy of *Sebastian* (1968), which he offers to put on to video for me, and Tony Palmer's epic *Wagner* (1983), in which Gielgud, Olivier and Richardson are on screen for the only time together. It's six hours long, so I think I may pass on that one.

Wednesday 18 March
I finally start writing. It's a terrifying moment, facing this 100,000 word mountain. My aim is to get down a minimum of five hundred words a day, but aim for a thousand. I'm definitely starting with his first Old Vic season in 1929. I reel slightly at the thought that this was nearly seventy years ago, and that he's still here, pottering around just fifty miles away, but quite out of my reach. It's an absurd, surreal situation.

Tuesday 24 March
So far the writing is coming surprisingly easily. It helps that length is not yet a consideration. I'm already settling into a rhythm: in the morning an hour or two assembling and reading the source material, then scribbling thoughts, phrases, quotes, headings etc, with maximum ease for crossing through, chucking out, etc. In the afternoon I convert it into rough prose on the word processor, and gradually the sequence begins to become clear. I can see the main challenge will be to avoid merely hopping from production to production.

Wednesday 25 March
I've reached his first major success at the Old Vic, in *Richard II*, and realise I've never seen or read the play. I repair the omission immediately, and am surprised to find it quite poor: disjointed, very little characterisation, much too much time spent on political rivalries. I don't think it would get more than three nights at the Battersea Arts Centre if Shakespeare submitted it today. On the other hand there's the poetry, half a dozen wonderful speeches for Richard, which even as I read I

hear being spoken in Gielgud's voice, as in the recording of his *Ages of Man* recital.

Thursday 26 March
Lunch at her home in Holloway with Cordelia Monsey, theatre director (she's been assisting Peter Hall with his Piccadilly season), and daughter of Yvonne Mitchell and critic Derek Monsey. I read her mother's book *Actress* last night: an autobiography disguised as career guide, it's intelligently written, informative, and has several useful glimpses of Gielgud.

Cordelia was a child when her mother was acting with Gielgud in *Ivanov* (1965). 'He was the most chivalrous and generous person,' she recalls. 'I would frequently knock on his dressing-room door and ask him to sign my programme, and he would always do it with great charm. He was never too busy, and never gave me the brush-off.' She shows me the inscription he wrote in her copy of his book *Shakespeare - Hit or Miss?* 'Dear Cordelia, So many happy memories of you and Yvonne. *Les années passent si vite, si vite.* All my love, John.'

She has some shrewd thoughts about the nature of his talent. 'He was always the character on stage that you fell in love with. You felt you understood his pain, and that's what audiences loved. It was an extraordinary achievement for the least chameleon of all actors. But maybe that's the thing, you always see John Gielgud, his vulnerability and fragility and spirit.'

Friday 27 March
I declare *The Unsinkable Hermoine Baddeley* joint winner with Roland Culver's autobiography for Worst Theatrical Memoir of the Twentieth Century. Self-obsessed, her mind stuffed with trivia and snobbery, she manages to make herself seriously unlikeable. Her sister Angela, a stalwart of Gielgud's 1930s companies, seems by contrast very appealing and genuine.

Monday 30 March
One of the delights of doing this work is the need to read plays I've not seen or read. Today it was Molière's *Le Malade Imaginaire*, Gielgud's first non-Shakespearean part at the Old Vic. I remember being bored stiff when I read it at university; now it strikes me as a wonderfully vicious satire on the medical profession. I must have matured a little.

March Progress Report
The writing is well launched, though I'm overwhelmed with the mass of detail I have on Gielgud's two Old Vic seasons. I shall have to cut severely on the second

draft, but better to pack it all in now, and select later. I realise there's too much of the Vic's director Harcourt Williams, who had such a strong influence on Gielgud. The problem is, his book *Four Years at the Vic* is such a brilliant source, almost a blow-by-blow account of the season.

Hopes: Peter Shaffer has agreed to meet me. I've had a postcard from Elaine Stritch from a New York hotel (does she live there?), inviting me to get in touch 'nearer the deadline'. Odd request, but I'll do so; I'd welcome her thoughts on *Providence* (1977), in which she featured.

Disappointments: More than usual. No response from Richard Bebb or Jason Robards. Silence too from Brian Bedford, Ariel to Gielgud's third Prospero, and apparently much under his spell offstage as well as on. Anna Ford says she has no documents relating to her mother Jean Winstanley, who was in his 1934 *Hamlet*. I find that Daniel Massey has died: obviously he was already ill when I wrote to him. Sadly and surprisingly, George Byam Shaw says he has nothing that would be relevant.

Wednesday 1 April
I've just read *Androcles and the Lion* for the first time, avoiding Shaw's preface, which is three times as long as the play. He has some good fun at the expense of religion and other idolatries. It's easy to imagine Gielgud enjoying the silliness of the part of the Emperor. It's certainly useful to have the text fresh in your mind as you write about it.

Friday 3 April
To Patsy Ainley's house, set in a beautiful Gloucestershire valley. I'm returning her diary of the *Ages of Man* tour, which has been invaluable, and am hoping this time to pin her down to an interview. She tells me she was due to have lunch with Gielgud yesterday, but had to postpone it because Eleanor was unwell. If she knows about my recent troubles with him, she's not letting on, and I'm certainly not going to mention it..

She's about to move house after forty years here, and we sit amid piles of books, and walls denuded of pictures. One item in the upheavals proves a jewel. 'I came across these, they might be of use,' she says casually, handing me a big packet. It's a host of letters from her and Gielgud to Eleanor, from the same American tour as the diary. I try not to look too thrilled. I finally get her to my tape recorder, and we fill in some gaps in the American adventure. 'He was a wonderful person to be with, a very good friend, very loyal,' she remembers. 'He never stopped talking; I didn't have to say much.'

We touch briefly on her father, Henry Ainley: 'He was tall and square so they thought he ought to declaim and be tragic, but he was really a very good comedian.' And then on Olivier: 'Dead common, but I suppose we're not allowed to say that nowadays.' She also reflects on Gielgud's friends: 'A lot of them are difficult, and not entirely good for him. But it's his life, so you leave it be, don't you think?'

Saturday 4 April

I catch a lively production of *Tartuffe*, a Molière play I don't know, at the Theatre Royal in Bath. It's an excellent translation by Christopher Hampton, but the production is spoilt by a great deal of 'look-at-me' comic business by Stephen Tompkinson as Tartuffe. It's hard to imagine Gielgud as Orgon: playing such a stupid character was just not part of his armoury.

Sunday 5 April

Michael Billington's biography of Peggy Ashcroft is a welcome contrast to Garry O'Connor's: he concentrates on her work without neglecting the personal side, combining readability with responsibility. I'm sure he had access to similar material to O'Connor, but he's been discreet with it, even after her death. It has excellent material on the productions she and Gielgud starred in together during the 1930s.

Monday 6 April

A day digging around the Bristol University drama department's theatre collection. It has a wonderful library, with several books I've been searching for, so the photocopy machine works overtime. But its Old Vic archive is disappointing: there are virtually no photos or reviews until the mid-1930s. There are a few valuable back numbers of the *Vic-Wells Magazine*, one of which has what may be Gielgud's first effort in print, a piece on 'Tradition in Shakespeare' (he's all for breaking it). The helpful archivist Sarah Morris asks if I would like to see the Gielgud scrapbook. The what? This turns out to be stuffed with Gielgud cuttings, seemingly a fan's lifetime collection. But with so many interviews and articles and reviews already in the bag, I'm not sure without my notes which of them are new to me. I obviously need to make a second visit.

Tuesday 7 April

I'm nearly through James Harding's biography of James Agate, which is even better than his life of Gerald du Maurier. He really is a star biographer: sympathetic, widely read, witty, yet he wears his learning lightly. Of course Agate is a gift: a total maverick, outrageously larger than life, who wrote millions of words about the theatre, most of them entertaining. His private life seems shocking, even in 1998.

Wednesday 8 April

I talked briefly on the phone earlier in the week to Peter Shaffer, who's here for rehearsals of *Black Comedy*. I've never seen it, and feel I should do so before we meet. I caught it yesterday in Richmond, and fell about laughing: an ingenious plot, exquisite timing by the actors, a farce in which you somehow care about the characters. It's brilliant stuff. The other half of the bill, *The Real Inspector Hound*, is amusing but seems lacklustre in comparison, though Stoppard has a wonderful sharp eye for a critic's cliché.

Thursday 9 April

I catch the film of *The Winslow Boy* on television. Rattigan wrote the part of the barrister Sir Robert Morton for Gielgud. Odd that he turned it down: maybe he felt it was not a large enough part? Robert Donat is very fine in the role, but I could imagine Gielgud capturing the essence of this haughty, clever man.

Monday 13 April

I watched a very poor documentary on Noël Coward, spread, amazingly, over three nights. It centres around three biographers talking over a meal in the Ivy. Morley is there, looking overfed; Philip Hoare, whom I thought pretentious; and John Lahr, the only one to say anything original. Much of the film consists of aerial shots of Coward's various houses, and Hoare taking a bus along the route Coward took in his youth. It's fatuous stuff. Its value to me is Gielgud talking about and reading from Coward's play *The Vortex*, in which he understudied Coward in the 1920s. He seems frail while reminiscing about the production, but as he reads a scene from the play the energy suddenly flows back, and he becomes young Nicky Lancaster once more. I find it very moving.

Thursday 16 April

Diana Devlin comes to lunch in Barnes, to collect her father William's scrapbook that she lent to me. Having written her grandfather Lewis Casson's life, she's very helpful on the matter of the influence on both him and Gielgud of William Poel and Granville Barker. She has a revealing anecdote via Sybil about Malcolm Sargent's response to Gielgud's arrest. And a charming one from Lewis' memorial service, when Gielgud recalled watching the Sputnik on television with the couple, and Sybil saying, 'Oh if only we could be the first actors on the moon!'

Friday 24 April
Coffee and recollections with Bill Gaskill, late of the Royal Court, in his Kentish Town flat. I'd expected from his reputation someone fierce and abrasive; instead he was friendly and thoughtful. Though he never directed Gielgud, he was running the Court with Lindsay Anderson when the famous partnership of Gielgud and Richardson appeared together in David Storey's play *Home* (1970). He remembers that as 'a beautiful piece of work played by class artists. The idea of two great actors being in such close harmony was very rare.'

He has long been an admirer of Gielgud, and is eloquent on his art. 'John is a very intuitive actor, not at all a technician like Larry was. He's much more of an artist, he does it on the feeling of it. In his lyricism and rhetoric he's unparalleled, and I don't think he'll ever be matched. His greatness for me is his amazing feeling for the writing, which has dominated my ear for as long as I can remember. I've never seen a Hamlet I've liked better than his last one.' He's clear about the difference between Gielgud and Olivier, who recruited him to help launch the National. 'Larry was so ungenerous, you never heard him speak well of other actors, he was not interested in them. He was a very closed man. John was the opposite, surrounding himself with all those people, who became part of his world, then went off and made their own theatres. If he hadn't brought in Michel Saint-Denis, who was such a big influence on George Devine, I think the Court may never have happened. I don't think he was conscious of a mission, he just chose interesting actors and directors, and that fed into the theatre as a whole.'

He muses on why Gielgud could relate to *Home*, but not to Edward Bond's *Bingo*. 'John had no idea how to do, for example, Dostoyevsky's Inquisitor; he's not made for that kind of hardness and irony. Whereas he could relate to David Storey, who in a funny way has quite a sentimental side. An actor has to make contact, and there's something rather hard about Edward.'

Sunday 27 April
I talk on the phone to Pauline Rumbold, daughter of Hermoine Baddeley. She reveals that the oldest Baddeley sister is still alive aged 97, in a nursing home. Tantalisingly, it's round the corner from my house in Barnes. Is it worth a visit? Probably not.

Monday 28 April

To Kensington for one of my best interviews yet, with actor, director and playwright Jerome Kilty, whose hit play *Dear Liar* was based on the letters of Shaw and Mrs Patrick Campbell. A shrewd, humorous man, with a wry take on the foibles of theatre people, he's thoughtfully photocopied his correspondence with Gielgud while they worked on *The Ides of March* (1963), his play about the last days of Caesar, which they co-directed. Even at first glance I can see these letters will enable me to document Gielgud's volatile emotional state during this disastrous production.

Kilty remembers an incident after the first night in Brighton. 'We knew Larry was in the audience, and John had gone to his dressing-room to wait for him to come round. Larry arrived, saw me on the stage, and we talked about the play for some ten minutes. John finally appeared in the wings, obviously seething. "Larry! What did you think of it? Tell me!" He sulked for a long time about that. I think Larry did it on purpose. '

He reflects on how hard it was as an actor to avoid Gielgud's influence. 'I remember seeing him in *The Circle* during the war, and playing the same part straight afterwards. All I could do was play Gielgud. It was the same whenever I acted in Congreve or Wycherley. But who *didn't* imitate him in those days? He had such a wonderful sense of style, he was born to act in those plays.' He talks of Gielgud's impetuosity, and recalls how he came to choose the designer for *The Ides of March*. 'He was passing Tiffany's window in New York, and saw some stage settings in which the jewels were displayed. He went in and said, "Who did those sets? I must have him for my play." So that's how Charles Gene Moore arrived. John never asked me about it; but in fact there was no problem.'

He saw many of Gielgud's productions in America, including his celebrated *Much Ado about Nothing* (1959). 'His Benedick was perfect, such splendid disdain.' The company included the magnificently unpredictable Irish actor Micheál MacLiammóir, playing Don Pedro. 'I was in the wings one night, and John was saying very loudly: "What's he doing? I want it to be like silk. He's ruining it! He's killing it!"'

April Progress Report

April is a good month, with plenty of solid reading, and very fruitful sessions with Gaskill, Devlin and Kilty. Patsy Ainley's material on the American *Ages of Man* tour is manna from heaven.

Hopes: Film director Fred Schepisi (*Plenty*, 1985) has agreed to talk to me on the phone from America.

Disappointments: No response from Glynis Johns, John Frankenheimer, Sidney Lumet.

Thursday 6 May

To the Royal Geographical Society, to hear writers Claire Tomalin and Victoria Glendinning talk about 'The Art of Biography'. Both are very stimulating, giving me plenty of ideas to chew over.

I like Victoria G's description of nineteenth-century biographies as 'extended tombstones', and her definition of the biographer's work as 'like trying to get hold of an ocean in a teaspoon'. She thinks you need to research the context first, so you know how the subject fits in with or differs from it. I decide this is my excuse for my sloth in starting to write. I'm also encouraged by her criticism of writers obsessed with their subject's sex lives (as I intend not to be). She recalls reading a biography of Osbert Sitwell. 'Not until you reach page 103 do you gather he's homosexual. That's smart.' She dislikes having to kill off her subjects, and confesses she wanted to end her Trollope book before he died, while he was old but happy. On her latest subject, Jonathan Swift, she says: 'I've never been intimate with such a screwed-up man.'

Claire Tomalin likens the biographer's task to having a long piece of string in your hand: you never see the end of it. She's interesting on the difference between French and English sources for biographers. In England, she says, everyone has material in boxes in their attics; in France it's all in archives. (I prefer the attics myself; it means less red tape.) She talks of the difficulty of being critical of someone whom you admire. 'In researching Katherine Mansfield's life I discovered that she habitually told lies. I just had to take a deep breath and say it, but I wondered if I wasn't presenting her too unsympathetically.' She says she would never write about a living or recently dead person. Six months ago I would have wondered what the problem was. Now I know all too well, and agree with her totally.

Friday 8 May

To the National Film Theatre with forebodings, to see Jane Campion's version of *The Portrait of a Lady* (1996). Alas, poor Henry; forebodings correct. The film is pretentious, phoney, and dull. Cast as Mr Touchett, Gielgud plays a couple of gentle scenes in a wheelchair, during which he smokes a cigarette, we get close-ups of his nose and forehead, he yawns, and expires. Even in this brief scene, with minimal dialogue, he avoids the self-consciousness of the other actors. I've never seen him die on screen before, and it's a strange feeling. I wonder how he feels, rehearsing for The Last Moment.

Monday 11 May

I've been enjoying Fabia Drake's autobiography *Blind Fortune*. Her forceful, spirited personality comes through clearly, as does her passion for the stage, especially Shakespeare. There's useful material for me on Marie Tempest, with whom Gielgud appeared in *Dear Octopus* (1938), and on Komisarjevsky. She claims to have been 'in love with' Gielgud in the late 1920s. I'm not sure if I believe her account of a half-swallowed kiss in a taxi.

Tuesday 12 May

Another good day at the Mander and Mitchenson collection. Among a great mound of material I unearth an interview Gielgud gave while making *The Whistle Blower* (1986), in which he stars with Michael Caine. 'I first met him when I had no trousers on,' he explains. 'I was at Doug Hayward's, the tailor, trying on some clothes. Michael didn't seem to mind.'

Thursday 14 May

I've been reading *The Lost Summer*, a curious but absorbing book by Charles Duff, part history of West End theatre in its heyday, part biography of Frith Banbury. It cleverly mixes serious analysis of Ackland, Rattigan, Whiting etc, with good gossip on the Tennent days, and on what Tynan called 'hostess acting'. He quotes Gielgud as saying there was poor attendance at the first night of his 1935 production of *The Old Ladies*, because 'either there was fog or the king died'. Good excuses, neither of them true.

Monday 19 May

A brief second meeting with Jerome Kilty, to return a picture he lent me, and pick his brains about a few American actresses both he and Gielgud worked with. He's had tea with Frith Banbury since our first meeting, and the subject of the Morley biography comes up. He asks me whether I think a biography can be truthful while the subject is alive. There seems to be an implication that he hopes mine will be published after Gielgud's death, but he doesn't press me on the point. I sense he's slightly concerned at having told me of Gielgud's prevarications over *The Ides of March*. He talks amusingly about Gore Vidal taking over from his biographer, declaring: 'I'll tell my own lies'.

Later, in preparation for meeting playwright Charles Wood, I watch *The Charge of the Light Brigade* (1968), for which he wrote the screenplay. Gielgud is delicious as the semi-detached Lord Raglan, somehow making him dotty without caricaturing the part. I also read Wood's play *Veterans* (1972), in which the main character is a wickedly accurate and affectionately humorous portrait of Gielgud himself. Reading of the hostility that greeted the swear words, it seems weird to me that it shocked audiences back then, at least in the provinces. Attitudes to strong language have certainly changed dramatically.

Wednesday 20 May
A superbly fruitful day, beginning with a stimulating interview with Charles Wood in the garden of his Oxfordshire home near Banbury. He's very acute on Gielgud's theatrical intelligence: 'He reacts to rhythms and emotions he gets from other actors as if he's an instrument. His brain is the most important part, which is not always so with actors. There isn't anything you can't ask him to do.'

He offers some delightful memories of Gielgud on the set of *The Charge of the Light Brigade*, filmed in excessive heat in Turkey. 'He got hot with the rest of us, but nothing seemed to bother him. Trevor Howard kept himself to himself, but John was always around, immaculate and considerate whatever the situation. He was marvellous with the children, always asking about their tummy upsets.' I get a rare glimpse of Gielgud's relationship with his partner Martin Hensler. 'John was invited to do *Ages of Man* in Ankara. Martin was fed up with the recital, and didn't want him to do it. But he said he had to, there were so many people there who wanted to hear it. So he did. Martin was so cross he took to his bed for a week.'

We talk of *Veterans*, on which he says the character played by John Mills was *not* as everyone assumed based on Trevor Howard, even though he co-starred in the *Light Brigade* film with Gielgud. But he won't tell me who the model was. He's sure the play will never be done again, because Gielgud is too heavily engrained in the character. 'People have often wanted to do it, we've even had a theatre ready and the money, but we can't get an actor for it.' He was horrified at a suggestion that Robert Morley should play the part. They had lunch together, Morley asked him to read it out loud, then after five minutes fell asleep.

Pursuing my inquiries on Gielgud's seasons at the Oxford Playhouse, on a trip to the city I call in at the Oxford County Archive (total blank), and the Playhouse itself (some useful fragments). Then on to see Don Chapman, former theatre critic of the *Oxford Mail*, who's compiling a history of the Playhouse. I'm staggered to find he's photocopied 60 pages of his book, covering Gielgud's four seasons at the Playhouse, and is happy for me to draw on them. A further surprise: during his researches he tracked down JB Fagan's daughter Gemma. So I've found her at last. But will she help?

Thursday 21 May

To his penthouse flat in Kensington to meet director John Schlesinger. Small, nut-brown, dressed unexpectedly in shorts, quietly spoken, he talks about directing Gielgud in the National's *Julius Caesar* (1977). 'Working with him was wonderful, I loved his grandeur, the way he played seemingly without effort. But the cast was an inexperienced one, and a lot of the performances were not good. The critics lambasted it, and it put me off for life doing Shakespeare, I felt I had failed. John was totally loyal to the production, and very supportive, he never expressed an opinion about the other actors.'

He picks out a quality in Gielgud's acting that he first noticed in *The Lady's Not for Burning* (1949). 'His stillness was remarkable, he was a wonderful reactor to others. You watched him even when he was still, he just commanded your attention.' Talking of Gielgud's willingness to try out any idea, he recalls the contrast with Olivier, whom he directed in the film *Marathon Man*. 'Dustin Hoffman was always wanting to improvise, while Olivier was saying, "I find it hard enough to learn the text. Can we just stick to the words?" It was a tricky umpiring match.'

I ask him if he's only interested now in doing films. 'I'd do theatre any time if I liked the play. But I think there's a black mark against me at the National. Maybe they think I'm a bit of a dilettante?'

Wednesday 27 May

Two interviews, both in Kent, both with former child actors in famous theatrical families, who met seventy years ago, and have not seen each other since. It's a strange life, the theatre.

I go down first to her house near Canterbury to talk to Mary Casson, daughter of Lewis Casson and Sybil Thorndike. As I sit down she says I look like my mother, whom she knew. The same is true of her in relation to Sybil. As we talk her voice and expressions are uncannily Sybiline: like her mother she's warm, bubbly and intelligent. She tells me JM Barrie himself picked her to play Wendy in *Peter Pan*, which she did for six years. I find it difficult to grasp that she acted with Gerald du Maurier, the original Hook and Mr Darling, who had a sudden urge late in his life to play the parts again. Her Peter then was Jean Forbes-Robertson, whose brilliant career was destroyed by drink. Mary remembers: 'She was a lovely, very mysterious actress, she only had to come on the stage and you felt the electricity.'

She recalls being in the first modern play Gielgud directed, Rodney Ackland's *Strange Orchestra* (1932). 'I was eighteen and such a fan of his, I was paralysed with fright for the first three days, but then I enjoyed it.' She knew Ackland slightly: 'An odd little man, with a funny squeaky voice, and terribly enthusiastic.' She herself gave up acting early, and became a musician. After an unexpected lunch invitation I persuade her to play a short piece on her virginal, which she does extremely beautifully.

Then it's on to Tunbridge Wells, and the newly discovered Gemma Fagan. It's forty years since our paths crossed in my youth. She reckons her father created a miracle at the small and dilapidated Oxford Playhouse, where Gielgud had his apprenticeship, and where her mother Mary Grey was the leading lady. 'He did everything himself: the lighting, the sets, the overseeing of the costume design. He liked to run the whole show. The theatre was rotten, which was very sad. But such conditions can bind you together. There was always a marvellous feeling of being a company there.' She herself joined it soon after Gielgud left, and played in *Dear Brutus* with Val Gielgud during his brief spell as an actor: 'He wasn't easy to know, he was rather reserved, always more interested in directing. But John was a natural Terry: we all thought he was wonderful at Oxford.'

She remembers Mrs Patrick Campbell, who was her godmother: 'A ghastly woman, she enveloped you! She asked me what I wanted for my birthday. I said "Paints", and she gave me an enormous set of professional oil paints.' She kindly lends me a copy of her father's play *The Wheel*, which gave Gielgud his first professional job, touring in 1922. She also promises to dig around for pictures of her father directing him in *The Cherry Orchard* in 1925. Over sherry she tells me the inside story of her parents' elopement, a famous scandal of the day, as they were both already married.

May Progress Report
A rich month indeed, after immensely helpful sessions with Schlesinger, Wood, Mary Casson and Gemma Fagan.

Reading: Fabia Drake's memoir entertaining. The Banbury/Duff volume offers useful, off-beat material. The Oxford Playhouse book by Don Chapman has given me some terrific background.

Disappointments: None, for once.

The Tomalin/Glendinning biography session has spurred me on: there's something very encouraging about hearing other biographers' problems. But I'm struggling with the sample material. I feel I'm not yet inside Gielgud's head. Maybe I'll only get there once I've gone back to the early years? Also, these are chapters with little of my own interview material in them. Perhaps I should have done the sample chapters on the 1960s, for which I have material galore? Too late now.

Health check: I hear from several people that Gielgud is still filming now and then, but only takes on work for one or two days. Apparently directors try to ensure that his scenes are done in one take. Gielgud to director Richard Lester: 'You have to remember if you cast me in a film I might drop dead in the middle of a scene.'

Monday 1 June
News on Gielgud's first four films from Kevin Brownlow. *Who is the Man?* (1924) is lost, so all I have to go on visually is a photo of Gielgud, playing a morphine addict, lying anxiously on a sofa, his head of hair still intact. There's also no sign of his first 'talkie', the colonial drama *Insult* (1933), so I'll have to make do with stills of him looking suave in Moorish dens.

Kevin doubts if Gielgud was actually in *Michael Strogoff* (1926). This is odd, as it's in Robert Tanitch's chronology, where Gielgud's early mentor Komisarjevsky is named as the director. Perhaps it never actually got made? However, Kevin has access to a copy of *The Clue of the New Pin*, which he describes as 'ghastly', but kindly agrees to screen for me. His interview with Gielgud is wonderfully rich, not just for Gielgud's comments on his own films, but his memories of his youthful film-going during the silent era. He free associates like mad, which was obviously difficult for Kevin ('Could we just go back for a moment...'), but is invaluable for me.

Friday 5 June
Coffee in her flat near Marble Arch with Margaretta Scott, once a leading actress and now 86. I had thought her a bit intimidating from her photos, but find her gracious and welcoming. Frustratingly, she remembers little about playing Ophelia to Gielgud's radio Hamlet in 1932. But she gives me useful snippets on contemporaries such as Marie Tempest, Robert Atkins and 'Harry' Ainley. She was clearly head over heels in love with Ainley: she calls him 'the pin-up boy of all time', and waxes lyrical about walking with him in Hyde Park and hearing his lines. We talk of his voice and, covering up my tape recorder for a moment, she whispers: 'It was even finer than John's!'

Saturday 6 June
In a second-hand bookshop I come across Ned Sherrin's diary for 1995. In it he reports a conversation with Morley, who tells him Gielgud keeps ringing him

up to ask him how he's getting on. Morley claims he's only got to age 21, but Sherrin thinks he's actually finished. An alarming thought if true, that for the last three years he's possibly been poised and ready to publish whenever the bell tolls for Gielgud.

Latest health news, from an actor who saw him at the Garrick on Christopher Fry's ninetieth birthday, is that he's frail, a little stooped, and wears a hearing aid. I send a silent message to his agent to find him plenty of work.

Monday 8 June
After months of pursuit I run Peter Ustinov to ground, in a smart Knightsbridge hotel. We spend the first minute or two crawling around on hands and knees looking for the mislaid remote-control device to switch the television off, so that breaks the ice nicely. He's smaller and rounder than I expected, but also more genial. From the start my role is more audience than interviewer. He quickly switches into performance mode, and I get a reduced version of his one-man show, covering directing at the Bolshoi, playing King Lear, the Crimean War, acting in *Spartacus* with Olivier – oh, and some memories of Gielgud.

He has a wonderful way with language, his mimicry is brilliant, and it's difficult to keep the questions coming while I'm doubled up with laughter. We touch on the film of *The Charge of the Light Brigade*, and I fall into a trap: 'Did John play Cardigan?' he asks. 'No, Raglan,' I reply. 'Ah, I knew it was some kind of sweater.' His quirky, richly entertaining observations flow unceasingly.

On Gielgud's flexibility: 'He had an entirely open mind, which can be blamed for being too open, or open too late, or open to too many things. But if you have to have a fault I'd rather that than, "Look left before you open your mouth, and not after."

On Gielgud's social skills: 'Peter Jones went up to see him in the Tennent office in the Globe. John was lying on the sofa like Madame Recamier, and said to Peter: "We've never met, but I've often seen you in the street." He had this tremendous gift of making remarks which were equivocal and strange, and in the long run very funny.'

On Gielgud and Shakespeare: 'He's particularly gifted with difficult texts, such as Prospero has. He has an automatic sense of contrast, so nothing he does is bereft of changes of colour. It's like clouds passing. He never takes a stretch of dialogue and says, That's that. The whole thing is permeated with all sorts of different skeins of colour and emotion.'

On Gielgud the film actor: 'No one who saw him do Romeo would ever think he could possibly adapt to films. Yet there he is, full of his particular integrity, suddenly absolutely magical as Polish conductors and God knows what else, playing a whole line of absurd characters that you would have thought beyond his range.'

On Gielgud's politeness: 'He came on to my boat one summer, and just sat on the edge of the seat. I said, "John, we've laid out lunch on board, but you're obviously not happy." He said, "I can't swim." It was so typical, to be so absolutely polite, demure even, and then to blurt out this terrible truth.'

On Gielgud and old age: 'We always thought John was the most vulnerable, but Larry's gone, and Ralph's gone, and here is this extraordinary character who obeys a rule which is frightfully consoling to people getting old, that in their dotage they become better actors than they've ever been, as though like fine wine they've matured in a certain way.'

Wednesday 10 June
I'm forever coming across tantalising snippets of information that I'd love to follow up if only there were time. Today I came across one where even time wouldn't help. According to a biography of Margaret Rutherford, her husband Stringer Davis was buried with a treasured letter from Gielgud in his pocket. No one knew the contents. What could *that* be about?

Thursday 11 June
A surprise letter from the great Polish film director Andrzej Wajda, who directed Gielgud in *The Conductor* (1979). His English is unsteady, but I get the drift: 'Whatever part he plays, whether it is a part of a rascal or an honest man, Sir John fills it with the whole intenseness of his individuality. It is like the actor suffers altogether with a villain he plays and is doubtful as a noble man with the same intensity.' Helpfully, he sends me extracts from a book about his films, which spells out more coherently his thoughts about Gielgud.

Sunday 14 June
A fruitless search for Gielgud's prep school near Godalming. I drive around this part of Surrey for ages, trying to find the building. Several times I pass Charterhouse School, its baths the setting for Gielgud Minor's failure to learn to swim. Finally I decide the building must have been demolished. A wildly frustrating trip, especially as I'm clearly not going to get into Westminster School now.

Thursday 18 June
I'm reading Emlyn Williams' autobiography and his essay in the celebratory book

The Ages of Gielgud, published to mark his eightieth birthday. He paints some wicked portraits of Gielgud, first at the Oxford Playhouse, then in his *Richard of Bordeaux* heyday, when they were both part of what was clearly a very fey group circling around Gielgud's flat in St Martin's Lane. I have to remember he's a writer, and that his Celtic impishness sometimes runs away with him.

James Harding's biography of Williams is fine stuff, and deals well with his gayness. Gielgud says Emlyn was 'frank and generous and a very faithful friend'. One example was Williams' willingness to act as carrier for 'a few small gifts' which Gielgud asked him to deliver to his cousins in Poland. I hadn't realised he liked to keep up with this section of his family.

Tuesday 23 June

A fantastically valuable chat with playwright and novelist David Storey, in his home in Kentish Town. Friendly and quietly spoken, he's supremely eloquent about Gielgud's talents, and how he used them playing alongside Richardson in his play *Home* (1970). He remembers Gielgud's apprehension about coming to the Royal Court. 'He was very aware that he and Ralph were bringing a theatrical tradition to a theatre which they suspected was highly sceptical of it. The Court at that time was, if not doctrinaire, at least polemical: the audience was there not to be entertained, but to be instructed. John voiced his anxiety, he felt his and Ralph's job was to serve the audience. I thought that made for a very good dynamic, the meeting of the two traditions. They got their characters through pure concentration and fear, really not knowing if they were stepping into the abyss.'

He's fascinating on the contrast between the two men. 'Ralph was a much more graphic, extrovert actor, very physical and lit by an extraordinary eccentricity. John was more introverted, more shy and empirical, he worked from the inside out, which is a much more vulnerable way of working, much more exposed. So it was a marriage of two contrasting temperaments, and it gave a quality to the performance that wasn't necessarily in my text.'

He was often struck by Gielgud's detachment. 'One night I was in the wings, and a man had a heart attack and died in the aisle, and the curtain was brought down. He and Ralph remained sitting at the table in silence, and as I approached them I heard John say, "Was it *your* cue that was missed, or mine?"' On another occasion Mona Washbourne had fallen and badly bruised her leg. 'When John came into her dressing-room she was half conscious, and her leg was bleeding. "Oh dear, how ghastly," he said. "A car knocked into us just now, and do you know, the chauffeur said it would cost £400. It's spoilt the whole evening." Then he went out.'

He also remembers with amusement Gielgud's total inability to relate to working-class people. This unease was evident when he introduced Gielgud to his coalminer father backstage. 'I've never seen two people less able to comprehend each other. It was like a Martian meeting a Venusian.'

Saturday 27 June
To Finchingfield in Essex, in search of the country house Gielgud owned in the 1930s. I'm not sure of its exact location, but the woman in the post office comes to my rescue. It's well outside the village, an exquisite whitewashed house with a long narrow garden, set in beautiful open countryside. The tennis court Gielgud had built has gone, as have some of the trees, but otherwise the place seems much as it was pictured in magazine photographs of the time. And it still carries its ghastly name: Foulslough.

I debate knocking on the door, but my courage fails me, and I make do with taking discreet pictures from various angles. I stand and stare and try to conjure up distant scenes...Edith Evans reading the part of Lady Bracknell for the first time in the low-ceilinged sitting-room...Gielgud and a young, unknown Terence Rattigan working furiously on adapting *A Tale of Two Cities*....Gielgud sitting in the garden in shorts and sandals with his two Schnautzer dogs.

June Progress Report
I'm almost ready to send off the first four chapters. But I fear they are rather plodding, that I haven't yet found the essence of the young Gielgud. This makes it difficult to editorialise, which I need to do. I remind myself that this is only the first draft.

Reading: Richard Findlater's book on Lilian Baylis, well worthy of the eccentric woman who gave Gielgud his Shakespearean break at the Old Vic. Also Thomas Kiernan's book on Olivier, a scrappy piece of work, full of sources 'requesting anonymity', who oddly all seem to speak with the same voice, which makes me sceptical about the rest of it. There's reference to a planned season of the four great Shakespearean tragedies, which might have brought Gielgud and Olivier back together in 1939. But this is mentioned in no other biography. Why not?

Problems I've discovered that one well-known married actor on my list for possible interview had an affair with Gielgud. This news inhibits me from approaching him, though I feel it should have the opposite effect.

Hopes: Greatly encouraged that Edward Albee has agreed to see me soon.

Disappointments: No reply from Richard Johnson, who was in Gielgud's 1944 Haymarket season. A shame, as witnesses for that period are thin on the ground, and in most cases under it.

Friday 3 July

With a mixture of hope and dread I send off 25,000 words to agent Derek, for forwarding to Michael Earley. I enclose a somewhat defensive letter, explaining that the first draft just tells the basic story of ten years, acknowledging that for the second I will need to add more comment, analysis, context and speculation. I also feel Gielgud needs humanising: at present it's strictly the on-stage story, and too reliant on quotes from Agate, Trewin, Darlington and other critics. I also boldly suggest I should be allowed a further 50,000 words, and another six months, to do justice to my subject. Hope to God Michael wears it, preferably with some extra money (though I'd still do it without).

Tuesday 7 July

Another fruitful day at Mander and Mitchenson. I find a cutting about the memorial service for Richard Findlater, Gielgud's first biographer. It seems he had only just got started when he died. Gielgud is quoted as not being very keen on a biography. I also find a piece by John Mortimer, written on location while shooting a TV adaptation of his novel *Summer's Lease* (1989), which I remember for Gielgud's delicious performance as the wicked elderly journalist Haverford Downs. Mortimer catches him reading a book about Lord Lucan: 'Could you really get someone to do a murder for £3000? I suppose Donald Wolfit might almost have paid that to get rid of me. He did *hate* me so much.'

I return home to a message from Derek, saying he thinks the sample chapters are great, that the material and the tone are just right, etc etc. Wonderful! I execute a little jig around my desk, and glance slyly at a postcard of Gielgud on my wall. The sense of relief is huge; just a little praise can mean so much. Then I remember that it's the publisher's views that count. Derek is a perceptive critic, and I value his judgement; but the real jury has yet to give its verdict.

Wednesday 8 July

I've finished reading Richard Huggett's massive biography of Binkie Beaumont. I approached it with some caution, as several people have said it's hopelessly unreliable. Though it's desperately over-written, it's extremely readable, packed with vivid detail and, for my purposes, one of the best documents going. Huggett researched the thing exhaustively, though I can see his source references are rather vague. And something made John Perry, who was initially helpful, withdraw his cooperation, refusing Huggett permission to use letters, the copyright of which he had inherited from Beaumont. I note also from the acknowledgements that Scofield changed his mind, telling Huggett he wanted to keep his memories for a book he would write himself one day. In my case he's just kept quiet, so I imagine he's one of many who have been warned off by the Other Biographer. It's all so *unfair*.

Friday 10 July
An unexpected windfall: through my good friend Ann Queensberry I've found one of Val Gielgud's former wives, alive and well and living in St John's Wood. Lively and humorous, Monica Grey seems amusingly unsure where she came in the sequence of Val's wives, but thinks she was either third or fourth.

I ask about the relationship between the two brothers. 'He and Val weren't close, but he was very kind and sweet to us. We weren't very well off, we had a very simple, rather run-down flat in Long Acre. John had this lovely house in Cowley Street, beautifully furnished, with a manservant called Bernie who ran his whole life. He used to lend us his silver, and ask us to his parties. I sat once with Edith Evans, expecting wonderful theatrical lore to come out, but she spent the whole time telling me how to make a rice pudding.'

She talks of Gielgud's dislike of illness and suffering. 'He was a great offloader of responsibility. Bernie and I used to visit an old and infirm aunt of his, but he couldn't bear anything like that, he used to just burst into tears. When she died Bernie and I had to sort out her belongings, he didn't want to know. And he never went to Val's funeral, it would have upset him too much.' She gives me valuable thoughts on Val's character, and tells me about an extraordinary, not to say sensational, confrontation between him and Binkie Beaumont the day after Gielgud's arrest. This was certainly not in Huggett's biography of Beaumont, nor anywhere else, though I can see that it would explain Val's vituperative comments on Binkie and HM Tennent, as reported to me by Peter Cotes.

Tuesday 14 July
I watched the Otto Preminger film of Shaw's *Saint Joan* (1957), with Gielgud as the Earl of Warwick. It's a very static film, but he gives a light and airy performance, touched with authority and nobility. It's a relatively small role, apparently heavily cut from the original, and for much of the time he seems quite detached from the action.

Friday 17 July

A note from Michael Earley, promising a response to the sample material within a week. He says he'll talk to Derek about my request for more time and words. He seems to imply he might make some more money available.

Later, at the end of an interview I do for the National's magazine *Stage Write* with Helen Mirren, about her Cleopatra at the NT, I mention Gielgud. She turns out to be a fan. 'I'm a great admirer of his personal courage as an actor, his lack of preciousness in taking parts. He doesn't just sit back, he makes sure he uses his talent. Whenever I have to make a difficult professional decision, I think to myself, What would John Gielgud have done?' She recalls with a chuckle the pornographic film *Caligula* (1979). 'We both had the courage and the stupidity to be in a film like that.'

Wednesday 22 July

A phone call to Charles Wood's father Jack, who was stage manager on Gielgud's 1945 tour of *Hamlet* and *Blithe Spirit* to India and the Far East. He says he can't remember anything, but then happily fills the next hour with his recollections. Strangely, he has no memory of the epileptic fit allegedly thrown by the actor playing Horatio in Cairo, during Gielgud's very last performance as Hamlet. This seems to throw some doubt on the story, but then Gielgud is the source for it, so why should he bother to invent such an odd incident?

Thursday 23 July

Michael Denison has died. He's the first of my interviewees to do so; there will inevitably be others. And he seemed in such rude health a year ago. The news story in the *Guardian*, in an unfortunate phrase, reveals that 'Dulcie Gray was being consoled by her friend Sir John Mills'.

Monday 27 July

Tyrone Guthrie's *A Life in the Theatre* (1959) is an excellent source, full of mainstream theatre history as seen by one of its heavyweights. Interesting that he dissented from the majority view that Olivier murdered the verse when he alternated Romeo with Gielgud in 1935. Also that he traces the 'pale, wavering, Werther-like Hamlet' in a direct line from Goethe's influence on German theatre, through Irving, to Gielgud, 'whose Hamlet has dominated and incalculably influenced all his immediate successors'. This makes me realise that I need to get more concrete evidence of this influence. I note one significant omission: Guthrie's much-criticised production of *The School for Scandal* (1937), in which

Gielgud scintillated as Joseph Surface.

Wednesday 29 July
In town I meet Sheila Ronald, another walk-on in the Gielgud story: she was assistant stage manager on several of his productions. An amiable woman, she brings along some useful documents, notably a rare programme for his 1953 *Richard II* in Bulawayo. She tells me of a bizarre-sounding event, a masque written for the first City of London Festival by John Betjeman. Gielgud and Tommy Steele were two of the participants, an intriguing combination. She has a recording, but it's on reel-to-reel tape, so there's little chance of my hearing it.

In the National Portrait Gallery afterwards I find a 1984 portrait of Gielgud by David Remfry, hanging between one of Alan Ayckbourn (very lifelike) and Peggy Ashcroft (totally off beam). It's a good portrait, catching both his shyness and his fastidiousness and, in the slight curve of his mouth, his humour. It's a relief that for once he's not surrounded by all that red plush and gilt in his grand Buckinghamshire home.

Thursday 30 July
To the Old Vic, to see Kevin Spacey in Eugene O'Neill's *The Iceman Cometh*. It's my first time in Gielgud's theatrical *alma mater* since I started the book, and for the first ten minutes his ghost hovers over the stage, as I imagine him there as Hamlet, Richard II and Benedick. But soon the riveting power of O'Neill's story and the first-class acting by Spacey and the company takes over, and the ghost vanishes.

July Progress Report
A quiet month, so I've been catching up with my reading. Anthony Holden's biography of Olivier is a model of intelligence, readability, and judicious opinions. Garry O'Connor's take on Guinness is quirky, irritating and contentious, but contains some valuable material. John Mills in his memoirs is fascinating on his early years, but otherwise rather humdrum and hearty. Peter Ustinov's *Dear Me* has an amusing glimpse of Westminster School which might be of use, but his humorous stories, so witty when heard live, fall flat on the page.

Tuesday 4 August
A surprise letter from Michael Earley, sent to all Methuen authors, announcing that they've broken free of Random House, and become an independent company again. That's the second upheaval since I joined their list, and I hope

it's the last for a while. Michael suggests the move is good news for authors as well as Methuen. That remains to be seen, though I'm all in favour of small publishing houses escaping the clutches of the conglomerates. Meanwhile, what about my sample chapters?

Monday 10 August

I'm deep in Ann Thwaite's fine biography of AA Milne, whose plays were so popular in Gielgud's youth. Her book is brilliant: written with a deceptively light touch, it catches Milne's virtues and limitations with unerring insight. It's sad to find that he should want desperately to be recognised as a novelist and playwright, rather than as a writer of children's books. In her introduction she touches on the pros and cons of a biographer meeting their subject. If you do, does your personal perception get in the way? I'm sure it must do, but in my case, sadly, the question is now academic.

Thursday 13 August

An agreeable chat with a very friendly Keith Michell in his north London studio (he's also an accomplished painter). He offers useful recollections on Gielgud's Stratford *Twelfth Night* (1955), in which Olivier played Malvolio. He talks of the effect Gielgud's verse-speaking had on his own acting, and how much he learnt from him while playing Orsino. 'Being Australian, I had always tackled Shakespeare as ordinary speech, which was the antithesis of John's way. So I was just blotting-paper at the time. You grew up imitating John, though I think my voice sounds more like Coward's.'

Unlike many actors, he found Gielgud's darting mind very stimulating. 'John loved experimenting, and so did I, so I took to his way of directing like a duck to water. It kept you on your toes, and I loved it. But you really had to concentrate to know what he was up to.' Unfortunately he's hazy about Gielgud's clash with Olivier during rehearsals, which he says went on behind the scenes. I need to pursue this further, as it's clearly a pivotal moment in the Gielgud/Olivier relationship.

Friday 14 August

A delightful hour in Hampstead with Peter Barkworth. An intelligent, polite and very witty man, he remembers as a schoolboy seeing Gielgud's 1944 Hamlet at the Manchester Opera House. 'We were sitting in the gods in this vast theatre, and he was completely and effortlessly audible. I couldn't understand why everyone else seemed either to be shouting or be almost inaudible. His performance was overwhelming, it made me cry.'

He gives me a vivid description of Gielgud rehearsing *The School for Scandal* (1962), and his own unhappiness in it. 'It was very much a surface approach, he didn't talk about the deeper things within the characters, or the society in which we lived. But he did give us wonderful ideas, only to be frustrated the following day to see them put into malpractice by nervous actors nowhere near as talented as he was.'

Having written a book on acting and taught at RADA, he has some precise thoughts about the Gielgud voice. 'I prefer it when he doesn't put any vibrato into it. I thought he was better without the heightened speech, when he was just a bloke, as in *No Man's Land*. I thought him a great actor then, whereas sometimes when the voice ruled, I though he wasn't.'

Monday 17 August

I finally track down David Spenser, Gwen Ffrancgon-Davies' biographer, only to be disappointed. He tells me she was unbelievably private about her career and the people she worked with, and her diary is full of nothing but flowers and the weather. But he promises to keep a lookout for anything significant. He says he wrote to Gielgud, who declined to help. I wonder why? Usually he's very cooperative, at least at first.

Still no response from Micheal Earley. One week since I sent him the chapters has become four.

Tuesday 18 August

An entertaining session with Roy Dotrice, over here for his annual 'sabbatical' from Hollywood. He had suggested meeting at the Garrick Club, where he says Gielgud used to give wonderful poetry recitals at Christmas time. I'm very curious to see the place, but in the event we meet in his London flat.

He's a great imitator of voices, and as we talk I get a rich selection of them, ranging from Sam Wanamaker to Michel Saint-Denis. He says he still blushes to think of his performance as Firs in *The Cherry Orchard* (1961). 'I was doing awful Method stuff, fussing around John's magnificent Gaev the whole time. I'm amazed he wanted to talk to me afterwards. But he was very generous and kind, the height of good manners. Or perhaps he just didn't notice me.' He thinks you can't analyse Gielgud's acting. 'It's one of those magical things. I don't think John himself knows the secret of it either, which is why he doesn't like talking about it. He just gets up and does it. And when he's on stage there's an aura there, you can't look at anyone else.'

He recalls an example of Gielgud's lack of manual dexterity and his antipathy to any kind of sport. 'John was demonstrating Gaev's billiard shots as if he were using a toothbrush, so George Murcell, who was playing Lopahin, said: "Why don't we have a game this afternoon and I'll show you how to play?" John said: "Don't be so silly, dear boy, I don't want to do that."'

Afterwards he plays me an extraordinary tape, now apparently a collector's item. It's a thespian 'Christmas Carol', written by Anthony Hopkins, who also does all the voices. So we have Burton as an *Under Milk Wood*-style narrator, meeting the ghost of actors past at the former National Theatre, now a car park: 'Johnnie' and Larry and Ralph and Albert and Peter are all there. Apparently Hopkins wrote it overnight while doing a radio play, and performed it the next day in the studio. It's brilliant, and historically spot on. Cue letter to Hopkins?

Thursday 20 August
Another day on the background trail, this time a journey to Gielgud's childhood in Kensington. I begin at his first home in Gledhow Gardens, a large Victorian building, now split into flats, looking on to a square full of those distinctive London plane trees. I take down the names of the occupants: perhaps I can persuade them to give me access to the nursery where young Jack Gielgud played so intensely with his toy theatre?

I move on to other landmarks: his nursery school round the corner, still being run as a school; the 'Mathilde Verne Pianoforte School' in Cromwell Road, where at the age of eleven he played one of the sailors in *HMS Pinafore*; and his parents' first home, in Earl's Court Square, a narrow but handsome building. I also managed, I think, to identify the site in Pembroke Gardens of his first drama school (now demolished), the Benson Academy. Seeing these places is a real bonus, not least because now that they're real to me it should be easier to make them come alive for the reader.

Tuesday 25 August
I've read Claire Bloom's two memoirs *Limelight and After* and *Leaving a Doll's House*. One of her first parts was in *The Lady's Not for Burning* (1949), when she played opposite a very young Richard Burton. Gielgud was then her idol ('the most beautiful man'), she'd been overwhelmed by his Hamlet ('the greatest we'll ever see'), and was terrified of him. Her account of rehearsals during the Fry play provides a useful snapshot of a rather less well-mannered Gielgud.

He was, she says, so desperate to succeed that he became very short-tempered with the company, causing one actor to develop jaundice and leave. She herself eventually took to her bed, after he had continually told her how studied and tense she was compared to the supremely relaxed and natural Burton. He could never remember her name and, since her dressing-room was above his, often referred to her as 'the little girl from upstairs'. She remembers how unnerving it was for the actors having to act with their director: 'He watched us all, those blue eyes missing nothing.'

Friday 28 August
Coffee in his London hotel with Edward Albee, over in England for rehearsals of his new play. He seems surprisingly amiable and easygoing, though I sense a toughness and rigour underneath. He tells me he has a memory like a sieve for incidents, but that he remembers visual things. He then sends a message via me to Gielgud, with whom he had a huge row over the lengthy final speech in his play *Tiny Alice* (1964), which Gielgud was sure was too long. 'Sorry John,' he grins into my tape recorder. 'We've just done another production, and you were right. I apologise for all the fun I've been having at your expense.'

I said I found the play baffling to read, and to my surprise, since I know he hates doing this, he talks a little about its meaning, then adds: 'I'm sure all these things had something to do with its construction, but how precisely they did I don't know. When I move a play from my unconscious mind on to paper, I get so involved with the reality of what I'm doing, it would be dangerous for me to start thinking of what's behind it. I stop thinking, so to speak, because you have to if you're working creatively.'

Despite his row with Gielgud, he remains admiring of his skill as an actor. 'Any playwright who concentrates on language is very happy with an actor like John, who can handle it so expertly. His feeling for the music of words, his sense of rhythm, is awesome.' We talk more generally of theatre. I'm intrigued to find that with his own plays he's always had casting control and director choice, to which he later added control over set and costume design, and even publicity. 'It's my stuff, and I stand or fall by it,' he says firmly.

He's scathing about The Method, especially what he sees as the negative influence of Lee Strasberg: 'His ego was transcendent, and so many actors used the studio for therapy.' He tells me that when Geraldine Page was offered the part of Martha in *Who's Afraid of Virginia Woolf?* she insisted that Strasberg attend rehearsals – which is why Uta Hagen ended up being cast in the role. Likewise Shelley Winters, who said she'd be happy to act in *The Death of Bessie Smith*, but that they could only open when she was 'ready'. They opened without her.

August Progress Report
Excellent interviews with Barkworth, Dotrice and Albee. Suddenly for the first

time I feel very comfortable with the 1960s.

Reading: You'd never know from Basil Dean's autobiography *Seven Ages* that 'Bastard Basil' was the most hated and feared man in the business. Gielgud suffered at his hands in *The Constant Nymph* (1926), in which he was very unhappy. Significantly, Dean makes only one reference to him, which must be a record for a book covering that period.

Disappointments: No reply from Richard Widmark, Jenny Quayle, Richard Huggett. I can't help feeling that most if not all of my recent non-responders have been got at by the Other Biographer, since previously everybody had replied to my letters.

Tuesday 1 September
I've read Rattigan's play *Harlequinade*, supposedly based on his experience of being directed by Gielgud while a student at Oxford. It's a creaking little farce, with Rattigan making silly swipes at 'theatre with a social conscience'. The director character certainly has echoes of Gielgud, constantly changing his mind and dropping bricks. But it's less useful than I had hoped; the mockery is very tame.

Still no word from Michael Earley, and tomorrow I'm off to Umbria for ten days. It's now six weeks since I sent him the material: something's up. Morley again? I ring Derek, who promises to get a response from him for my return.

Monday 14 September
Back from Italy to continuing silence from Methuen. Derek is in the States at the moment, so I'll just have to sit and grind my teeth. I'm desperate to carry on writing, but quite unable to do so in this awful vacuum.

A call from John Miller, who's finished his biography of Judi Dench, and is happy to meet. He tells me he's dedicated it to Gielgud, but not yet had a response to the copy he's sent him. Apparently he always uses a second-class stamp: 'One of his little economies.'

Thursday 17 September
I've finished Elizabeth Sprigge's biography of Sybil Thorndike. It's a grave disappointment, being little more than a thinly disguised autobiography, with large chunks of Sybil's recollections interspersed with her story. Author comment is minimal, and wincingly gushing. She makes Sybil out to be a near-saint, instead of the complex ragbag of virtues and vices that she clearly was. I recall Mary Casson saying that Sprigge quite failed to find her more hard-edged quality when

she interviewed her mother. It shows.

Friday 18 September

Coffee in his Twickenham house with John Nettleton and his two beautiful cats. He's debonair, cultured, and very well-informed about the theatre.

Fresh out of RADA in 1952, he played in Gielgud's Stratford production of *Macbeth*, with Richardson and Margaret Leighton. He remembers it as 'weird, quite Kabuki, with a black set and dark grey Samurai costumes', and recalls Richardson's misery at his failure in the part. He remembers too Gielgud's hopelessness with accents: during rehearsals he tried but failed abysmally to demonstrate cockney to help the actor playing the Porter. I'm reminded of the famous occasion when Gielgud was playing Sherlock Holmes on the radio, with Richardson as Doctor Watson. Holmes/Gielgud, supposedly disguised as a rough coalman, says in his mellifluous voice: 'I brought you a sack of coal, matey.' He then reveals his true identity, prompting Watson/Richardson to burst out: 'Good God Holmes, I'd never have recognised you, the appearance, the voice, it's just perfect!' The tape of this episode apparently prompts helpless mirth in all who hear it.

Saturday 19 September

A dressing-room interview for a change, at the Albery (formerly the New), where Barbara Jefford, in fetching black kimono, is between performances of Racine's *Phèdre*. Mightily experienced in Shakespeare, she was Isabella to Gielgud's Angelo in Peter Brook's production of *Measure for Measure* (1950) at Stratford. 'I was nineteen, and to work in such an august company was stunning,' she recalls. 'Young actors today don't hold their elders in awe as we did then. We really did call them Miss Ashcroft or Mr Gielgud, until given permission to do otherwise. So one day it was: "Do call me John."'

She remembers his generosity on stage, to a novice only one year out of drama school, and his willingness to listen to Brook, then only twenty-six. 'It was probably the first time John had stepped away from leading with that beautiful voice. Peter, who was quite jolly then, helped him make Angelo a complex, psychological character. It was a very fine performance.'

We discuss the rival merits of the Olivier and Gielgud legs: 'John had very good legs, not nearly as thin as Larry's,' she says. As I return to the stage door I experience a small shiver: sixty years ago, when this was the New theatre, all four of those legs were striding around the nearby stage, taking Romeo and Mercutio in turns. This was also the theatre where in 1934 Gielgud played possibly his greatest Hamlet.

Afterwards I walk the short distance up St Martin's Lane to find his old flat, which was his home when he first came to stardom at the Old Vic. But it's gone, replaced by offices and a garage. Ironically, the adjacent flats are still standing: tall, attractive, weathered Victorian buildings. Distance from the New, 400 yards. Distance from the Ivy, 200 yards.

Monday 21 September

A stimulating morning with Jane Howell, who directed Gielgud as Shakespeare in Edward Bond's *Bingo* (1972) at the Royal Court. 'He was very easy to direct,' she says. 'He worked very simply and honourably with Edward's very difficult text.' She remembers his frightened reaction when she asked him in the first scene to look out into the auditorium, as if it were Shakespeare's garden. 'He said, "Oh I shall hate doing that, my concentration is bad at the best of times, and I shall just know everyone who is out there." Which he did: "So and so is in tonight," he would say. But he was very sweet, he said: "I'm sure you're right, I'll do it." I thought that was an amazing thing for someone of his experience to say to someone who had so little.'

She recalls an encounter with him two years later at the BBC. 'He was coming out of the lift, and I was coming down the stairs. When he saw me he ran back into the lift. I realised he knew he knew me, but couldn't remember my name. But at the ground floor we met again. "Ah Glenda!" he said. "Wonderful speech in the House last night!" Then he dashed off, not quite sure if he had put his foot in it.'

Tuesday 22 September

I've been reading Cecil Beaton's diaries, which contain several fascinating titbits, including Gielgud's visit to a poverty-stricken Mrs Patrick Campbell in a New York hotel. When he wept at her situation and offered to lend her money, she told him he was too hysterical. Wiping his eyes he said: 'These are Terry tears.'

He and Beaton fell out at one stage (I need to get to the bottom of this), so I wonder how accurate the remarks are that Beaton attributes to him. Self-critical as he was, did Gielgud really say, 'I'm spoilt, I'm niggardly, I'm prissy, I come home in the evening and count the books on the shelf to see if one is missing'? It doesn't sound quite right.

Wednesday 23 September

A Morley missile. In a letter to Methuen he says I am still going round posing as the Official Biographer. He then claims that he has a file containing at least a dozen letters, including one from Gielgud, all of which assert that I have no authorisation to do the book. Many of the letter-writers, he says, state that, as I lied to them and obtained my interviews under false pretences, they now want to withdraw permission for me to quote from their interviews, either directly or indirectly. He adds that Gielgud is keen to withdraw any reprint permission he has given. He ends with a threat: that if I make any claim in the future to be publishing a Gielgud biography, he will invoke those letters.

All this is clearly just bluff and intimidation. But I'm still worried by the suggestion that Gielgud might withdraw his permission for me to use his books and letters. That would be really serious. It's probably a fantasy on Morley's part; certainly Gielgud has never raised the matter himself. But it highlights his determination to undermine my book.

There's one priceless sentence, in which he says that he has been working on the authorised Gielgud for more than a decade, and feels like a portrait painter who suddenly finds someone with a polaroid camera trying to rob him of his work. Well pardon me, Augustus John, but how is it that after nearly ten years you still haven't completed your masterpiece? Clearly Morley is worried that I may have covered the ground at least as thoroughly as he has, and possibly more so, and that my book will appear first. These perfectly legitimate anxieties don't excuse his disgraceful behaviour.

Tuesday 29 September

I talk over the legal position with my lawyer and publisher friend Charles Clark, who is *the* expert on copyright. He's appalled at the 'sorry mess' I describe. It's nice to have some objective sympathy. He confirms that Morley's letter is libellous; that material gathered from interviews can't retrospectively be 'unpermitted' if it was gathered in good faith; and that Gielgud can't legally withdraw his copyright permission. He suggests that a meeting between Micheal Earley and Ion Trewin, who commissioned Morley's book, might help to clear the air, and offers me the name of a good solicitor as a fallback. A friend indeed.

September Progress Report

My three solid and fruitful interviews with Nettleton, Jefford and Howell are quite overshadowed by the latest Morley moves. But if he thinks I will give way in the face of his threats, he's quite wrong. They just make me more determined than ever to carry on. His bluff will be called, if necessary in court, though I hope it never comes to that. I shouldn't be thinking such thoughts, but if Gielgud can hang on until the new millennium, it could be a close run to the finishing line.

Thursday 1 October

A rattling good session with Richard Briers in his London house. He's geniality incarnate, and also a very good listener, so we have a proper conversation. He's thoughtfully dug out an old 78 record of Gielgud reciting poetry, and an old *Theatre World* interview from 1935. He's a serious theatre history enthusiast, and clearly held his own with Gielgud when the talk turned to Irving, Forbes-Robertson *et al*, as it so often did.

We discuss acting styles, and I get some amusing impressions of Tree, Milton and Ainley. At RADA in his youth he used to imitate Gielgud (apparently Albert Finney did Olivier, even down to the false noses). He says Gielgud inspired him as a young actor. 'I could hardly move at all, and he didn't move terribly well, yet he was at the top of the tree, so that gave me hope.'

He mentions Gielgud's 'lovely humility, with a steely quality of course, but always appreciating other actors'. We talk about what makes a great actor; he suggests one mark is a capacity sometimes to be truly bad. 'Both Gielgud and Olivier could be atrocious, but then they suddenly do something which is far and away superior to anything that we little people can do. They're doing something else, as one critic said about Irving, something higher somewhere in the ether.'

He's worked with Gielgud comparatively recently, on Kenneth Branagh's film of Chekhov's *Swan Song* (1993), about an old drunken actor recalling past triumphs. 'Branagh wanted to get him on celluloid in the evening of his life, doing snippets of all those great Shakespearean roles. Whenever he forgot his lines, he would go, "Oh dear, how maddening!" He would never get across anyone else, like others do, he was just annoyed with himself, which was very endearing.' He remembers Gielgud's dissatisfaction with the radio Lear he did for his ninetieth birthday. 'He's always telling himself to be better, which is such a wonderful thing when you've ruled the theatre for sixty or seventy years.' Unlike me, he hopes Gielgud won't last much longer: 'I'm sorry he's getting so old, I wish he'd pop off. He's so bored, he has very few interests, apart from lighting bonfires.'

Friday 2 October

A two-hour session with Michael Earley, too much of it devoted to Morley. At first I detect a slight wavering of support on Michael's part, so I make it clear I am continuing with the book, come what may. I pass on Charles Clark's idea of a meeting between the two editors, which Michael thinks a good one. Finally he agrees to write to Morley to confirm that my book goes on.

We eventually get round to my sample material. He says he likes the tone, the readability, but wants more colour, more extensive sketches of directors such as Fagan, Komisarjevsky, Basil Dean, and more historical context. This is fine, not least because it will require more rather than fewer words. So he has little choice but to agree when I ask for an extra 50,000-75,000, plus a six-month extension to my deadline. What a relief: there wasn't a hope in hell of sticking to the original terms.

On the train I read that Marius Goring has died. I recall with sadness that poignant day at his country home in Sussex. Edward Thompson rings to ask for Gielgud's phone number, so he can ask him to speak at the memorial service. I wonder if he will?

Saturday 3 October
I catch Gielgud in his latest film *Elizabeth*, in which he has a tiny part as the Pope. His roles seem to be shrinking rapidly: this one is only about thirty seconds. Soon perhaps he will pass soundlessly in front of the camera, *à la* Hitchcock. Then maybe just a voice? Actually his voice seems tired and feeble, which makes me wonder how much longer he'll be able to work.

Tuesday 6 October
The latest Mander and Mitchenson visit produces a cutting with a useful clutch of Gielgud thoughts on some of today's leading actors:
  – On Judi Dench: 'She is extraordinary, her range is immense, and the way she goes on putting in four or five new performances each year is fantastic.'
  – On Ian McKellen: 'I'm a bit embarrassed, he keeps on asking me to join him in all sorts of demonstrations.'
  – On Vanessa Redgrave: 'She is perhaps our greatest actress. One wishes she were a cosier character.'

Thursday 8 October
An intriguing session with Margaret Wolfit, daughter of Donald, Gielgud's life-long enemy. Her father's gross features have softened in her to handsome: she seems very unWolfitian, and willing to talk frankly about her father and his hostile relationship with Gielgud.

She was in her father's company for a while, playing Jessica in *The Merchant of Venice*. 'He was a powerful figure to have to combat to keep your end up,' she says. 'He treated me dreadfully, which I thought was a bit much, since he left my mother when I was two.' She ascribes his dislike of Gielgud to several factors, including his antipathy to homosexuals, and his being 'a little boy lost from the provinces, who felt people with a theatre background had an unfair advantage'.

Gielgud, she recalls, was the polar opposite to her father. She understudied Diana Wynyard as Beatrice in *Much Ado about Nothing* (1952), and one night had to go on and play opposite him. 'I was very shy, but he knew I'd had a hard time with my father, and was very encouraging. He was so generous, giving me the curtain call, sending me flowers, he was just lovely.'

Friday 9 October

A *rendez-vous* – I decide to call it that – in a quiet Kensington hotel with the still very beautiful Virginia McKenna, now in her mid-60s. As well as specific memories, she makes several perceptive observations on actors and acting. Like so many others she recalls Gielgud's kindness to her when young. At eighteen she played Perdita in *The Winter's Tale* (1951): 'He was so kind to us nervous, overwhelmed, insecure actors. He put you at your case, he made you feel that what you did was fine, whether it was or not. He was never grand, he didn't want to be set apart. He'd say to you "Call me Johnny."'

She remembers his tendency to giggle, and how infectious that was on stage. She also enthuses about the subtleties and intelligence of his verse-speaking, and tells me that when she was a guest on *Desert Island Discs* one of her choices was Gielgud speaking a Shakespeare sonnet. 'I could listen to him reading the telephone directory,' she sighs.

Saturday 10 October

A letter from Derek, who has talked to Michael, who seems to have been happy with our meeting. Derek hopes his firm but conciliatory approach with Morley will result in a truce between us. Me too: I can do without such a distraction. The bad news is that Michael won't release the next part of my advance until the sample material is in 'a more finished state'. This is a shock, since at our meeting last week he never even hinted at such an opinion; on the contrary, he was very positive about the chapters. I feel let down.

Derek suggests that a revised version of those chapters, taking into account Michael's points, would release the money. I'm sure he's right, but I now have an urge to start at the beginning. I'm sure it will be easier to polish and improve post-1925 once I've picked up the main strands of Gielgud's early development.

Monday 12 October

A jolly session in his house in Hampton with actor and caricaturist Clive Francis, who produced *Sir John: The Many Faces of Gielgud*, an affectionate anthology of anecdotes and observations sprinkled with his own delightful drawings, and published on Gielgud's ninetieth birthday. He tells me Gielgud initially agreed to him doing the book, but a few months later couldn't remember anything about it. Sounds worryingly familiar.

He recalls the nightly suppers he and Edward Fox had with Gielgud during the making of the TV version of *Quartermaine's Terms* (1987), when his memories of the past were in full torrent. 'You only have to say, "Martita Hunt, 1932," and he's away, that's the meal taken care of. But I've never heard him take the theatre and acting seriously: when you're talking with him about the business, it's always fun. His remembrances are always uplifting, he never gets heavy.'

He says Gielgud influenced him enormously as an actor. 'I used to imitate him when I was a kid, I bought the *Ages of Man* record when I was around thirteen, when other boys were buying Acker Bilk. He opened doors for me, made me feel I needed to be part of the theatre. Later I learnt from his phrasing, the beautiful way he spoke Shakespeare. He was a beacon to a young actor, and I would go to everything he did.'

I'm not sure how, but he knows about the state of play on the Morley book. He says Gielgud occasionally rings Morley up to ask him how he's getting on. He also says that the book 'seems to be very much on the back burner'. My spirits rise. Long may it stay there, simmering without coming to the boil.

Tuesday 13 October

I've been reading Marguerite Steen's book on the family, *A Pride of Terrys*. It's a frustrating volume: she was a novelist, and it's full of fanciful speculation combined with lashings of Mills & Boon mawkishness. She's good on the individual personalities, especially Fred and Ellen, but since there are no notes it's hard to know how much of the material is reliable.

Preparing to write again, to begin at the beginning, I spend a long time pondering on the right opening. I want to avoid the conventional 'Arthur John Gielgud came into this world on...' or 'The Gielguds originally came from Poland'. There is of course the theatre-focussed beginning: 'On the night when John Gielgud was born Mrs Patrick Campbell was thrilling West End audiences', etc, etc. It's hackneyed, but tempting. But at the moment I favour zooming in on him getting his toy theatre at the age of seven, then panning back through the various characters in the family tree.

Thursday 15 October

I spend most of the day in Ealing with Gervase Farjeon, son of the critic, wit and Shakespeare scholar Herbert Farjeon, whose sister was the children's writer Eleanor Farjeon. He generously leaves me free to roam among his father's papers which, by a happy chance, he's been sorting and cataloguing during the last few months. A charming, gentle man, he's touchingly pleased that someone should want to dig around in the family archive.

I find there some invaluable early Gielgud reviews, notably of his Trofimov in Fagan's ground-breaking production of *The Cherry Orchard* (1925), and of several Old Vic performances. But it's a long business wading through bound volumes of Farjeon's columns in the *Sunday Pictorial*, in amongst the pictures of chorus girls kicking up their legs in the latest revue. Later Gervase's partner Anne Harvey arrives, and tells me that the poet Elizabeth Jennings has corresponded with Gielgud. I must get in touch.

Monday 19 October
A courteous letter from Richard Todd, with a couple of recollections from the Otto Preminger film of Shaw's *Saint Joan* (1957). It comes as a surprise, as in my paranoia and the passing of time I assumed he was among those who had either been got at by Morley, or who had contacted Gielgud and been asked not to assist me. So perhaps all is not quite lost.

Tuesday 20 October
Lunch at the Barbican with Chattie Salaman who, at a remarkably advanced age – on the phone she described herself as 'small and ancient' – is still teaching and directing at the Guildhall School of Music and Drama. 'I'm just of the fan-club persuasion,' she says modestly. She's actually an ardent and knowledgeable Shakespearean, inspired originally by Gielgud's 1934 Hamlet. 'It was so romantic, I fell in love with him, with the play, and with Shakespeare. I bought all the editions of *Hamlet* I could lay my hands on, and read all the notes.'

She gives me some invaluable recollections of Michel Saint-Denis, who taught her at the London Theatre Studio; at sixteen she was the youngest student there. 'He was horrible to most people, but not to me, I was so young. I got to know him well: he was enormously funny, witty, intelligent, a *bon viveur*. I thought he was the greatest man alive.' We get on to other actors of the period, including her brother-in-law Alec Guinness. 'His Hamlet was very modern, I don't think he's been appreciated enough as a Shakespearean actor.' She adds, to my surprise: 'I thought he was much more rigorous about the verse than John, he stuck to the structure, and made things wonderfully clear.'

Thursday 22 October

A brief but not unfriendly letter from Edward Bond. He gives me a couple of thoughts about Gielgud's performance in *Bingo*, but declines my suggestion that I come and talk to him, suggesting he would have nothing to say. I find that hard to imagine of a man with such fierce opinions about the theatre. Still, at least I have Jane Howell's recollections of the production.

Friday 23 October

Sitting in the foyer at the National Theatre, I become aware of a familiar voice booming across the tables. Lo and behold, it is the Other Biographer. He's sitting with a small man – at least small by comparison – and swamping him with theatrical anecdotes. I listen for a while, relishing being so close to the great portrait painter without his knowledge. I assume he's come, as I have, to hear Judi Dench talk about her life to John Miller, in a Platform linked to his biography of her. In the dress circle I am surrounded by the Judi Fan Club, mostly smartly dressed elderly women. It's impossible not to warm to her: what you see is what you get. She admits cheerfully to having skipped a page of *Filumena* a few nights ago, and says no one in the audience noticed – though Michael Pennington did on stage.

I try to imagine Gielgud and me doing a similar joint Platform, but somehow my mental screen goes blank.

Saturday 24 October

A card from Clive Francis, telling me he has the unpublished notes made by Gielgud during the 1940 *King Lear*, directed by Barker. More buried treasure? Also some pictures of the war-time *Macbeth*, including a shot of the mincing Ernest Thesiger as one of the three witches. This I must see.

Tuesday 27 October

A phone call from my friend Charles Clark, just back from the Frankfurt Book Fair, where he met Ion Trewin. Charles told him there was no question of my behaving in the kind of dishonourable way that Morley had suggested. It's a typically kind and helpful gesture.

Wednesday 28 October

A morning at the National Theatre archive in Brixton. What a contrast it is to the gloom of the Theatre Museum: light, space, new carpets, photocopy machine to hand. There are eight files to work through, the fattest being for the American tour of *No Man's Land* (1976), which every local paper in Canada and the US seems to have reviewed. I have to be ruthless and skip a great deal, which I find painful.

I find two references by Gielgud to Ronald Hayman's biography. In one he says he asked him to write a chapter on his failures, because 'they are much more interesting than one's successes', but Hayman 'didn't see the point of that'. The other is a brutally blunt verdict on the book given to a Canadian journalist: 'Boring. I gave him two years of my life, access to all my papers, and he missed it completely. I should have written it myself.' I have no problem with charting his failures, but the second remark I take as a challenge.

Thursday 29 October

Another day at Mander and Mitchenson, this time *à la recherche de* James Agate. I find there are some nine volumes of his *Ego* diaries: fortunately most of them have an index, but even then it's a slog. But I'm rewarded with several reviews of early Gielgud productions, and several pungent observations on his art. There's also an excellent 1947 essay by Agate's side-kick Alan Dent, assessing Gielgud's stature and reputation at the time. Such pieces are rare, and invaluable.

Friday 30 October

Three weeks ago I wrote to Ted Hughes about his translation of *Oedipus*, hoping for his thoughts on Gielgud and the production at the National. Today his death is reported. I'm horrified to find that my first reaction is, 'Damn it, now I won't get a reply.' I fear I am becoming obsessed with my quest. But perhaps it's impossible *not* to be with such a project?

October Progress Report

A reasonably good month. After the bombshell, it's been all quiet on the Morley front, where no news is definitely good news. The Briers interview was top-notch as well as great fun, while Francis, McKenna, Wolfit and Salaman were all very fruitful encounters.

Hopes: Sarah Miles rings, to say she can see me in December. Daniel Thorndike and Hugh Whitemore both delighted to collaborate. All very positive.

Disappointments: Patrick Garland has been collared by Morley, and doesn't feel keen to repeat the exercise. At least he's good enough to reply to my letter. No response from Warren Clarke, James Bolam, Timothy Bateson, Polly Adams, Peter Jones and Natasha Perry. Morley has presumably warned them of the imposter. This would explain the increasing silence from the profession. Silence also from

Peter Shaffer, who I suspect has returned to the States now that *Amadeus* is re-launched in the West End.

Health check: Gielgud was apparently depressed by Michael Denison's death, and declined to go to his memorial service. Who can blame him?

Tuesday 3 November
I drop in on the private view for Clive Francis' *There is Nothing Like a Dane!*, a delicious collection of his original cartoons of actors playing Hamlet, now also published in book form. The two of Gielgud, wonderfully glowing humorous drawings, have pride of place at each end of the room. Clive wonders if I might like one for the cover of my book, which is a kind thought. But my instinct is that it would give it too light a flavour.

Wednesday 4 November
A smashing interview with Hugh Whitemore about Gielgud's last stage appearance, in his play *The Best of Friends* (1988), which also starred Rosemary Harris and Ray McAnally. A serious man always ready for a laugh, he's friendly, informative and entertaining. He muses on the paradox of Gielgud's acting. 'On the one hand he's enormously accomplished, on the other naturally vulnerable. He didn't have that great barrage of confidence that Olivier seemed to have. Olivier would bash out at the audience, whereas Gielgud invited you to care, so you reached out towards him. That's why he's so good in the sadder, more introspective roles.'

He recalls Gielgud's fears of returning to the stage after an absence of ten years, his struggle to remember his lines – he once forgot his final one, so the curtain had to be brought down – but also his supreme musicality. 'Plays are like music, the rhythm is so important. I used to be astonished at the brilliance of his phrasing.' After repeating the role of Sir Sydney Cockerell on television and radio, Gielgud dropped him a postcard: 'Next time on ice?'

He wrote the screenplay for *A Dance to the Music of Time* (1997), and recalls Gielgud's involvement: 'When he was filming it was rather touching, everyone gathered round just to catch a glimpse, they were so pleased he was there. He was very enthusiastic about doing it, although he hated Anthony Powell's books. "I can't stand them, they're so snobbish, I can't read them," he said.'

By chance I mention *Othello* and my lack of a response from Zeffirelli, and he offers to try to fix a meeting when he sees him in London next month. 'But be warned, he's never punctual,' he adds. I say I'm prepared to wait as long as it takes.

Friday 6 November

The autobiography of Gielgud's mother, Kate Terry Gielgud, is a total delight. I began reading it for possible material to mark, but quickly put my pencil away and just read. Her Victorian childhood amid the theatrical Terrys is wonderfully evoked, as are the various members of the family. Her account of her marriage to Gielgud's father is frank and honest. I can see that Gielgud inherited her shyness, her sensitivity to beauty, and her total absorption in theatre.

The book stops in the 1920s, and Gielgud's debut at the Old Vic: the intensity of their relationship, the proud mother and the ardent theatregoer are all there in her closing sentences: 'How fervently I wished for him success and happiness: the power to hold an audience in thrall, to whisper and be heard throughout a mighty house! Today I know that he found his vocation from the first, and found in it great happiness.' I must return and study it more carefully: it's a marvellously rich source.

Sunday 8 November

I watch Gielgud in what was only his second talkie, *The Good Companions* (1933), in which he plays a music teacher turned touring revue artist, opposite Jessie Matthews. Contrary to the rude things he says about his early films, he plays the light-hearted, impulsive, pipe-smoking Inigo Jollifant with relaxed charm. I'm fascinated to hear his singing voice for the first time: a pleasant, Cowardesque tenor. He also plays the piano with obvious dexterity. I enjoy the scene in which Jessie Matthews tells him he's feeble, and he responds by kissing her: '*That's* the sort of chap I am!' It's meant to be masterful, but isn't. I'm intrigued to hear the prologue read by one of his boyhood idols, Henry Ainley: the voice melodious certainly, but light and precise, rather than the booming resonance I had expected.

Wednesday 11 November

A strange couple of hours at Ellen Terry's house in Smallhythe, Kent, now owned by the National Trust. It's closed for the season, but the curator Margaret Weare kindly opens up the small library for me. Here I sit and look through the minutes of meetings of the Ellen Terry memorial committee (Gielgud was president), and programmes and pictures of performances in the theatre in the garden.

It's difficult not to be distracted by the surroundings, by the knowledge that Ellen Terry died in the next room. Afterwards Anthony Weare shows me the Barn Theatre, a charming little building made entirely of wood. I notice on one of the pillars someone has scratched with a knife the names, including Gielgud's, of the actors who performed here in the early days.

I drive on out to New Romney in the Kent marshes, to talk to Daniel Thorndike, nephew of Sybil. A merry, modest man, he has two links to Gielgud: Rosina Filippi, his grandmother, was Gielgud's first teacher; his father, Russell Thorndike, was leading man at the Old Vic in 1921-22 when Gielgud, then a drama student, walked on in several productions. He delights in showing me his theatrical memorabilia, including the original programme for *Peer Gynt*, which lists (and misspells) Gielgud among the 'extras', and his grandmother's book *A Hint to Speakers and Players*, which is dedicated to Gielgud's great-uncle Fred Terry. I'm struck once again by the apparent smallness of the theatre world at the turn of the century.

He also acted with Gielgud at the National, and recalls a moment during *Julius Caesar* (1977) when Gielgud forgot to come on: 'Someone had to go and get him from his dressing-room while we sacrificed a few more goats.' He remembers also his amiability: 'We had to carry the bier with the body of Caesar on it, and twice we went through the backcloth. He didn't seem to mind at all.'

Thursday 12 November
Another session at the Farjeon archive, which yields more early reviews. I'm impressed by Herbert F's wit and wisdom, his ability to write light, semi-jokey stuff for the tabloids of his day – imagine the *Sun* having a theatre critic – then switch to the role of Shakespeare scholar to write serious reviews in the *Listener* and the *New Statesman*. It's hard not to be diverted from the main Gielgud highway into all the irrelevant but delightful side-roads down which he beckons me.

Friday 13 November
I start to write again, this time about the family background. This part of a biography can quickly pall if there's too much detail. But it's hard to encapsulate in a few paragraphs all that has been written on the Terrys, among others by Gielgud himself, his mother, Ellen Terry, and Marguerite Steen, especially when I'm impatient to get the man himself born.

Sunday 22 November
To St John's Wood, where I locate without much difficulty the two separate blocks of flats off Avenue Road that Gielgud lived in during the second half of the 1930s. At the time they were brand new and the last word in elegance. Now they seem dreary, rundown and without character. Then it's on to Mayfair, to find his wartime homes. I walk down Piccadilly looking for number 142 - and find that it's gone, and on its site stands the Inter-Continental Hotel. I have better luck in Park

Lane, where the ten-storey block in which he shared a flat with Binkie Beaumont for some months still stands. Very bijou.

November Progress Report
I'm pleased to have got back to the writing. It's probably still too impersonal, but I don't want to intrude much in these early pages. Overall I feel more confident with the material. I'm able to relax and inject some humour into it, which I've been wary of doing up to now. I'm less hung up about cramming in all the facts, and able to focus more on what actors like to call 'the emotional journey'.

Tuesday 1 December
I've been wrestling with the question of the authenticity of certain Gielgud anecdotes. There's the one about him sitting next to Mary Wilson at a lunch, and asking her where she lives, to be told '10 Downing Street, of course.' Or was he talking to Clement Atlee, as one actor told me? Or was it Atlee's daughter, at a Shakespeare celebration in Stratford, as in another version I heard this week?

Then there are all the variations on the classic 'Not you Athene/Edith/Clive/Edward' gaffe. The latest, told me by someone present there, has Gielgud at a party in New York he didn't want to attend, sitting on a couch with a fellow-guest. *Gielgud*: I understand the person to avoid at this party is Mrs Higginbotham. *Fellow-Guest*: But I *am* Mrs Higginbotham. *Gielgud*: No no, I mean the *other* Mrs Higginbotham.

Friday 4 December
I'm absorbed in Eric Salmon's fine life of Gielgud's guru Granville Barker. I realise I hadn't appreciated before the extraordinary depth and power of Barker's influence in the theatre, which goes some way to explaining Gielgud's hero-worship. Oddly, he himself told Salmon that Barker was a rather cold man, a point missing from his enthusiastic accounts of being directed by him. I notice from the book that Barker wrote a short story called 'The God of Great Bricks'. Is this another connection?

Saturday 5 December
I've just caught up with a piece in the *Observer* on Morley's biography, tastefully titled 'Long life locks secrets of sex in the closet'. Astonishingly, Morley admits he's 'being deliberately slow' with his book, to have a better chance of dealing more frankly with Gielgud's sexuality. This, he says, is because Gielgud has the right to veto anything he doesn't like – but obviously not if he is dead.

Other 'facts': he claims he was made official biographer five years ago, when it was actually nearly ten; to admit this would of course make his progress seem even slower. He also says he's done more than a hundred interviews, which makes me wonder why he claimed on the phone to me to have done over two hundred. I'm intrigued to read that he's 'already written a few chapters on Gielgud's early life'. I muse on what prompted the article, and wonder if it was Morley himself, keen to remind the world that he is the official biographer. In fact, the effect is merely to show up his obvious intention to make a meal of Gielgud's private life.

Monday 7 December
Morley has replied to the *Observer* article. He now denies being 'deliberately slow' in writing the book, but admits he is still only in the 1930s, adding that 'by Holroyd standards that is not slow'. He adds disingenuously: 'I have agreed that John will see the book when it is complete.' He refers to Gielgud's 'immense generosity and the time he has given me over the years'. I wonder how this squares with Gielgud's remark that he has yet to ask him a single question. He also suggests that, since Gielgud will probably live to be a hundred, that would be the appropriate time to publish what he calls 'a life story, not just a career study'. Is this a sly reference to the man with the polaroid?

I see he calls Gielgud 'the greatest actor in world history', which I find a ludicrous claim. How can you possibly measure such a stature? He also mentions that he has 'outlived two authorised biographers, and may well outlive a third'. I still don't know who the other one was besides Findlater – unless this is another Morley error.

Tuesday 8 December
A relaxed chat in his stylish London flat with Waris Hussein, who directed Gielgud in the TV *Saint Joan* (1968), and also at the National in his penultimate stage appearance in Julian Mitchell's play *Half-Life* (1977).

'I was very young when we did the Shaw, and very much in awe of him,' he admits. 'But he loved to work with young people, I'm sure that's one of the things that kept him so youthful. He gave me a lot of respect, and was very kind.' He remembers Gielgud's initial shyness in rehearsal. 'We started rehearsing in a hall in Fulham. When lunch came he opened his copy of *The Times*, and we were just tiptoeing out when suddenly this voice rang out: "Isn't anybody going to invite me to lunch?" Of course that broke the ice.'

On *Half-Life* he recalls Gielgud's hatred of the National building, and his nervousness at tackling a part that seemed to him as long as Hamlet. 'It was a very acid character, but John can never be totally unsympathetic, and he pulled off the breakdown scene wonderfully well. We never had a chance to run it in properly, and I was very frightened on the first night. He himself was very nervous, but he carried it, he just used his own technique and great experience.'

Thursday 10 December
While finding some extremely useful material at Mander and Mitchenson, I come across a letter from Coward, in which he enthuses to Gielgud's mother about her son's witty and authoritative performance as the butler in *Nude with Violin* (1956). Unfortunately I shan't be able to use it: Morley's involvement with the Coward estate makes me feel there's no point in applying for permission to do so.

Monday 14 December
Margot Peters' biography of Mrs Patrick Campbell is superb, and very illuminating about her friendship with Gielgud. She makes it clear what a monster Mrs Pat could be, but also her fascinating quality that held Shaw, Du Maurier and many others in thrall.

I discover Gielgud first met her when her career was on the wane, and she was playing *Hedda Gabler* on Brighton Pier. ('A *tour de force* now forced to tour,' she wittily confessed.) He was bewitched by her beauty and formidable intelligence, but also amused by her scurrilous wit and defiant humour, and her refusal to take the theatre too seriously. 'The famous *bon mots* are quoted with appropriate relish', he enthuses in a review of the biography, quoted on the cover. His loyalty to Mrs Pat in her sad old age is impressive, as is the obituary he wrote for *The Times*, which balances praise with discreet criticism. He's very good at these: my growing 'tributes' file includes fine examples of them that he wrote on the deaths of Komisarjevsky, Esmé Percy, Rex Whistler, Lilian Braithwaite, Sybil Thorndike and Edith Evans.

Tuesday 15 December
I drop in again on Gervase Farjeon, to borrow two hefty volumes of his father's theatre criticism. He's listening to a programme about changing attitudes to homosexuality in radio programmes, and suddenly there's a reference to 'Sir John Gielgud being caught cottaging'. I can't help wondering if Gielgud is listening, and if so whether he still feels wounded by such references. Or is he too old to care about them any longer?

Wednesday 16 December
I send the first four chapters to Derek. I feel they're much stronger than the

first batch, even though I have very few personal sources to work from for this period: his autobiography *Early Stages*, his mother's *Autobiography*, and a handful of letters. The most valuable material, which I've been plundering heavily, is his youthful theatre criticism, covering the years 1917-1925. They range from his naive schoolboy comments on revue and pantomime, to his shrewd critiques of Eleonora Duse, Mrs Patrick Campbell, du Maurier, Barrymore and many others. Reading them in sequence, it's fascinating to see his obsession growing, his mind developing, his literary style gradually sharpening. Had he not been an actor, I reckon he could easily have been a theatre critic.

Friday 18 December
A frustrating fax from California. I thought I had tracked down Alan Napier, who was with Gielgud at the Oxford Playhouse in 1924, at the same time as James Whale, later a celebrated director, but then a fledgling actor. But Whale's biographer James Curtis, with whom Kevin Brownlow had put me in touch, tells me that Napier died twelve years ago. Apparently there's an unpublished autobiography in one of the university collections, but Curtis doesn't know which one. Tantalising, but to pursue such long shots is now a luxury.

Monday 21 December
Derek rings to say he likes the first four chapters very much – more background, much richer texture, etc. – and that he'll make sure Michael gets them before Christmas.

In the evening I go to hear Dulcie Gray give a talk at the National, only to find that the ubiquitous Other Biographer is introducing her. It's the first time I've seen him in action, and I find him appallingly gushing and self-promoting. 'This is my twentieth Platform'... 'My grandmother Gladys Cooper'... 'My forthcoming production at the King's Head', and so on. Whose talk is it, for God's sake? He giggles and guffaws a lot, constantly interrupts his guest, and refers in passing to 'John G', as if everyone knows who is meant. Surprisingly, he doesn't mention 'my forthcoming biography'. Dulcie Gray still looks amazingly youthful; she's soon to go on the road in *The Ladykillers*, which is not bad in her eightieth year. She tells the story of husband Michael Denison's last illness, which is brave of her, and could have been mawkish, but isn't.

Tuesday 22 December
I check to see what's on the internet on Gielgud. I've not used it before, and find that it's full of the most amazing trivia, including his alleged autograph collection, which ends with the cheery message: 'If you've got questions or anything else,

mail me! (Arthur John Gielgud).' I'm amused by one biographical detail: 'Actor Laurence Olivier is one of his best friends.' Really?

Year 2 Progress Report

Looking back to the start of the year, I have to be pleased. I've done 75 interviews, amassed a full collection of reviews, interviews and features, and got a fair proportion of Gielgud's films from television on to video. The writing is at last beginning to flow, and I'm getting a grasp on his character, rather than merely his acting and directing achievements. My disgust with his extraordinary attitude to the book has evaporated, leaving me I hope with a greater objectivity.

I find it hard to think that, all being well, I will have finished this time next year. Right now I have a mountain to climb: the trick I suppose is not to look up at the summit.

– THREE –

Is There an Editor in the House?

Thursday 7 January 1999

To the National for *Peter Pan*, the opening event of NT2000, a year-long series of discussions and rehearsed readings from the 'best hundred plays of the century'. Barrie's play was the first Gielgud ever saw. And which biographer is that in the chair yet again?

Friday 8 January

Back to the National, this time for a reading of scenes from *The Voysey Inheritance* by Barker, Gielgud's favourite director. One of the actors is Frank Thornton, who I notice from the programme worked in Shakespeare at the start of his career with both Gielgud and Wolfit. I rush home to discover he was in the 1942 *Macbeth*, for which I have no living witnesses. Excellent, especially given the Wolfit connection.

Wednesday 13 January

I catch Gielgud in *The Elephant Man* (1980), David Lynch's moving film about the famously disfigured John Merrick. It has subtle performances by Anthony Hopkins and John Hurt, fully matched by Gielgud as Carr Gomm, the house governor of the London Hospital. He acts with restraint and sensitivity, hinting with just the occasional inflection at the warm heart beneath the aloof exterior of the man. It's a small part, but definitely not a cameo.

Friday 15 January

I feel I should have had a response to my chapters from Michael by now. I hope we're not in for another saga of editorial dithering. I leave a message with Derek asking him to find out what's happening.

Friday 22 January

Another fruitful day in the theatre collection of Bristol University's drama department. I bury myself in the two bulging Gielgud scrapbooks, lovingly kept from 1930 onwards. Where would theatrical biographers be without these obsessive fans? Several reviews, news items, and articles by Gielgud are new to me.

I browse again in the collection's bookshelves, and find an excellent interview in a commemorative book on Guthrie, where he talks in unusual depth about the technique of acting. After all this time I still get a thrill from such finds.

Saturday 23 January

I phone Patsy Ainley to arrange to return her diary and letters. She tells me Eleanor died just before Christmas, quite suddenly, and that Gielgud was terribly upset. Apparently he had caught flu, which at 94 could have carried him off. But he recovered and ploughs on, still looking for work, which is good news.

Tuesday 26 January

I speak to Derek, who's still not had any word from Michael. I find this discourteous, especially after all that nonsense after the management buy-out from Random House about how greatly Methuen cherishes its authors. But it's also alarming: such a silence inevitably provokes fears that he's having doubts about the book. At least if he asks for more material I have the first eight chapters (around 50,000 words) in very fair shape.

Leslie French, aka Puck/Ariel, has died. I hadn't realised until I read his deservedly long obituary today how amazingly varied his career had been. It ends with the classic euphemism: 'He never married.' I hadn't realised that either.

Wednesday 27 January

Philip Hoare's biography of Coward is streets ahead of Morley's, and very stylishly written. But I became a little weary of his social diary, and the bronzed sailors he had in nearly every port. Yet Hoare does pin down the butterfly very effectively. The problem is that Coward becomes increasingly unbearable as a man – selfish, spoilt, ruthless – and tedious as a writer, his wit dwindling into self-parody. It's not the biographer's fault, but you eventually lose interest.

Gielgud was one of his interviewees, but there's surprisingly little from him, or about his relationship with Coward. Do I detect a certain coolness between them in Coward's later years? I check in Coward's *Diaries* for possible enlightenment, but find little. He raves about Gielgud's productions of *Much Ado About Nothing* (1950), *The Way of the World* (1953) and *The Cherry Orchard* (1954), and finds him an amusing house guest. On the other hand he is quite rude about his comedy playing, and his fussy direction of Coward's own *Nude with Violin* (1956), but effusive about his humility and willingness to accept criticism. His criticisms of Gielgud productions seem fair and not bitchy, though he seems unable to appreciate the *Ages of Man* recital. I'm amused to read that *Nude with Violin* had to be postponed because Gielgud had a surtax problem, and had to take a part in *The Barretts of Wimpole Street* to pay for it. The film was duly slated.

Thursday 28 January

Many of the people I interview start by saying they don't have much to offer, and then the memories come flooding in. But not today. I interview a very friendly actress who'd worked with Gielgud in the 1950s. On the phone she'd made the usual protestations, but unfortunately she proved to be telling the truth. The problem is she gave up acting years ago, so it no longer matters to her. Result: total amnesia, and my only failed interview to date. I can't say I wasn't warned.

Friday 29 January

Coffee and a long chat in a stylish cafe in Portland Place with radio producer John Theocharis, a merry man who, by contrast with my last witness, seems to have almost total recall. He worked on several poetry broadcasts with Gielgud, and recently put together the excellent 'John Gielgud at the BBC' cassette. In it there's a tantalisingly brief two-minute interview, in which Gielgud talks more personally than usual, among other topics about death. John T says the interview, done on his ninetieth birthday, is much longer, and elsewhere in it Gielgud says he regrets not having had children. This I must hear.

He's good on Gielgud's radio technique. 'A lot of actors think if you take a passage more slowly, you make it more comprehensible. In fact it does the opposite, and Gielgud knows that. He's a great technician the way he uses speed.' He remembers his initial anxiety about working with such a celebrated actor. 'When John comes into the studio, he doesn't come in alone: Prospero comes in, Hamlet comes in, the unmentionable Scotsman comes in, and it can be intimidating. And you say to yourself, Shall I actually tell him how to read this line? The secret is to realise such people are not always confident themselves.'

He recalls a moment of social uneasiness: 'As we were leaving Broadcasting House, we came across some professional autograph hunters of a certain age. John signed, then presumably felt he had to say something else, so he asked them, "What else do you do?"' At the end he mentions a recent phone call to Gielgud, who complained about 'getting old, and all the aches and pains'. Theocharis says that he mentioned my name to him, presumably checking on my credentials, and was certainly not warned off. All very curious, but encouraging.

January Progress Report

A month remarkable for the total silence of Michael Earley. I'm speechless, but not wordless: I've spent much of it writing solidly. Revising the two Old Vic chapters, the first ones I wrote, has been tricky. Gielgud is in one place most of the time, with the same director, and devoting himself almost entirely to Shakespeare. It's hard to avoid focussing in detail on the productions, because so many were key performances: his Romeo, Hamlet, Benedick, Macbeth, Lear and Richard were all first shots at parts he was to tackle again later.

Yet now I know what came before, it shifts my perspective, for instance on his aspirations to direct. Knowing him so much better, I begin to see the links with his younger self. My first draft now seems scrappy, without much colour or variety, with too many superlatives from the critics. I assume recognising this is a good sign: this is what second drafts are about, isn't it?

Tuesday 2 February

Letter to Derek: 'It's now exactly four months since I met with Michael Earley, and six weeks since he was sent the first four chapters of my book. In all this time I have not heard a word from him, and the silence has now become deafening. Is he still alive? If so, is he still planning to publish my book? If not, perhaps he will now pay me the £5000 he owes me, and I'll take it elsewhere. I have been shabbily treated by Morley, then Gielgud, and now Earley. I have completed 60,000 words, about one third of the book, and know that I have a good property. I am not prepared to be ignored or to work in the dark any longer.'

Wednesday 3 February

A good interview with Dilys Hamlett, in the hamlet of Ham. And the play she was in with Gielgud?...No, it was *Twelfth Night*, in which she walked on, and understudied Vivien Leigh. 'I was a handmaiden, and for a long time he just called me "the girl in black". One day Vivien said, "Really Johnny, you must learn their names." The next day I heard him say, "Where's Dilys?" He'd gone home and learned them all.'

An intelligent and thoughtful woman, she recalls Gielgud's constant changes in rehearsals. 'He was so full of ideas, they just poured out of him, and he had to be restrained.' But like Keith Michell she has no recollection of his being excluded by Olivier from the final rehearsals. Surely this can't be a Larry fantasy? After all it's in his memoirs. I need another source.

Thursday 4 February

I've tracked down Frank Thornton, who was Angus in Gielgud's wartime production of *Macbeth* (1942), and who tells me among much else that Gielgud had none of the usual superstitions about 'the Scottish play'. He produces an unexpected primary source, a scrapbook/diary he kept at the time. He reads me a few extracts, providing good contemporary evidence of Gielgud's unselfishness on stage, and recalls his popularity with the actors: 'He was very modest, thoughtful and approachable, we'd all do anything for him.' He treasures a moment from the technical rehearsal. 'The murder of Duncan had just been discovered, and John suddenly stopped and said, "Oh my God, you're all so *English!*"'

He's acute on Wolfit, whom he worked with just prior to *Macbeth*. He says he was a bully unless you stood up to him, but praises his ability to tour Shakespeare without ever getting into debt. He's also concise about the Gielgud/Olivier contrast, asserting: 'Olivier served himself, Gielgud served the play.'

Monday 8 February

I stumble across several revealing Gielgud letters in *Power Play*, Stephen Fay's admirably even-handed life of Peter Hall. I'm fascinated to discover that it was Gielgud who suggested he play Othello at Stratford in 1961; I had thought it was Hall who had offered it to him. Gielgud spins out of control in discussing the casting of Iago, chopping and changing ideas almost daily, and coming up with some wildly unsuitable suggestions – including Harry H Corbett and Rex Harrison!

Wednesday 10 February

A quick half-hour in his dressing room at the National with Michael Bryant, between performances of *Peter Pan*, in which he's playing the Narrator. An unpretentious, down-to-earth man, he recalls Gielgud's vagueness as a director, and some 'friendly tangles' with him during *Five Finger Exercise* (1959), Peter Shaffer's first play. Most of these are about Gielgud's usual *volte-faces*, but also his desire to cut certain speeches. 'John kept Shaffer locked up, re-writing all the time. He was never happy, he always thought the writing was wrong.' We talk about his assets and limitations as an actor. 'He can only play what he can find in his own soul, in what Stanislavsky calls his "emotion memory". Most star actors play themselves, so it's hard for him to play evil, he's so sweet and kind. He's a good character actor within limits, but I can't somehow see him as a Mafia man or a gangster.'

I ask about HM Tennent and their alleged favouring of homosexuals: 'I was part of the scruffy jeans and sweatshirt gang, and not of their set at all. They knew I wasn't gay, but they were very fair, they took me on, and were wonderful to me.' He also reveals a quirky side to Binkie Beaumont. 'He insisted his plays should run for no more than two hours and ten minutes: anything longer you had to cut, since he believed an audience became bored after that. He'd also go round the theatre with a thermometer to see if the temperature was right. He said if it was too high, they stopped laughing.'

Thursday 11 February
I open an envelope marked 'Methuen' with keen anticipation, but it's only a standard letter to authors, confirming the contract arrangements following the split from Random House. I enjoy the claim that 'we have the experienced staff and resources necessary to perform our duties in a professional and competent manner'. I just manage to restrain myself from sending a rude reply about the performance of Michael Earley (who I've now predictably dubbed Michael Late).

Thursday 18 February
An interview with John Miller, who helped Gielgud put together his autobiography, based on taped interviews. He's interesting on the delicate art of getting him to discuss Olivier. 'When I talked to him on radio, I asked him direct questions, and got very little. So later, when I interviewed him for television, I didn't ask a single question about Olivier, and he kept bringing him in.'

He touches on Gielgud's thoughtfulness and dislike of bad manners. 'My wife and I were talking with him at the Theatre Museum, on the day he opened their Gielgud Gallery. Suddenly Roy Strong rushed up and said, "John dear, I've come to rescue you from these boring people." Sir John went bright pink, and rolled his eyes at me. The next morning he rang to apologise for Roy Strong's behaviour, adding: "I hardly know the man, and we had the most *terrible* meal."'

Friday 19 February
A call from Derek Granger, who tells me Gielgud's companion Martin Hensler died a few days ago. What a blow, especially coming so soon after his sister Eleanor's death. I can't imagine what he will do. As far as I know there's no immediate family to step in. He seems to have been totally dependent on Martin to organise his life. Derek says there was another view among some of his friends, that Martin was a monster, and imprisoned Gielgud in the country so no one could get at him.

In the evening I have a lively interview with Anna Carteret in her dressing-room at the Savoy theatre, where she's playing Queen Margaret to Robert Lindsay's Richard III. Friendly, amusing, immensely attractive, she has vivid memories of Peter Brook's production of *Oedipus* (1968), 'the most exciting I've ever worked on'. She remembers Ted Hughes, who did the translation, at the first read-through. 'He insisted on reading the whole play himself. Writers are usually rather shy and inhibited, but he was very forceful about the way it should be done and spoken. He gave it absolutely everything.'

She recalls Gielgud's unhappiness during Brook's pre-rehearsal exercises: 'I think he found a lot of the physical part difficult and irrelevant, and he was very uncomfortable. You felt he would have been happier in a conventional production. But the end-result was very exciting, a combination of Peter's experiment and John's expertise.'

She works occasionally with drama students, and wishes there was a recording of *Oedipus*, so she could let them hear how Gielgud used his voice. 'His range was astonishing, he would go up and down the octaves in just one or two lines. That's what you need to aim at, that's the pinnacle.'

Monday 22 February
A note from John Miller. Following Martin's death Gielgud is apparently in a state of shock, seeing no one and not taking any phone calls. He recently had to go into hospital after a fall, at exactly the moment when Martin became seriously ill. I fear Martin's death may be fatal for him, especially if he's unable to work. What else does he have to live for? I would like him to see my script, if he survives that long, but not if it's going to create more problems. What I need is a sympathetic go-between. Perhaps Patsy Ainley might be the right person? We get on well, and she's a friend of the family.

Tuesday 23 February
Back on the film trail, I watch *Around the World in Eighty Days* (1957). I'm bored to distraction. It's more of a travelogue than a narrative, with endless absurd cameo performances, including Gielgud's as a gentleman's gentleman, a part originally offered to Olivier. He looks ill at ease in his one scene with Coward who, despite looking rather like a frog in a silver wig, walks away with it. The film was released the same year as *The Barretts of Wimpole Street*, so I assume Gielgud's surtax was still not sorted out.

Wednesday 24 February
A good hour with Michael Feast in a quiet corner of the National's foyer. He's eloquent about playing Ariel to Gielgud's last Prospero, in Peter Hall's production of *The Tempest* (1974). 'Even though he was steeped in the part, he was at pains not to reproduce his earlier performance. We had long sessions working on the rhythm and metre, and I learnt a lot from him then, much more than I did at

drama school. I loved working with him, it was incredibly exciting to feel part of that tradition that went back to Garrick and beyond.'

He was also with Gielgud in *No Man's Land* (1975): 'From close to, his performance was astonishing. I couldn't imagine what he would do with the part, and then he created this seedy, potentially quite vicious old sponger. It was a miracle of transformation.' He recalls an odd quirk of Gielgud's on stage. 'He had a tendency to focus slightly above your eyes a lot of the time. It wasn't off-putting, you didn't feel he wasn't concentrating on you; I don't think he was even aware of it.' During the run he was asked to play with Gielgud in the television version of Dostoyevsky's *The Grand Inquisitor*. He thought he'd been cast for his acting ability, but Gielgud soon disillusioned him with a typical gaffe: 'I asked for you as I couldn't bear looking at a stranger's face for all that time.'

Thursday 25 February
A brief telephone interview with a leading director, who worked with Gielgud on a television play. I'd interviewed him before at the National for *StageWrite*, when he was directing a Shaw play, but I had forgotten how supremely arrogant he was. He brusquely suggested that there was no point in talking about the film 'if you haven't done your homework' i.e. seen his masterpiece. After five minutes I give up. It makes me realise even more clearly how extraordinarily helpful most people have been.

Friday 26 February
I've gathered more details of Martin's death. It seems the gardener came to the house on Monday morning, found the door locked and nobody answering. Eventually he broke a window, and found a macabre scene: Gielgud lying on the floor with a broken leg, Martin dying on the sofa. It's terrible just to imagine it.

February Progress Report
More solid interviews, filling obvious gaps. I read Mark Gatiss' biography of Gielgud's gay friend James Whale, which throws useful light on the raffish 1920s scene. But the month is dominated by Martin's death, and the continuing silence from Michael Earley.

Monday 1 March
To Sarah Miles' beautiful old house near Petersfield in rural Hampshire. She sits cross-legged on the floor, looking ridiculously young, drinking what appears to be seaweed. Having read her extraordinarily candid memoirs I'd been nervous about

interviewing her. But she proves an easy witness, one who simply says what she thinks, which is probably one of the reasons for her chaotic life. 'Everything I do turns into a catastrophe,' she says in passing.

Gielgud provided her with her first West End part, in *Dazzling Prospect* (1961), which she calls 'a bit of old twaddle; they threw tomatoes from the gallery on the first night'. She remembers his directing method: 'There was no psychology, it was all "Try moving up to the sofa, see if that works. No, sit on the pouf, no, oh God, take a drink of water from the carafe." There were no insights into why the character was saying what she was saying.'

She recalls his terror at the prospect of having to seduce her in the television version of Anouilh's *The Rehearsal* (1963). 'He was very sweet, he had a great purity of heart. I felt his *faux pas* came from a kind of innocence, and I've always thought innocence one of the finest qualities.'

After lunch I drop in on Christopher Fry, who lives nearby in West Sussex, to return a set of records of *The Lady's Not for Burning* that he'd lent to me. As I walk up the path I get a lovely glimpse of him through the window, serenely writing his diary. He has a bad cough, and is worried about being well for the reading of *The Lady's Not for Burning*, which is being staged at the National as part of NT2000, so I don't linger.

Friday 5 March
I've finished Ted Morgan's biography of Somerset Maugham. He's a monster, unattractive in almost every respect, which can of course make for an absorbing biography. Morgan catches his essence well, though the torrent of detail eventually becomes tedious. Biographers so often seem to drown in the depths of their material. But there's first-rate stuff on Gielgud directing Maugham's last play *Sheppey* (1933), as well as on contemporary attitudes to homosexuality, and Maugham's desperate efforts to conceal his.

Wednesday 10 March
Continuing silence from Earley. I talk to Derek about pressing him on the money question, but he advises waiting for his editorial comments, then using them as a basis for negotiations. I defer reluctantly to this suggestion, but it's all *so* frustrating.

Friday 12 March
I've been reading Gielgud's lengthy 1937 essay on costume, scenery and stage business in *Hamlet*, printed at the back of Rosamond Gilder's book *John Gielgud's*

Hamlet. I'm astonished yet again at his industry, his passion for detail, and his determination to honour Shakespeare's text. There are shades of the Barker *Prefaces to Shakespeare* that he so admired, and used extensively, though I see this was written before Barker's one on *Hamlet* was published.

Monday 15 March

Last night I watched Gielgud's sole Hitchcock film, *Secret Agent* (1936). His reviews were mostly negative, but I find him convincing as the novelist turned unwilling secret agent. Debonair but austere, he's very much at home with the crisp dialogue. I'm interested to note how gracefully he dances with Madeleine Carroll.

I'm amused to find him claiming in an interview that he couldn't sit through any of his films, and describing in detail what's wrong with his performance in this one. I see also that he suggested three of the cast to Hitchcock: Michael Redgrave, who appears for a few seconds in what was his first film; Florence Kahn, Max Beerbohm's actress wife; and Michel Saint-Denis, who was visiting Gielgud on the set, and was roped in to play a coachman. It's useful to see that meticulous director in action: his joviality in his tiny scene undermines my image of him as stern and lacking in humour.

Friday 19 March

A memorable evening in the Cottesloe, with Christopher Fry, his cough now conquered, introducing a reading of scenes from *The Lady's Not for Burning*. Shyly at first, he offers a little background to the writing of it, chuckling at the memory of the Lord Chamberlain's insistence that he remove the euphemism 'mucking' from one speech. During the reading he sits sideways on to the actors, listening but not looking at them. Alex Jennings (in Gielgud's part) and Juliet Stevenson play his romantic/poetic/comic lines with wonderful intensity. At the end there's a warm ovation for him, in which the actors join. It's a sell-out occasion for a lovely man. Maybe it's time for the National to revive the play?

Tuesday 23 March

Prompted by a puff on the cover from Gielgud – 'Tempestuous, vivid and shrewdly characteristic' – I read Enid Bagnold's *Autobiography*. He's wrong: it's fragmented, tedious and self-indulgent. But for me it's worth reading for the backstage material on his production of her play *The Chalk Garden* (1956). There's also a glimpse of Gielgud and Richardson rehearsing her dire piece *The Last Joke* (1960). She found Gielgud amusingly adaptable: 'Would you like it this way or that way?' But she was less amused when, sensing disaster, the two actors radically revised her play during the pre-London tour. It was still a disaster.

March Progress Report

I've run out of words to describe Earley's continuing silence. Yet despite the vacuum, the writing goes well. With a dozen chapters in draft I'm beginning to see the arc of Gielgud's life, starting to make connections between its different elements, and discreetly inserting my interpretative comments.

Reading: Michael Hordern's autobiography *A World Elsewhere* is flat and unprofitable, rather laddish, and full of extracts from his fishing diary. Maybe it's time to stop bothering with such memoirs, and stick to biographies, done by real writers.

Hopes: Judi Dench has agreed to see me, but not until August. Her letter is a great morale-booster.

Monday 12 April

A valuable and delightful hour with Dorothy Tutin at her house in Barnes. She was the pin-up of my youth, so there's an extra frisson, which I hope I conceal.

Effervescent, intelligent, with her exquisite smoky voice, she is eloquent about Gielgud's Benedick in *Much Ado About Nothing* (1952), in which she played Hero. 'His timing, his knowledge of what was truly witty, was just immaculate. His antennae for judging the audience was perfect, and he brought the house down. He did it with the minimum of movement and facial expression, which only added to it. He was the funniest Benedick I've ever seen. He was not a romantic figure in a way, but he could exude a romantic wit and sharpness. To me it was a complete miracle.'

She remembers with sadness his Othello at Stratford in 1961 with Zeffirelli (she was Desdemona), when what promised to be a fine performance was ruined by the cumbersome sets and costumes, and a disastrous first night that lasted four and a quarter hours. She remembers how Gielgud saved the production by reverting to a more rhetorical style, to match the sets and costumes. 'There was no self-pity or blaming others. His resilience and natural courage were incredible.'

Tuesday 13 April

I've been reading Valerie Grove's *Dear Dodie*, an absorbing biography of the playwright Dodie Smith. She's not a very sympathetic character, being hugely self-absorbed, but certainly a lively subject to write about. The book is weighed down with too many of her own writings, endless autobiographical notebooks etc, charting her every move and emotion, but otherwise it's stylishly and meticulously done. Today, if Dodie Smith is read at all, it's for *One Hundred and One Dalmatians*. But the biography has handy backstage details on *Dear Octopus* (1938), in which Gielgud took refuge after his exhausting classical season at the Queen's. Gielgud's arrest is treated in some detail, though quite discreetly. I wonder how painful it is for him to read now of that traumatic occasion?

Wednesday 14 April

Gielgud is 95 today. How many more birthdays will he see? At least one more, I selfishly hope. I celebrate from a distance by listening to a tape of his *Desert Island Discs* programme. I hadn't quite realised how much music meant to him. His taste is mainly romantic – Delius, Mahler, Brahms, Fauré – but he also goes for Mozart, Bach and Purcell. In passing he drops snippets of family information new to me, and re-tells the famous Edward Knoblock story; so at least one of the gaffes is true. His choice of book is predictable: a book of crosswords plus a dictionary, or perhaps a complete Proust ('They're so expensive to buy these days').

Derek has again got nowhere with Earley, who fails to return his calls. He suggests I ring him myself, so I do so, only to be told that he's in the States. I write a short, angry letter. Probably unwise, but I'm absolutely fed up with being ignored.

Thursday 15 April

In the evening to the Gielgud Theatre, to interview Michael Pennington, currently playing Oscar Wilde in *Gross Indecency*. In the foyer I study the large Snowdon portrait of Gielgud. Did *he* choose it to hang there? It's very severe, and doesn't seem to me to capture the essential Gielgud.

Michael P is highly articulate, humorous, thoughtful and, unlike some actors, sensitive to what would be of most use to me (i.e. *not* endless details of their own career). Last night I read the opening and closing chapters of his excellent book on *Hamlet*, so I ask him about his playing of the part in 1980. Ironically, though he was said by some to have assumed Gielgud's mantle, it was apparently Olivier who influenced him most. 'John Barton wanted what you would loosely call a Gielgud Hamlet, the sweet prince, the romantic Hamlet. But I was pulling in a more passionate, violent direction.'

He disputes the idea, voiced by Olivier and others, that Gielgud 'sings' Shakespeare's verse. 'Listen to his Clarence from *Richard III*, the terror and the starkness of it. His voice is a God-given instrument, but what he's brought to that natural gift is fleetness of thought, mercurial feeling, emotions he can access swiftly, and a slightly impatient intelligence, always wanting to move on. That's why he's so dazzling in Shakespeare.' He played Oedipus alongside Gielgud as Teiresias in the TV *Oedipus the King* (1985), and remembers being astonished at the physical strength of his acting at the age of eighty. 'It was all coming as it should do, right from deep in his belly. It was diaphragm power, which is emotional power. There was nothing weedy about his Teiresias.'

He recalls Gielgud's genuine interest in the careers of younger actors, and his willingness with Peggy Ashcroft to be a patron of the English Shakespeare Company, co-founded by the two Michaels, Pennington and Bogdanov. The productions became remorselessly modern dress – Mohican haircuts, tommy guns and battle fatigues – and after seeing one production the two eminent patrons decided it was time to end their association. 'In the sweetest way Peggy extricated the two of them. It was she who made the call; he would probably have left it.'

While he and Gielgud were filming John Mortimer's *Summer's Lease* (1989) in Tuscany, Gielgud tried in his own way to give him a helping hand: 'He asked me what I was doing next, and I said I didn't know. He said, "Call Richard Eyre, tell him to put on *Faust* for you." I said, "John, it's changed a bit nowadays, that's not how it's done." But that was his offering: he was very considerate.' He remembers how, when news of Olivier's death reached them while they were filming in Italy, Gielgud talked generously of his talents, and his ability to play parts beyond his own range.

As I leave the theatre he says with feeling: 'One begins to wonder whether John might not be immortal. My experience of him is that if he's working or talking, he's indestructible. I dread his going, he's such a national resource, such a magnet for people's affections.'

Friday 16 April
Over again to Mander and Mitchenson. Richard Mangan's personal Gielgud memorabilia, which I thought were simply a few early programmes, turn out to be *eight* bulging folders full. So I spend the whole morning on them, and find new and invaluable details on several early productions.

In the afternoon I plough through volumes 2-6 of Agate's *Ego*. My, didn't he have one! This brings me several small jewels. I also dig up a ten-page pamphlet published in November 1953 by the *Sunday Times*. It contains its liberal leader on homosexuality published immediately after Gielgud's arrest, and a selection from the many letters it provoked. I hadn't realised the incident had caused quite such a stir. The readers' letters provide a fascinating glimpse of attitudes of the time, ranging from tolerance and understanding to that of the conductor John

Barbirolli, who is relieved 'that this pernicious and pestiliential problem may at last be squarely faced, for it has for too long now been a canker eating into the so-called intellectual and artistic fabric of our society'.

Back home I discover that there was panic in Fleet Street this week, as reports circulated that Gielgud had died. One reporter at a press conference given by Elizabeth Taylor was told to ask her for a comment, but by the time she arrived an hour late he'd been paged with the message, 'He's alive, alive, alive!' Comic, especially as no one seems to know what caused the false alarm. I imagine Gielgud rather enjoyed the fuss.

Wednesday 21 April
I watch a video of John Miller's television interview with Gielgud. Most of the material is familiar, but he's more relaxed than I've seen him before. I find myself understanding his personality better, and warming to him again. What comes over most strongly is his sheer enjoyment of ideas and of people, his delight in the absurdities of human behaviour, and his modesty, which I still believe is genuine. It's useful also to see his house, and what looks like a stunningly beautiful formal garden. But will I ever see it, or him, in the flesh?

Thursday 22 April
I've been reading Melvyn Bragg's slim volume on Olivier. It's sentimental and over-written, but catches Olivier's complex character well. So too does Gielgud, who in it describes without any obvious malice the many offstage parts Olivier played – landowner, squire, gardener, host – when he visited him and Vivien Leigh at their grand country home, Notley Abbey. Bizarrely, Bragg suggests that like Olivier, Gielgud 'longed to be a priest'. Actually he just liked sniffing the incense and watching the theatrical rituals at Brompton Oratory.

Monday 26 April
An excellent session with Oliver Cotton in his dressing-room at the National, where he's a member of Trevor Nunn's new ensemble. He acted in five productions with Gielgud, and offers me many pertinent observations, as well as amusing snippets of offstage conversations.

He remembers Gielgud's anxiety during the Peter Brook production of *Oedipus* (1968). 'The script was very late, and that worried him; he fluffed a lot in rehearsal. He has such a fine ear he can't bear saying the wrong thing, so he'd go back and correct himself, where others would go on. I was young and stupid and arrogant, I thought he represented the old-fashioned school of acting, but I began to realise he was doing something very extraordinary.'

He admits to being heavily influenced by Gielgud. 'He more than anybody has taught me about speaking. As a young actor I didn't understand phrasing and cadence, I used to chop it up and mangle it. It took me twenty years to realise what he was doing. What he did was the best of the nineteenth century taken into the twentieth.'

Like many others he's amused by Gielgud's lack of political sophistication. 'While we were doing *Julius Caesar* the Grunwick strike was on. One day he said: "Why do people have to behave like that?" And I said: "Actually, John, the police are behaving like pigs." And he replied: "But that's what they're there for, to keep order."' We talk about the ubiquitous mimicking of Johnny and Larry and Ralphie, and the interview descends into semi-hysteria on both sides as he does all three of them, then re-enacts a story he devised involving Gielgud, the ghost of Ralph Richardson, Marlon Brando and a singing pig.

Tuesday 27 April
Lunch with my friend Charles Clark, who's astonished to hear the latest twist, or non-twist, in the Methuen saga. He advises me to make sure to get on the record all verbal agreements with Earley about extra time and length, and to do so before my contractual deadline, which is now only four days away. He also suggests I contact the Society of Authors for advice.

Wednesday 28 April
To Brighton, for a lengthy and giggly session with Derek Granger, Olivier's latest biographer. I had imagined someone rather large, grand and wearing a cravat; instead he's short, twinkly, and dressed in jeans and trainers. Sitting high up in his seafront flat, with nothing visible outside but sea and sky, we soon get into the inevitable Gielgud/Olivier comparison. Having known both, he is very helpful.

'John is very unLarry like, much more cool and detached, which can be disconcerting, even though he's also charming and kindly. Compared with Larry he's very unambitious, there's no sense of personal struggle. Perhaps that's his inheritance? Socially he didn't want to dominate, unlike Larry, who got very annoyed if anyone faintly had a conversation away from him. John is the most civilised and educated of actors, he always seems to have a lot of time for living and cultivating his friends. He seems a very whole person, whereas with Larry you have a sense that everything is directed to his work.'

Wednesday 5 May

I talk to Richard Eyre on the phone. Though he'd originally agreed to help, he feels he's too busy to meet right now, and fears anyway he'd have little to say that would be original. I'm sure the latter's not true, but how can I argue? He offers to send me some pages about Gielgud from his forthcoming book on the history of British theatre, which is a nice gesture.

In expectation of meeting him I've been reading his eloquent memoir *Utopia and Other Places*, one of those books you hope will never end. It's full not just of shrewd observations and colourful incidents from his life in the theatre, but also wonderful evocations of his Dorset childhood. He gives a moving account of his lifelong discord with his father who, when he died, 'looked like a patriarch, like Gielgud – all nose, and all English'. It's interesting to read that his actress grandmother worked with Du Maurier, and that like Gielgud he's a huge admirer of Barker.

Thursday 6 May

A disappointing talk with Clive Francis about Gielgud's notes on the 1940 Barker *King Lear*. He can't show them to me at present as he's decided to try and get them published, which is perfectly reasonable, but frustrating for me. He sends me one tantalising page, with Gielgud's ingenious solution to the arguments over the 'And my poor fool is hang'd' line from *Lear*. He tells me he wrote to Gielgud recently to commiserate about Martin's death, and got a reply back in a crude envelope, written in what he describes as 'a cleaning lady's hand', and misspelling Wilde. Gielgud signed it, but that was all. It's a worrying development.

Sunday 9 May

Dirk Bogarde died yesterday. His life can't have been up to much these last few years, so a heart attack was surely the kindest way. Coincidentally, yesterday his editor Tony Lacey was telling me he had got some feeling back in his arm. In the evening I watch the video of *Sebastian* (1968), the only film apart from *Providence* that Bogarde made with Gielgud. He had warned me that it was dreadful, and it is, though he himself as always gives an interesting, sensitive performance. Gielgud plays the head of intelligence, and is much too bland in a part that calls for more menace. Only in his one scene with Bogarde, in Blackwell's bookshop in Oxford, does he come anywhere near the character.

Wednesday 12 May

A reply from Kate Pool to my letter to the Society of Authors. She's at a loss to explain Earley's behaviour, and offers to contact him on my behalf if necessary. I hope it won't be, but it's good to know there's a fallback. I fax Derek with copies of my two recent letters to Methuen, in the hope that he can break through the wall of silence.

Thursday 13 May
I've just read Morley's biography of James Mason. It's a poor, lazy effort: too often he just throws chunks of his interview transcripts into the story e.g. the section on *Julius Caesar* consists almost entirely of reminiscence from director Joseph L. Manckiewicz, Gielgud, and producer John Houseman. He also has an odd, irritating habit of calling his subject 'Mason' in one paragraph, and 'James' in the next. Mason was an interestingly sad and offbeat character and a skilful, under-used actor who was ruined by Hollywood. He deserved better. One passage puzzles me. Morley says George Rylands tempted the young Gielgud from London into the Marlowe Society in Cambridge. It's very curious that nobody, including Gielgud and Hayman, has ever referred to this occasion.

Saturday 15 May
The pages from Richard Eyre's book arrive. His take on the Olivier/Gielgud rivalry is succinct, but fair. Interesting to see that he highlights Gielgud's radicalism. He writes like an angel; I envy his ability to sum up the essence of an actor's talent in a sentence, something I find hard to achieve.

Monday 17 May
A short interview with Cicely Berry, voice director of the RSC, who I know from the days when she was teaching with my mother at Central School. Before we start I play a brief excerpt from my *Ages of Man* tape, hoping it doesn't seem too didactic a gesture. She scribbles some notes, and then talks interestingly on the quality of Gielgud's voice, and the reasons for its beauty and resonance. Elvis, she says, has an equally 'centred' voice that compels you to listen. She says she doesn't like music, and has no ear for it. Neither apparently does John Barton, a world authority on Shakespeare. It seems there's no connection between that faculty and having an ear for verse, which I find surprising.

Tuesday 18 May
A friendly postcard from Alan Bennett, who claims he has nothing to say about Gielgud that he hasn't already said several times; he mentions his book *Writing Home*. He says he failed to dredge up anything fresh for Morley, which is good if true. He adds that if he were to give his opinions on his performances they

wouldn't be interesting enough to publish. This of course is nonsense: his review of Gielgud's last volume of autobiography *An Actor and His Time* (1979) was full of astute and affectionate comments on his virtues as an actor.

Thursday 20 May
Derek's persistent prodding has finally worked, and Earley's comments arrive. After all this time, they're a huge disappointment. They seem to contradict what he told Derek verbally a while back: he's making exactly the same comments as before, about lack of colour, context, etc. He asks why there is nothing at all on the Terry family: there are three pages. He says nothing about the chapter on Gielgud's time at the Oxford Playhouse, which I revised extensively after our last meeting. All this makes me wonder if he's actually spent more than a few minutes reading the chapters.

He asks if I've been in touch with Morley who, he tells me, 'is still hoping to hear from you'. Is he joking? What is there to talk about? In any case, why would an esteemed portrait painter want to hobnob with a mere polaroid photographer? I talk to Derek, who suggests I take up Earley's suggestion that he and I meet; this might help to mend fences. He agrees that Morley is now irrelevant, and that I have no obligation to him.

Friday 21 May
I catch Kenneth Branagah's four-hour *Hamlet* (1996) at the National Film Theatre. It's a curious but compelling mixture of cinematic tosh and subtle acting in the intimate scenes, notably by Branagh himself, and Derek Jacobi as an excellent Claudius. Gielgud makes another thirty-second appearance, this time as King Priam, gesticulating wildly as Troy burns around him. I notice he's still wearing his large, pre-Trojan-War signet ring on his little finger. I hope it survived the conflagration.

Saturday 22 May
Back to the National Film Theatre, this time for a more substantial Gielgud role: 22 minutes of almost uninterrupted monologue in the film Richard Briers mentioned, Chekhov's *Swan Song* (1993). Also directed by Branagh, it gives Gielgud a chance to re-enact bits of Shakespeare from his past. It's immensely touching to see glimpses of his faraway youth in Romeo's last speech, and the still fiery energy of his Lear. It's a sparkling performance for someone aged 88, in which he catches both the melancholy and humour of the old actor. Branagh has done what no one else was able to do, and got Gielgud to play a drunk

convincingly, at least for the first five minutes. It's obviously time to contact him about a possible interview.

Tuesday 25 May
I've nearly finished a riveting biography of Kenneth Tynan by his wife Kathleen. It's a bold, generous book, exposing so much of their personal life, yet somehow not in a prurient way. Tynan was something of a monster, but also rather a sad case in his search for oddball sexual experiences, and his embrace of pornography. She's very perceptive on his development as a critic, and writes shrewdly about his tangled life at the National. I was hoping I'd discovered a book that was neither by Morley nor mentioned him. Alas, up he pops, telling us all that as an undergraduate at Oxford he used to cross the High Street barefoot in his pyjamas at eight in the morning to buy the *Observer* and read Tynan. How very exciting.

Thursday 27 May
I send a heavily revised chapter off to Earley, on Gielgud's early ventures with Coward and Chekhov. It feels good, a balanced blend of information, personal story and background theatre history. Perhaps anger is a valuable incentive, in which case Earley is subtler than I thought. In my accompanying letter I go through his points, leaving the implication hanging in the air that he hasn't really read these chapters. I also enclose my contents list, so he can see what I'm up against on the length, now looking to my horror like coming out at around 200,000 words.

Friday 28 May
Out of the blue comes an apologetic letter from Paul Scofield, wondering if he ever sent me the answers to my questions, and if not would I still like them. Would I hell! I fire off an enthusiastic reply. Good: that's one less lost to Morley than I had thought.

May Progress Report
However inadequate, Earley's response has given me something to grapple with. I hadn't realised until now how much I was missing proper, detailed feedback. I hope he'll see the need for it when we meet shortly. Then I'll feel I can speed on more confidently.

Disappointments: No response from Joan Plowright or Peter Jones. And Richard Eyre has finally eluded me.

Tuesday 1 June

I've been enjoying Michael Coveney's biography of Maggie Smith. Her spiky, mercurial personality comes over very sharply. I like his device of breaking off the narrative for the occasional 'Entr'acte', brief essays on her wit, her friends, her fellow-actors, and so on. Should I do the same? It might be handy to stand back from the flow of his life now and then. I will give it serious thought.

I know Maggie Smith never gives interviews about herself, but maybe she would do so about Gielgud? On the other hand, I learn from Coveney's book that her marriage to Robert Stephens was falling apart while he was directing them both in *Private Lives* (1972), so it might be a sensitive area. But it's worth a try.

Wednesday 2 June

A white letter day! Ten closely written pages from Paul Scofield, full of wonderfully shrewd, detailed and generous observations on Gielgud. If, as he claims, he's not articulate in an interview, he certainly redeems himself in print. He's even bothered, to my astonishment, to give me thumb-nail sketches of directors who I had asked him about. It's a jewel of an offering that's been well worth the wait.

Thursday 3 June

A constructive meeting at last with Michael Earley. We spend three hours going through my two most recently revised chapters, which he thinks a great improvement. He feels still more colour and background is needed, which is reasonable, and also more on the Terry connection, which isn't, and which I shall ignore. Happily, he agrees to a new maximum length of 200,000, and we talk about a possible delivery date of the end of the year, with publication next autumn. I leave to Derek the task of getting some of my advance shifted forward.

Michael tells me that Peter Brook, whom he also publishes, was in London last week for the launch of his memoirs in paperback. It seems he rang Gielgud and found him 'in a bad way'. No further details, but it's worrying news again.

Tuesday 8 June

This evening I watched Olivier's film of *Richard III* (1955), which I'd not seen for many years. His performance still has the power to terrify, though it now also seems very camp. Gielgud plays 'simple, plain Clarence', and in his one scene with Olivier steals the moment with a display of puzzled melancholy at his sudden arrest. His main scene in the Tower, in which he recalls his nightmare, is a fine example of his ability to combine lyricism with anguish, while keeping a tight grip on the flow of Shakespeare's verse. But much of it is shot in the middle distance:

was this, I wonder, deliberate on Olivier's part?

Tuesday 15 June
To the National again, for a performance of scenes from *Home* (1970). No Morley this time, thankfully. David Storey sends a message to say he'd rather have the play speak for itself than come along and talk about it. So there's just two long scenes, played with great poignancy by Edward Petherbridge and Oliver Ford Davies. The latter takes Gielgud's part, but can't manage the real tears at the end. Good as the two actors are, it's impossible for me not to hear Gielgud and Richardson speaking the lines with them.

Wednesday 16 June
Peter O'Toole's memoirs are totally unreadable. He thinks he's James Joyce, but he's not: it's the most self-obsessed work I've ever read, or rather skimmed, since after the first few pages I rush through, looking only for Gielgud nuggets, and finding few (alas, no index). After two volumes he's still only just left RADA, for God's sake! The book seems to be as much about Hitler and Edmund Kean as about O'Toole. Truly weird. Where was his editor at Macmillan?

Thursday 17 June
I'd given up on hearing from Joan Plowright, but now her secretary writes to say she's in America, and could she be in touch on her return? She can indeed.

Monday 21 June
I make contact with the actress Nan Munro's daughter Angela Gau, with whom I was at school. She's not hopeful about finding any material, but promises to look through the family archive. In passing she tells me that Mavis Walker, one of Morley's alleged 'refuseniks', has died. My first ungracious thought is, What has happened to her 'Travels with Gielgud' book that Penguin rejected? It would be an excellent source if I could track it down.

Tuesday 22 June
One of the many delights of working on this book is reading Agate's diaries. I've got as far as *Ego 8*, just managing to keep ahead of my own writing. This volume is full of learning, gossip, entertaining parody, and scabrous wit, but also excellent mini-essays on Olivier's Richard III, Wolfit's Lear, and Gielgud's Hamlet. Only one volume left: it will be a wrench when I finish.

Derek tells me there's unlikely to be more money coming from Methuen, that

Michael Earley says they've already been generous. He suggests I write asking for the delivery date to be extended to March, to allow me time to earn a bit from journalism. All very annoying.

This afternoon in an office at the National someone surfing the internet clicked on to Gielgud for me. First entry: The Death List! This claims that he's fourth in a list of the top twenty celebrities most likely to die this year. On closer inspection I see the list is a year out of date, so now perhaps he's top of it.

Monday 28 June
At my local theatre, the Orange Tree in Richmond, I talk to its director Sam Walters, who's keen to know how the book is coming along. It's soon apparent that he knows Morley quite well, so I'm a bit vague about my progress. We talk of Rodney Ackland, whose plays Sam helped bring back into fashion. He tells me he was bi-sexual, and that when he was in New York with Gielgud working on his adaptation of *Crime and Punishment* (1947) he was forever picking up young men, to an extent that shocked even Gielgud.

By a strange coincidence, a letter came this morning from a school friend, who tells me that Gielgud once tried to pick him up, 'in Fortnum's of all places!'

Tuesday 29 June
An annoying but pleasant enough letter from Kenneth Branagh's assistant, saying he's tied up for the rest of the year with post-production on *Love's Labour's Lost*, and then a new film in America; so he can't help, but wishes me luck. A great shame: I'd have welcomed a discussion about *Hamlet* and *Swan Song*.

Wednesday 30 June
A letter from Michael Earley, in which he expresses anxiety about the delivery date. He says I must deliver mid-January if they are to publish in the autumn. Damn it! I really feel I need that extra two or three months. On the other hand the alternative of postponing publication until spring 2001 doesn't bear thinking of.

He's scribbled comments on the latest three chapters. Some are helpful; yes, I need to explain more about certain movements in the theatre. Others are absurd: does it really matter how Gielgud's young gay friend Lord Lathom acquired his wealth? But I'm grateful that at last he's reading it closely. He actually says he *likes* one section, on Mrs Pat and Gielgud in *Ghosts*. This is his first really positive comment. It's ridiculous how a small compliment can be so encouraging. He still wants more on the theatre of the time (agreed), how Gielgud is developing as an actor (no, I think this is all right), and on the Terry family connections (forget it). He's worried that Barker's influence on Gielgud doesn't come though, but there's more in the 1930s chapters he hasn't yet seen, so that doesn't worry me.

June Progress Report
I've made fair progress on the writing, now nearly two-thirds done in first draft. But the crunch begins here, since while keeping up the pace I also need to flit back frequently to revise the early chapters, for Michael to comment on. But I shall relish the challenge now that at long last I have an editor back in action again.

Thursday 1 July
A note from Derek, saying Michael wants a new delivery date built into the contract, one that I'm confident I can meet. That's fair enough: he's clearly becoming worried that the writing could go on for ever. I know it won't, but that's no help to him.

Monday 5 July
I'm reading an intermittently interesting biography by Paul Ferris of Richard Burton, who owed his theatrical breakthrough to Gielgud. It conveys clearly Burton's casual, take-it-or-leave it approach to acting, the other end of the spectrum to Gielgud's dedication. It's fascinating to see how Ferris tried to get Burton to cooperate, but never finally penetrated his entourage. Burton's technique was never to reply to letters, which, whatever problems he might cause a biographer, Gielgud would never do.

Tuesday 13 July
A frustrating session at the Theatre Museum, where I'm suddenly told I can't have photocopies made of Gielgud's letters to Christopher Fry in their collection. When I query this ridiculous policy, I'm told it's because they are 'personal letters'. It's absurd: either they should give people proper access or none at all. The letters are good material, so I'm forced to waste three hours writing out the highlights by hand. I look up at Gielgud's portrait on the wall facing me: do I detect a hint of a smile?

Later, interviewing Fiona Shaw for *StageWrite*, I mention the book, and she adds a couple of stories to my collection. She tells me she and Christopher Lee and Ian Richardson were swapping Gielgud anecdotes only yesterday, while making *Gormenghast* for television. Good to know that the tradition continues.

Sunday 18 July
Last night I watched Gielgud in the Hollywood film of *Julius Caesar* (1953).
I'm startled by how tough he plays Cassius, catching the rampant bitterness and
jealousy of the scheming, acute politician. Dressed in a symbolically black toga, he's
convincingly brooding and intense, and his scenes with James Mason are riveting.

Mason is sombre, contained and guilt-ridden, and they match and complement
each other wonderfully. The tent scene, with its shifting emotions, is brilliantly
done, with Gielgud bringing out the essence of Cassius' fellowship with Brutus,
and the nobler side of his character, such as it is. Brando as Mark Antony looks
saturnine, and is effective in the early scenes, though his performance is slightly
spoilt for me by knowing that he's wearing jeans under his toga. Remembering
Gielgud's dislike of riding a horse, I watch the battle scenes carefully, and notice
that you never see him mounting or dismounting. Glimpsed once or twice in the
saddle, he looks less than resolute in the face of the foe.

Tuesday 20 July
Meeting Oliver Cotton again by chance, at a reception at the National, I learn a bit more
about Martin Hensler, notably that he came to Britain in 1956 after the Hungarian
Revolution. When Oliver was at the house he asked Gielgud what Martin did before
then: 'No idea,' he replied. In the distance I see Denis Quilley, to whom I wrote recently.
Pathetically, I'm unable to summon up the nerve to ask if he's able to help.

Sunday 25 July
I watch Tony Richardson's film of *The Loved One* (1965), based on Evelyn Waugh's
famous novel about the American 'death industry'. Gielgud has only a smallish
part, but a delicious one. He plays an elderly painter in Hollywood, wafting around
in a floral dressing gown. After half an hour, following scenes with Robert Morley
and Rod Steiger, he hangs himself. The film descends into mayhem: it's tedious,
gross, and badly edited. Then suddenly Gielgud reappears, on the mortician's slab,
being prepared for the hereafter. It's a lovely moment.

July Progress Report
A satisfying moment: 20 out of 30 chapters are completed. However most of them
are still in draft, and I'm very aware that each will need substantial revision.

Reading: Robert Stephens emerges from his memoirs *Knight Errant* as bombastic
and unlikeable. But the book has useful material on Gielgud's thoughts about
directing him in *Private Lives* (1975).

Hopes: A note from Maggie Smith's secretary, saying she's away and about to film, 'but if she can help you with any information, I will be in touch soon'. I think this is a polite brush-off, but you never know.

Disappointments: Nothing from John Moffatt, Jonathan Miller or Juliet Stevenson.

Sunday 1 August

While wandering around the grounds of Snape Maltings this afternoon, I suddenly hear a familiar voice floating out from an upper window, not Gielgud's, but the Other Biographer's. This is ridiculous: is there no escape? I find him in the restaurant, his chin wagging in profile as he holds forth non-stop. I decide not to eavesdrop, but just to enjoy again my role of unseen spy. I should have brought my polaroid camera. I discover later that he's hosting a Coward centenary event at the Maltings this evening. Good: the more of these he does, the less time he has for writing.

Monday 2 August

A friendly letter from Kate Fleming, Celia Johnson's daughter and also her biographer. One sentence in her book about her mother had intrigued me: 'She got on well with Gielgud, with whom she had a long heart-to-heart in a Glasgow cemetery; in later life they would occasionally remind each other of it.' This was during the war, when she was standing in for Peggy Ashcroft during the tour of *The Importance of Being Earnest* (1939). Although Kate F is able to help on other points, she knows nothing more about this tantalising fragment, which is very frustrating.

The biography is well put together, with lots of theatrical background to back up the unique personal material. I'm intrigued to see that Gielgud tried but failed to get Celia Johnson to play Ophelia in his 1944 *Hamlet* at the Haymarket. In fact she took on the role in his 1948 radio version: despite the genteel accent, she gives a movingly anguished performance.

Wednesday 4 August

I finish *Peter Hall's Diaries*. They're riveting in themselves, and pleasantly self-critical. But they are also a valuable source for cameo shots of Gielgud at the National, especially in *The Tempest* (1974) and *No Man's Land* (1975), both directed by Hall. I like his description of Gielgud as 'a thorough-bred horse'. He's both admiring of and amused and bewildered by him, which is pretty much my stance after all this time spent on his trail.

Thursday 5 August

I watch Gielgud in his second film of *Julius Caesar* (1970), directed by Stuart Burge. It's not a patch on the Hollywood version. Jason Robards is a horrendously wooden Brutus, while Charlton Heston as Mark Antony merely grimaces wildly in a ginger wig. Gielgud is a more reflective Caesar than most: he gets the character's arrogance, but also his weakness; you believe in his 'falling sickness'. He puts over with great subtlety Caesar's conflicting emotions in his reaction to the soothsayer.

Saturday 7 August

A sympathetic obituary by director Peter Wood of the designer Carl Toms, who was on my second-division hit list; he designed *The Complaisant Lover* (1959) and *Caesar and Cleopatra* (1971). I discover that he had emphysema for many years, and lived in Hertfordshire with a lot of parrots. I wish I had made contact.

Monday 9 August

I feed the two revised Old Vic chapters to Michael, hoping they meet his recent critical points. He's helpfully sent me a book he published recently on Craig, which has proved very useful on Gielgud's controversial cousin.

Thursday 12 August

Moving into second gear on Gielgud's film career, I watch *Aces High* (1976), a well-made film about pilots in the first world war, 'inspired' by the play *Journey's End*. As a headmaster sending his pupils off to war ('Play the game for the game's sake'), Gielgud gives an imitation of his role in Alan Bennett's *Forty Years On* (1968), but without the irony. He doesn't have much time to develop the character: he's on screen for all of sixty seconds.

Monday 16 August

An entertaining session in Pimlico with Ian Bannen, a gruff, twinkly, mischievous Scot who I take to at once. He was Iago in Zeffirelli's disastrous Stratford *Othello* (1961), so I get a villain's-eye view of everything that went wrong on that notorious first night. I also manage to extract from him the definitive version of his classic 'Cassio's dead - I mean he's nearly dead' blunder. He says there have been many variations, and that Richard Burton was the worst for elaborating the story.

He recalls Zeffirelli telling him that he and Gielgud were not close enough, and sending them out to have a meal together. 'He was a wonderful talker but very nervous, so all we talked about was Hamlet, which I was playing that year.'

He remembers the sheer emotion Gielgud engendered in rehearsal: 'Tears were running down his cheeks – "The weed that smells so sweet" – they were running down mine too – "Soft you, a word". It was marvellous. I've heard a lot of Othellos, but none that approached his for beauty.'

As a young actor he was the third murderer in Gielgud's Stratford production of *Macbeth* (1952). He recalls his inability to let the actors get started: 'At the first reading the witches began, "When shall we three", and he burst in, "No, no, *space* the words." So they tried again: "When shall we three", and then it was, "No, no, *much* too slow." It took them a while to get past that speech.'

He found Gielgud a joy to work with in the scenes they filmed together for *Gandhi* (1982). 'He didn't want to go to India, so we filmed his scenes in the Directors' Club. On the wall there were gigantic pictures of Victoria, and Albert when he was young. John said, "You can see why she adored him, he's got such a lovely little waist."'

Tuesday 17 August
To the National Film Theatre, to see Gielgud and Richardson in the television version of David Storey's *Home* (1972). It's wonderful to see the famous partnership in action. Richardson brilliantly suggests the layers of misery in his character's past, sometimes with just a flash of the eye. Gielgud is very funny, and fine with the pathos, but I feel he lacks Richardson's depth. It's a rare chance to catch the famous walk: in fact his ramrod stiffness suits the part.

Wednesday 18 August
Despite Michael's characteristic lack of response to the Old Vic chapters, I send him two more, on Gielgud's beginnings as a director in the early 1930s, and the *Richard of Bordeaux* chapter. I ask him pointedly if he would kindly acknowledge receipt of all four.

Tuesday 24 August
Michael apologises for failing to acknowledge the earlier chapters. He says he's enjoying the Old Vic ones. Goodness, a second pat on the back. This is becoming seriously encouraging.

Back to the video, and *Murder on the Orient Express* (1974). It's a creaky, convoluted plot, and ultimately a tedious film, hideously over-acted, most notably by Finney. Gielgud's performance stands out because of its restraint. As Richard Widmark's manservant he glides smoothly and deferentially around the train's compartments, making acerbic remarks, and somehow managing to suggest he knows this is all a lot of nonsense.

August Progress Report
I have been revising heavily the chapters covering Gielgud's 'Battle of the Romeos' with Olivier, his Hamlets on Broadway and at Elsinore, and the Queen's season, all in his golden period. Returning to them six months later, the writing seems to me very limited and pedestrian. I suppose the fact that I can see this clearly is a good sign. Gielgud is now emerging from the mist, and I feel more confident about bringing in the personal material. The difficulty is striking the right balance between diplomacy and honesty so that, if he does read the typescript, he won't feel tempted to scupper the whole project.

Hopes: An unexpected call from Denis Quilley, whom I'd given up for lost. Apparently he understudied Burton in *The Lady's Not for Burning* (1949), so there will be more than I expected to talk about when we meet.

Disappointments: 1. A letter from a leading actress, who says she admires and loves Gielgud very much, but 'finds it difficult to put into words what my true feelings are and in a way which will communicate them to others'. I feel this is an honest answer, and not a Morley-inspired one. 2. Having just heard from Judi Dench's assistant that it will be the New Year before I can see her, I read that her husband Michael Williams has cancer, which is tragic. An interview now unlikely, I feel.

Wednesday 1 September
A jolly hour with Pinkie Johnstone, who worked in five productions with Gielgud. She remembers a disconcerting habit he had while acting in *The School for Scandal* (1962), which he also directed. 'He was playing Joseph Surface, and in my scenes with him he said every single one of my lines under his breath to me. Sometimes at the end of a speech he would give me a kind of question-mark look, as if to say, You've done it a bit wrong.'

Although he sometimes made her cry at rehearsals, she says she never found him threatening as a director. 'He was so wonderful himself at acting, he was repellled when you made a complete hash of it, and he would say so. In *Private Lives* he ticked me off for getting vulgar laughs: "We're not in *No Sex Please, We're British*, you know." But he never held it against you personally. And he was quick to tell you if you'd done it well.' She remembers his dislike of seeing people lose control in public: 'He liked the gossip about it, but not the sight of it.' And she recalls with amusement his awkward attitude to women. 'He had no idea how to deal with them, so he would treat us a bit like an ornament, or a difficult child.'

Thursday 2 September
I watch a tape of 'Twilight of the Gods', one of the last episodes of *Inspector Morse* (1993). Gielgud obviously revelled in playing the unworldly, tactless chancellor of Oxford University. Typecasting or what? 'I like Wagner, you can eat between the acts,' sounds like one of his own *bon mots*. I notice he uses the old Edwardian actor's 'me' for 'my', as in 'I want me lunch.' I catch him once glancing at the camera. Naughty.

Friday 3 September
A fax from Michael, acknowledging the Hamlet and Romeo chapters. He feels I'm still covering too much production ground, and not getting enough personal material in, either about Gielgud or others such as Richardson. I think he's probably right.

Tuesday 14 September
Back from a week in Corfu, during which I had vowed to forget all about Gielgud. But I cheated slightly by reading *The Shooting Party*, Isabel Colegate's brilliant novel set just before the first world war, and filmed in 1984. Odd for once to read the story before seeing the film, but I can just see Gielgud as the earnest, innocent, blundering animal-rights activist Cornelius Cardew.

In my local library I find Morley's reference book *Great Stage Stars*. The entry on Gielgud is surprisingly accurate, though I enjoy the claim that he directed *Treasure Island* in 1949 (it was actually *Treasure Hunt*). I try, but fail, to imagine Lewis Casson as Long John Silver.

Wednesday 15 September
I attend a full-length, rehearsed reading of *The Lady's Not for Burning* at the National. It's superbly played by Alex Jennings, witty and strong in Gielgud's part of the disillusioned soldier Thomas Mendip, and Sally Dexter, sexy and romantic in Pamela Brown's role of Jennet Jourdemayne, the alleged witch. They gain a great ovation at the end. Then up from the row behind me bobs Christopher Fry. Chirpy as ever, he tells the story of a very nervous Richard Burton failing his first audition, but omits to mention that it was Gielgud who suggested he should be given a second chance.

The play stands up remarkably well, and infinitely better than Osborne's *Look Back in Anger*, which I caught in the Lyttelton last week. Fry's poetry and humour seem timeless: surely the National will give it a proper airing now?

Saturday 18 September
Back to Smallhythe, this time to look at the Ellen Terry museum as a visitor. I find a couple of items donated by Gielgud: a fan his great-aunt used while playing Beatrice in *Much Ado about Nothing*, and a handkerchief for Katharine of Aragon in *Henry VIII*. I wonder if she originally gave them to him? Re-visiting the Barn Theatre in the garden, I notice the chair that Gielgud donated stands between those carrying the names of the stalwart Shakespearean Ben Greet, and the king of revue CB Cochran, an apt reflection of his catholic theatrical taste.

Tuesday 21 September
I find in my local library a tape from the 1950s of Gielgud playing Sherlock Holmes on the radio, in four stories, with Ralph Richardson as Watson. He plays Holmes straight: debonair, cosy, but with a quick intelligence. Alas, the famous tale in which he attempts a coalman's accent is not included. But he has another go, when Holmes disguises himself as a bookseller and accosts Watson in the street. Once again, *nul points* for the accent.

Wednesday 22 September
Another NT2000 event at the National, involving scenes from Simon Gray's *Quartermaine's Terms*. Gielgud played in the TV version in 1987. Afterwards Jenny Quayle, articulate and strikingly like her father round the eyes and mouth, talks about the original production, which Pinter directed. I sit there wondering why she never answered my letter asking her about any Quayle-Gielgud correspondence. I think about sending a further letter.

Tuesday 28 September
A lively chat in his dressing-room at the National with Denis Quilley, who speaks resonantly of his admiration for Gielgud, especially his work in Shakespeare. He recalls his 1944 Hamlet, 'so light and quick and elegant, the meaning crystal clear; it reinforced my desire to be an actor'. Thirty years later he was in the audience for the National's last night at the Old Vic, a tribute evening to Lilian Baylis, during which Gielgud spoke Hamlet's soliloquy 'Oh what a rogue and peasant slave am I'. 'He was seventy, but he was spellbinding. All the fluidity and lightness were still there. I thought, Christ, put a wig on him and he could play Hamlet *now*. I was sitting next to Albert Finney, and I thought: "I hope you're watching, Albert, because this is the way to do it."'

He remembers vividly rehearsals for *The Lady's Not for Burning* (1949), in which as a young actor he understudied Richard Burton. 'John used to call Richard "Pretty Bottom"; they were very fond of each other, despite their very different backgrounds. Older actors like Harcourt Williams and Eliot Makeham found John's continual changes of mind very trying, but I loved it.' He recalls how helpful Fry was at rehearsals. 'John would say that a few extra lines were needed for a scene, and Christopher would go away, and come back in half an hour with four lines that did the trick for the plot, was in beautiful verse, and had two laughs in them. He was marvellous.'

He observed Gielgud at close quarters in Peter Hall's 1974 production of *The Tempest* at the National, when he played Caliban to Gielgud's fourth and last Prospero. 'His performance could have been harsher, but he hasn't got a harsh bone in his body. He was irascible, but there was a gentleness about him that you couldn't really erase. Every actor has limitations, things you can't change: with John it's his sweetness and gentleness.'

September Progress Report
I finally complete the revisions of the first three chapters, covering Gielgud's first twenty years. I'm appalled at how inadequate the first draft now seems. This time the material feels more coherent, more personal, and more informed.

Reading: John Elsom and Nicholas Tomalin's history of the National Theatre is lively stuff, and contains a beautiful description of the Hamlet soliloquy that Gielgud gave at the Lilian Baylis tribute evening. I'm amazed to learn that Harold Hobson put Gielgud on his personal shortlist (alongside Guthrie, Brook and Hall, but not Olivier) for the post of first Director of the National. Could anyone be less suitable?

Hopes: A nice letter from Juliet Stevenson, who apologises for the long silence, and agrees to meet me.

Disappointments: Phone message from Peter O'Toole's office; he's 'unable to help with the book at present'. I take that as code for 'I'm talking to Sheridan Morley'.

Friday 1 October
I send off the revised first three chapters, which are the first on which I feel absolutely confident that no more work is needed. I hope to God Michael agrees, otherwise the writing *will* go on for ever.

Sunday 3 October

After a considerable search I find the house Gielgud lived in with his lover John Perry before they bought Foulslough together. It's outside the village of Harpsden, in the middle of a woodland, on a hilltop above Henley. Quiet and secluded, it's heavily screened by hedges and tall fir trees. Walking right round it and peering through the gaps, I can see it's a substantial house. Here in the early 1930s Gielgud escaped from the London theatre, and gave weekend parties for his theatrical friends, an odd mixture of all-night gambling and table tennis.

It's impossible to under-estimate the value of seeing the bricks and mortar and general setting of the places in which he lived, and being able to fix them in my mind's eye.

Tuesday 5 October

More comments from Michael. He likes the 'Hamlet in America' chapter because it has 'some very lively commentary'. He thinks the first encounter with Olivier is not strong enough, and looking at it again I agree. In fact I realise I need to give Larry's background and the Romeo episode a whole chapter. Michael feels it's not too early to think about cover images, which is a pleasing sign of confidence. He favours, as I do, one of the early pictures of Gielgud in his 1930s heyday.

Sunday 10 October

Watching Gielgud's cameo film appearances means sitting through a lot of trash. Today it's *Gold* (1974), a glossy piece of rubbish starring Roger Moore and Susannah York. Thank God for Gielgud, playing the ruthless chairman of a mining company. In his four brief scenes he is acerbic, suave and authoritative, and utterly convincing. Only he and Ray Milland give this totally worthless film some quality and depth.

Tuesday 12 October

A meeting with Michael at Methuen. We're through the confidence barrier now: he likes the re-written early chapters very much, which is a huge relief. We talk about source notes, the index, permissions, and suddenly the book begins to seem real. I suggest the 1934 Hamlet as the cover image, and he agrees. It's one of the best-known photos of Gielgud, but I think that works in its favour. Most importantly, we agree on an extra three months beyond January. I was beginning to panic about finishing by then, so it's a great relief. I'm surprised he has suddenly become flexible on the delivery date, until I discover that he also has Stoppard and

Ayckbourn biographies coming up on the rails, and wants to avoid publishing all three too close together.

In the Theatre Museum in the afternoon I meet John Miller, who spoke to Gielgud on the phone recently. He says he sounded 'very low'.

Friday 15 October
Methuen have reissued Garry O'Connor's life of Ralph Richardson. I'm fascinated to read of Gielgud's role in 'helping' with the book. Initially he agrees to talk to O'Connor, then checks with Richardson and changes his mind, offering as excuse his fear that he will say something indiscreet. Richardson scolds O'Connor for 'bothering' his friend. O'Connor suggests as a compromise that he approach Gielgud again later, on the basis that he will not include in his book any indiscreet remarks he makes about Richardson. He does eventually see Gielgud, but carefully avoids any personal questions about Richardson. Gielgud then swings to the other extreme, reads the book in proof, and makes helpful suggestions. All very bewildering, but typical.

One apparent reason for his reluctance to talk was a tactless remark he made about Richardson's relationship with his wife Meriel Forbes, which appeared in Tynan's *New Yorker* profile of Richardson: 'He expected her to be the perfect hostess during dinner and then, after coffee was served, to kick up her legs like a chorus girl. It must have been difficult to reconcile those two demands.' I can see this would not have gone down well *chez* Richardson.

Friday 22 October
I send off to Michael the chapters covering Gielgud's war years. I can see that, given the huge volume of Gielgud's film work, I have to be very selective on what I cover. Overwhelmed by his screen appearances, I had wondered for a moment if his film career might have made a separate book. Michael swiftly knocks this crazy idea on the head.

I hate raising this matter, but I also ask if there's any chance of half the next part of the advance being paid when I deliver a complete draft in January.

Tuesday 26 October
I endure more celluloid nonsense in the shape of *Les Misérables* (1978), with Gielgud playing Marius' grandfather. It's a tedious film, with a lot of ham 'historical' acting, especially by Anthony Perkins. Gielgud, who seems uncomfortable throughout, uses a stick and walks unsteadily: is this acting, or was he getting suddenly old (he was actually only 74). He comes to life when he says to his grandson: 'Why don't

you make the silly girl your mistress?' It's obvious that he enjoys making gaffes on screen as much as off.

Friday 29 October
I've finally reached the difficult chapter involving Gielgud's arrest for, as they so nicely put it in those days, 'importuning male persons' in Chelsea. I'm writing it on the assumption he will read it, and am therefore treading very warily. I don't think I'll quote, for instance, the magistrate's description of men such as him as 'the scourge of the neighbourhood'. The main problem is that I have no direct evidence of his emotional state at the time, apart from one very short circular letter he sent to the many friends who wrote to support him after the incident. I'm trying to write about the episode briefly and factually, and not make a huge issue of it. It's obviously a traumatic moment, but it would be easy to get it out of proportion.

October Progress Report
In the light of his present frailty, I wonder whether I should now make contact with Gielgud. I have a growing list of questions, none of them on hugely significant points, but they're ones that only he can answer. Yet I don't want to upset him unnecessarily, or provoke him in any way that would jeopardise the book now that I'm so far into it. I would like to show him the finished text, so maybe I could offer him a few chapters now? It's just so hard to know what his state of mind is, especially after Martin's death.

Reading: Michael Darlow and Gillian Hodson's biography of Rattigan is rich in background, and very good on the moral climate and attitudes to homosexuality.

Hopes: A surprise letter from actor Trader Faulkner, who is happy to talk. I've also netted Alastair Bannerman, a late bonus, who goes as far back as 1937 and the season at the Queen's.

Disappointments: Although Trevor Nunn never directed Gielgud, I had hoped he might talk more generally about his influence on the theatre and the next generation of actors. Sadly, he feels he has no special insights or stories to contribute.

Friday 5 November
I'm shocked to read of Ian Bannen's death in a car crash in Scotland. When we met a few weeks ago in Dolphin Square he was so full of life, such a lively, ebullient man. I recall his delight in telling me how he and John Neville ran the Old Vic flag

up the mast on the roof of the theatre at Stratford. I find it ironic, after talking to him about playing Hamlet and Iago at Stratford, to read the headline 'Dr Finlay actor dies in holiday accident'. It's extremely hard to grasp that he's dead.

Sunday 7 November

I've finished a biography of Peter Finch by his fellow-Australian Trader Faulkner, who I shall meet tomorrow. It both gains and suffers from his being a close friend: plenty of good stories, not enough objective comment. There's a great deal of detail on Finch's extraordinary childhood, including his months as a street orphan in India. A fine, intuitive actor who screwed up his career with a turbulent personal life.

Monday 9 November

I pass an entertaining hour in Kensington with Trader Faulkner, who as a raw young actor replaced Burton on Broadway in *The Lady's Not for Burning* (1951). He felt Gielgud was 'a brilliant director if you had confidence, but totally destructive if you didn't'. He himself didn't, and tells some stories to prove it.

He's an unusual mixture: his mother was a ballerina with Diaghilev, and he's a flamenco dancer as well as an actor. He owes his stage name to Gielgud, who thought his father's description of him as 'a right little trader' – he sold illegal whisky at school – much more dashing. You can see his point: his real name was Ronald.

I like some of his verbal images: 'John had a mind like mercury, it would fly around like confetti, then all come together again, as mercury does. I was absolutely spellbound by it, his precision, his articulateness.' He talks of Gielgud's homosexuality, of 'that draconian 1950s hypocrisy' of which his arrest was a part: 'His manner was difficult, he had big emotional problems, as a homosexual there was great repression. But it's like Lorca, if he had been living in a free society, would he have written as he did? John's repression was his drive.'

Tuesday 10 November

A helpful letter from Valerie Grove. I'd asked her about the possibility of seeing the transcript of her interview with Gielgud for her Dodie Smith biography. In passing she tells me that Morley warned her that Gielgud would be furious that she'd mentioned his 'little embarrassment', but that in his charming letter to her after her book was published there was no sign of this.

Saturday 13 November

Lunch at the National with Alastair Bannerman, the survivor of the Queen's season, who I've unearthed from his Dorset home. It's another 'spear carrier' interview, yielding up several useful new fragments. He bears a slight resemblance to Gielgud, the shape of the head, the resonant voice, the old-fashioned manners. He tells me this was a handicap in his youth: people thought he was trying to imitate Gielgud when he was just being himself. But he admits he modelled some of his performances on him. His Joseph Surface in a production of *The School for Scandal* in a prisoner-of-war camp must have been a night to cherish.

Gielgud himself appears to have noticed the resemblance: 'When we did *Richard II* at the Queen's, he suddenly handed me the book and said, "Read my part." I did this on the stage, so he could see how his moves were working.' He also remembers Saint-Denis directing *Three Sisters* during the same season. 'He worked everyone very hard, he was tremendously keen on detail, and also on Stanislavsky; it all had to come from within. John was playing Vershinin, and Saint-Denis would say to him: "John, you're always a *king*!"'

Monday 15 November
Peter Cotes, one of my first interviewees, has died. I recall him telling me that when he wrote obituaries of theatre people in the *Guardian*, he would close his eyes for ten minutes, and then phone it through verbatim. Now *his* turn has come round, and the former critic Eric Shorter has stepped into his shoes.

I find a second message on my machine from Juliet Stevenson, who clearly wants to help. It's frustrating that I keep missing her. When I ring her agent and explain, she goes all bureaucratic, and insists on my sending her the original correspondence. Couldn't she just ring her client, who wants to contact me? Oh no. No money in it, of course.

Tuesday 16 November
Michael Darlow, one of Rattigan's three biographers, generously sends me a copy of the transcript of his interview with Gielgud which he made for the playwright's television obituary. It's full of illuminating detail, much of it new to me, and just what's needed to add colour to some of my more information-heavy paragraphs. Michael D tells me that a new edition of his Rattigan biography is imminent, and that it contains further details of Gielgud's friendship with Rattigan. What excellent timing for me.

Wednesday 17 November
I finally get to see Gielgud's Oscar-winning performance in *Arthur* (1981). The film has a plodding script, with Dudley Moore at his unfunniest, Liza Minelli

ditto. But Gielgud, in a variety of dashing hats and well-cut suits, is very funny as Moore's man Hobson. With what relish he delivers lines such as 'Go screw yourself!' and 'You little shit!', his timing as exquisite as if he were speaking Shakespeare. Unfortunately he dies half way through the film: he plays his death-bed scene with great simplicity, as if he were playing in a decent drama.

Thursday 25 November
A message on my machine from Pinter's assistant. She says he's seeing Morley in a couple of weeks' time, and doesn't feel he can do two interviews. Damn and blast! Why ever didn't I write to him six months or a year ago? At least I have other sources for *No Man's Land*, including my interview with Michael Feast, the Hall diaries, biographies of Pinter and Richardson. But I'm very annoyed with myself. However, the fact that Pinter is seeing Morley indicates he hasn't yet finished, which is a relief. On the other hand if he's got to Pinter and the 1970s, he may be nearer doing so than I thought. I feel I need a further health report on Gielgud.

November Progress Report
Only seven chapters to go. The one covering the *Ages of Man* tour of North America has been especially difficult, simply because of the richness of the material: Gielgud's letters home, Patsy Ainley's diary and letters, my interview with Patsy, and so on. I've had to be ruthlessly selective, and that really hurts.

Reading: Melvyn Bragg's *Rich*, a biography of Burton, has some handy first-hand material on Burton's debt to Gielgud, but the style is overblown, and I couldn't be bothered to finish it. Corin Redgrave's book on his father, on the other hand, makes only passing references to Gielgud, but I couldn't put it down. It's a poignant account of Redgrave's difficult personal life, and it includes good detail on homosexual law reform. Unfortunately Corin has been working with Morley, who's been directing him in a Coward play. It seems absurd, but this has inhibited me from following up his earlier helpful letter.

Disappointments: No reply from director Peter Wood. And my hunch about Maggie Smith was right: her secretary writes to say that 'Dame Maggie prefers not to talk about her work'. Actually it's not *her* work I'm interested in, but let that pass.

Wednesday 1 December
Suddenly Gielgud appears, being interviewed by Jeremy Paxman on *Newsnight*. Though he's dressed as dapperly as ever, it's a huge shock to see how much he's

aged. His mind has slowed, his voice is sadly diminished, and he pauses before answering, which he never did before. There's still the occasional smile, but it's very wan: the sparkle has gone. Paxman treads uncharacteristically carefully. He asks Gielgud about his thoughts on death, a question I hope he cleared with him beforehand. He seems astonished by Gielgud's admission that he feels guilty for not having done more outside the theatre. It's a point he's been making for twenty years.

This poignant interview makes me wonder again whether I should risk making contact with Gielgud before it's too late.

Friday 3 December
To the National Film Theatre to see Christopher Miles' film about DH Lawrence and Frieda, *Priest of Love* (1981). Gielgud is the man from the Foreign Office, determined to ban and burn *Women in Love*, and seize Lawrence's 'lewd', nude paintings. He has only two brief scenes, but catches the man's priggishness expertly. In one delicious scene he rushes around the art gallery, examining the paintings with a mixture of feigned horror and barely disguised delight. He's very funny.

Monday 6 December
I phone Derek Granger to check whether it's worth pursuing Joan Plowright any further. He thinks it is. I ask if Thomas Kiernan's biography of Olivier is as unreliable as it seems. God yes, he says: 'He even has Larry's parents talking to each other before they actually meet!' As for all those 'sources not wishing to be named'!

He tells me he's overwhelmed by the volume of material he's having to get through for his Olivier biography, and is impressed I've got so far, which cheers me up. At the end he urges me to see Keith Baxter, who's about to visit Gielgud. I move him to the top of my list.

Thursday 9 December
Reading two books devoted entirely to just one production is a touch overwhelming: you don't *want* that amount of material. But William Redfield and Richard Sterne's separate fly-on-the-wall accounts of Gielgud directing Burton in *Hamlet* (1964) are in different ways utterly absorbing.

Redfield especially, from the vantage point of Guildenstern, provides a remarkably shrewd and revealing picture of Gielgud at work. There are wonderful moments where the American actors are searching for a Concept and desperate for Motivation, and Gielgud refuses to provide either. Several actors are tearing their hair out because they can't pin him down on their characters: Redfield describes it as like being directed by the White Rabbit: 'He is late, he is late, and he is always on his way.'

Friday 10 December

I send two more chapters off to my supposed editor, who yet again is deafening me with his silence. Despite my having sent him chapters regularly for the last seven weeks, there's not even a whiff of an acknowledgement. I find this behaviour extraordinary.

Monday 13 December

Renée Asherson's agent has been in touch, telling me her client 'feels unable to contribute'. I only wrote to her recently, having stupidly assumed she was dead. She understudied Peggy Ashcroft in the Gielgud/Olivier *Romeo and Juliet*, so I'm really sorry not to have had the chance to meet her.

Meanwhile I've been reading Bill Gaskill's memoirs. They are laced with stimulating ideas on theatre, and contain invaluable background on the Royal Court, to supplement my fruitful interview with him.

Tuesday 14 December

Alec Guinness' latest volume, *A Positively Final Appearance*, includes a positively final nod to Gielgud: 'If I were to gauge lasting influences on my subsequent professional life I would head the list with John Gielgud (hero-worshipped).' Guinness is as gently caustic as ever, and rails at two critics who describe Keith Baxter's playing of King Henry in *Chimes at Midnight* as 'Gielgudry'. He adds: 'Why the greatest speaker of Shakespeare in our time should be held up as an example not to be followed I can't imagine.' To underline Gielgud's 'tenuous grasp of public events' he cites his remark about the barrage balloons tethered over London, made during the 1940 run of *King Lear*. 'I feel so sorry for those poor men sitting up there all day, they must be so cold,' Gielgud apparently said.

Friday 17 December

I send Michael Earley a state-of-play report, indicating I'm on course for a complete draft by the end of January. Then, trying to keep the tone light, I repeat my unanswered request for half of the next instalment of my advance. How I hate having to beg like this, especially after his continuing silence. I also enclose a copy of another possible cover image, inviting his response. Surely he can't continue to ignore me for much longer? Do all his authors get treated in this shabby manner, or am I just unlucky?

Friday 24 December
In the last post before Christmas shutdown, and after nearly three months' silence, I receive a letter from Earley. He's sorry not to have responded before, but gives no reason or excuse, which I find amazing. He hopes he will catch up on his reading in January. I am sceptical. He promises to 'review the situation' about the money when he has the complete draft. At least it's not a refusal, which in itself is a sort of Christmas present.

Wednesday 29 December
With no interruptions and everyone on holiday, I have at last got into a decent rhythm. The words are flowing, I know exactly where all my material is, and even Christmas has failed to disturb me. There are now only four chapters left to write, plus a fresh introduction, so the end of January is still a realistic delivery date.

Thursday 30 December
Last night I dreamt of Morley. God knows why, since I haven't thought of him for ages. We were both at a small dinner party, and I was aware that he didn't know who I was. He sat down next to me and said: 'Do you know much about *me*?' I replied: 'I've seen you several times at the theatre.' That was it. Very puzzling. Must be a touch of millennium fever.

Year 3 Progress Report
A key end-of-millennium question: To write or not to write to Gielgud? After his *Newsnight* appearance I'm torn about which course of action would be best. Perhaps his frailty will cause him to look more benevolently on the book? I decide finally on the cowardly option: to hold off making a decision until I have a complete draft to show to him.

– FOUR –

The Race to Publication

Wednesday 5 January 2000

I discover to my horror that the Theatre Museum has separate files on most twentieth-century productions staged in London. I kick myself for being so absorbed in the Gielgud boxes, and not realising this earlier. I manage to work through the 1920s files during the afternoon, but time is now precious, and I doubt if I can afford more than one more visit before my deadline.

Friday 7 January

Filling in the final film gaps, I sit through three hours of Richard Attenborough's *Gandhi* (1982) for five minutes of Gielgud. This time it's not just research, but a pleasure, for it's a very fine film. Gielgud is all steel and granite as Lord Irwin, and convincing in the imperial contempt with which he delivers lines such as: 'Mr Gandhi will find it takes a good deal more than a pillar of salt to bring down the British Empire.' I notice for the first time, in his scene with Ian Bannen and Michael Bryant, how good he is at listening on screen, as he was on stage.

Monday 10 January

Taking a deep breath, I plunge into the notorious *Caligula* (1979), the semi-pornographic film about the decadent Roman emperor, who is played in manic fashion by Malcolm McDowell. It proves as revolting as everyone says. Gielgud as the wise and good senator Nerva, clad in fetching black robes, looks understandably stunned at all the rude behaviour going on around him, though I'm sure he's inwardly giggling. For him it's an early bath, literally: after half an hour he slits his wrist and dies bloodily in his tub, thereby saving me from having to watch the rest of this nauseating stuff.

Tuesday 11 January

I finally get round to reading Peter Brook's memoir *Threads of Time*. It's an austere, rather chilling book, like its author, but full of good things, including a fascinating description of rehearsals for his famous production of *A Midsummer Night's Dream*. Surprisingly, there's little on Gielgud, and what there is I've mostly already heard from the man himself: same sentiments, different words. But what strikes me is the fact that in the 1950s Brook learned from Gielgud as much as Gielgud learned from him, that working with what he calls this 'unique and endlessly inventive mind' led him to question again what was meant by good and bad in theatre. Interestingly, he says that he felt close to Gielgud; few people would claim to have done that. With Olivier he was unable to be so, finding him false: 'Even his laughter was acted, as though he never ceased re-making and polishing his mask.'

Wednesday 12 January
The final three chapters are proving immensely difficult to write. Gielgud packed so much film and television work into these last twenty years, and the amount of interview material I have is out of all proportion to the space available. I need to cover the ground reasonably thoroughly without turning it into a mere cataloguing of his roles. I'm slightly perturbed to find that the four parts into which I've divided the book cover successively 25, 9, 15 and 47 years of his life. But his later work is so much better known, so I think the balance is about right.

Sunday 16 January
To the Middle Temple Hall off Fleet Street, thought to be the venue for the first night of *Twelfth Night*. Four hundred years on it's being used for the presentation of the Sir John Gielgud Award for Excellence in the Dramatic Arts, created by the American Shakespeare Guild. The recipient this year (Ian McKellen and Judi Dench were previous winners) is Kenneth Branagh. The evening rapidly turns into effusive tributes from Ken's friends, some given in person, some read out with increasing discomfort by Judi Dench, Derek Jacobi and Geraldine McEwan. Keith Baxter conveys a brief message from Gielgud, adding that he's just sacked his agent for getting him insufficient work. The occasion is partially redeemed by some fine 'Shakespearean Vignettes', notably Samantha Bond's Juliet and Keith Baxter's Henry V, and by Ben Elton sending up the whole event. Although he admires Branagh, Gielgud would I'm sure have been uneasy about this kind of public worship.

Monday 17 January
Back to the days of languid youth under the chestnut trees. Not mine, but Evelyn Waugh's, as I spend an enjoyable evening listening to Gielgud reading an edited version of *Brideshead Revisited* on cassette. I imagined I would only be able to think of him as Edward Ryder after his superb television performance, but I'm wrong: he manages skilfully to create a different feeling for each of the characters,

and as narrator his voice is perfect for the period. I note that Sebastian and Charles smoke fat Turkish cigarettes, as Gielgud does, and wonder if this began as an affectation during his Oxford (Playhouse) days, when he was effectively one of the Brideshead generation?

Friday 21 January

In my extensive reading over the last three years I've come across a huge number of errors, by no means confined to Morley's articles on Gielgud, though they lead the field. A recent favourite came in the *Guardian* on the history of the Royal Court, in which reference was made to one *Harry* Granville Barker. It conjures up a much flashier, down-market director, and one whom Gielgud might have found more difficult to worship. But at least it wasn't Harley Granville Davidson. Today I found a peach of a one in Patrick Garland's recent volume on Rex Harrison, which refers (both in the text and index) to Gielgud's appearance in *Normansland*. Perhaps a century hence academics will be puzzling over this lost Pinter masterpiece, and speculation will be rife as to whether it was a joint venture with Ayckbourn?

Sunday 23 January

I finally track down a privately taped video of the television version of *Quartermaine's Terms* (1987). Gielgud is magnificent as the not-as-eccentric-as-he-seems head of the seedy Cambridge language school, managing to offend all the staff with his smiling put-downs. He ages cleverly, from bow tie to deaf aid, and handles with great delicacy the suppressed emotion of the final scene, in which he announces the death of his male companion. Touching in itself, it seems even more so now in the light of Martin's subsequent death.

January Progress Report

A great moment: I have a complete draft. However, there's still an awful lot of information, incident and personal memories to go in, and I'm already 10,000 over the 2000,000 words limit. I can see I'll have to cut some of the early chapters ruthlessly, and not worry about covering all Gielgud's productions. It will be the devil of a task, though I find re-writing easier and more enjoyable than the original writing.

Tuesday 1 February

At the National Film Theatre I catch a period piece in both senses: the 1955 television version of *Richard of Bordeaux*, the play that made Gielgud a star back in 1932. The production is from the dark ages, when television plays were filmed live.

All the mistakes are left in, including a prop falling off a table, and the occasional fluffed line. This gives it an odd freshness, although the play now seems very ordinary, and soon palls when intrigue takes over from character.

Peter Cushing is Richard: I'm amazed to discover that he's a fine actor, and not just Horror fodder as I had thought. I detect shades of Gielgud in his pleasing light voice, intonation and manner: perhaps a deliberate influence? He also has the same cheekbones, which can't have been intentional. I'm glad to see George Howe in action. A friend of Gielgud from his RADA days, a reliable stalwart of many of his companies, he's less affected than many of the cast, who flounce around knowingly in their period costumes.

Thursday 3 February
Writing about Gielgud's partner Martin Hensler is proving problematic. My reticence in asking people about him has left me with very little material, and what there is turns out to be very impressionistic. Someone told me that Gielgud picked him up on the Embankment after seeing him at an exhibition at the Tate. Yet I can't be sure this is true, so I'll have to leave it out. Much the same applies to other recollections or 'facts' about him.

Friday 4 February
A meeting with Michael Earley, to which I bring a complete draft. I tell him there are still a few chapters that need more context, and more personal material. I also suggest I need to grasp more firmly the nettle of homosexuality. I offer to have a final draft of the text ready by the end of April if he can now react swiftly. He promises to do so, and we agree to meet again in a fortnight. Publication is now definitely to be early in 2001 rather than this year, which is a pity. But after such a marathon I don't want to rush the final lap.

Monday 7 February
Rounding up the last few Gielgud films, I sit through two hours of Al Pacino's *Looking for Richard* (1993) to catch two 15-second glimpses of him being interviewed by Pacino. Along with those of Branagh, Jacobi, Peter Brook, Vanessa Redgrave and Rosemary Harris, his words are swiftly intercut with the play and the documentary elements. The film, a self-indulgent ego-trip masquerading as a quest to make the play more accessible, is surprisingly effective. Pacino makes a convincingly evil Richard, though he lacks Olivier's silky subtlety, but Alec Baldwin shines out among the supporting cast as Clarence, just as Gielgud did in the same part back in 1955.

Wednesday 9 February
An unusually formal letter from Michael summarising the state of play. He confirms the end of April delivery date for the text, but to my dismay adds that this should include everything: bibliography, sources, chronology, even all permission clearances for text and pictures. This was certainly not what was agreed, and I have no intention of applying myself to such matters while I'm grappling with the final text.

Thursday 10 February
An admiring piece about Morley in my local glossy magazine. The writer describes him as 'the critic's critic' and the 'theatre world's champion', which I imagine will be news both to the critics and the theatre world. At least she didn't label him the biographer's biographer.

In the evening I catch another Gielgud film, *The Tichborne Claimant* (1999), at the Waterman's Arts Centre in Brentford. He plays a judge, and with considerable gusto, which cheers me momentarily – until I realise the film was made over a year ago, before Martin's death, and certainly before that *Newsnight* interview.

Thursday 17 February
Michael has cancelled tomorrow's meeting: apparently he has to be at home next week for domestic reasons. This is annoying – I need his comments fast if I'm to meet the deadline.

Thursday 24 February
Another film, another cameo. *First Knight* (1994) proves an execrable Hollywood take on the Arthur/Launcelot/Guinevere story. It's full of authentic medieval dialogue, such as: 'Nobody moves or Arthur dies', 'Come on, the party's starting', 'Launcelot, just a thought' and (my favourite) 'I'm sure you'll find Arthur will come round to the merits of compromise'. Fortunately Gielgud, playing a village elder, has virtually no lines. A Prospero-like figure with staff and trim white beard, he wanders amongst the looting and pillaging, looking seraphic and amiable, as if he's on the wrong set. A week's work, no real demands: thank you, that's the new roof on the house paid for.

Friday 25 February
I have saved until nearly the last what is generally thought to be Gielgud's best screen performance, in Alain Resnais' *Providence* (1977). I find the film pretentious in the extreme, the other actors, including Bogarde, devoid of life. But Gielgud

is magnificent as the dying writer, trying to create a last work in his mind during a night of heavy drinking. It's a roaring, swearing, bravura performance, full of humour and self-loathing. In the elegiac conclusion he has a brief scene with Ellen Burstyn that is almost romantic. I think it's the only time on film that he has played such a scene with a woman, and he plays it with great sweetness. It's a real triumph.

February Progress Report

I'm working at high speed now, cutting merrily and with less agonising than I had expected. An imminent deadline does wonders for the blue pencil, and scores of reviews have bitten the dust. I think I shall get there just on time, though I now urgently need Michael's thoughts on the concluding chapters.

Thursday 2 March

To the Theatre Museum, for probably my last session there. I manage to rush through the 1930s production files, after which date I'm well covered for material. I take a last glance at the Gielgud portrait above my desk, but he remains impassive. No hint of Dorian Gray here.

Afterwards I visit the Edward Gordon Craig exhibition upstairs. The highlight for me is a five-minute video of Craig himself, speaking from Vence in the south of France in 1955, when he was 83. He's sitting on a sunlit terrace, wearing a straw hat, which he takes off to reveal a mane of long, white hair. I'm fascinated by his rakish appearance and melodious, resonant, very Edwardian voice, so much so that I fail to take in what he's talking about, and have to watch it again.

Elsewhere I notice a small display case devoted to Gielgud, a pitiful collection of six items, one of which is missing. Surely the museum can do better than this? I notice that the Gielgud Gallery is now inhabited by Mole, Ratty, Toad and other *Wind in the Willows* creatures who appeared recently in Alan Bennett's version at the National.

Friday 3 March

Yet another bombshell: Michael Earley has left Methuen. A letter from their managing director tells me he has left to 'pursue his other publishing interests'. Just like that. No warning from Michael, which suggests the sack, or at least a row. Someone called Max Eilenberg is temporarily taking over the drama list. My immediate worry is that he'll want to feed in views on the book that may differ radically from Michael's. Though Michael has generally been a real pain to work with, his departure could hardly come at a worse time for the book. I'll just have to keep a steady course and hope for no further squalls.

Friday 10 March

A standard letter from Max Eilenberg, who wants to 'reiterate our absolute commitment to maintaining Methuen's best publishing traditions', and stresses that 'it's a great honour to be associated with your work'. The usual publishing bullshit: we'll see what his words mean in practice. He talks about meeting soon, so I leave a message on his voice mail, saying the sooner the better.

Wednesday 15 March

I read today that the latest trend in writing biographies is to just make it up where you have no evidence. Andrew Motion seems to have done this with *Wainewright the Poisoner*, but the most spectacular example is Edmond Morris' life of Ronald Reagan, into which he inserts himself as an imaginary character in the story. I recall someone not long ago quoting AS Byatt's view that the future of writing lay in fictionalised biography. At the time I assumed it was a joke.

No comeback from my message to Max Eilenberg. It must be something in the Methuen water supply.

Monday 20 March

Another Gielgud cameo ticked off. *Shining Through* (1990) starts as a tense, interesting thriller about Nazi Germany, but then descends into bathos and absurdity. As a world-weary spy (codename Sunflower, which he would have enjoyed), Gielgud tries hard to be stern, but his heart clearly isn't in it.

March Progress Report

Write, write, write, and I'm getting there. I keep seeing places where there is room for improvement, but I'm trying to leave the early chapters alone as far as possible. It's frightening standing in the last-chance saloon, knowing that this, finally, is what people are going to read, Max Eilenberg willing. I've still had no response to my message, so perhaps after all it's not such an honour for him to be associated with my book. I refuse to pursue him at this moment: I need to save all my energy and focus for the final revision.

Wednesday 5 April

I talk to Derek, who is having lunch with Max Eilenberg next week. We agree this may be the time to raise the thorny question of the cost of the pictures, and whether Methuen would now be prepared to share it.

Thursday 6 April

I see from a press report that the Olivier archive is going to the British Library, which already has the Pinter, Tynan and Rattigan collections. The deal is still going through, so it's too late to be of any use to me. I'm not sure whether to be dismayed or relieved: the archive must be a vast one.

Wednesday 12 April

The revisions are proving more complex than I had hoped. I'm determined not to rush it at the last moment, but I can see that I'm not going to finish by the end of the month. Fortunately no one's pressing me to deliver, so I'm just keeping my head down, in both senses.

Friday 14 April

Gielgud is 96 today. No celebratory features this time round, I see. Strange what a difference just one digit can make. I wonder if he's spending it alone, as I gather he did on Millennium Eve. This is my self-imposed deadline for deciding whether to make contact with him. I've been debating the pros and cons ever since I completed the second draft. Now I decide to wait until I've completely finished.

Monday 17 April

Meriel Forbes, Ralph Richardson's widow, has died aged 87. I see she was once engaged to Morley *père*. This reminds me that I've heard nothing from Morley *fils* for several months. All that may change once the book goes into production, when he gets wind of its completion.

Tuesday 25 April

In my continuing pursuit of Judi Dench I ring her secretary, who kindly promises to put my request back at the top of her list. I feel there's still a modicum of hope of an interview, though the chances are diminishing rapidly as my deadline approaches. She will almost certainly be my last interviewee.

Wednesday 26 April

I get a nasty shock on opening the obituaries page of the Guardian, to see a large picture of Gielgud. Opening it further I see Vivien Leigh next to him, then realise that he's still breathing: the picture is being used for an obituary of the American producer Alexander Cohen, who produced the two of them in *Ivanov* in America.

April Progress Report

My revision rate has slowed, but for a good reason: I've belatedly decided to reorganise the last five chapters. Initially I had dealt with the bulk of Gielgud's film and television work in the two penultimate chapters, but now I see that some of his 1960s films sit better in the right chronological position, which is where they were originally. I'm furious with myself for not seeing this earlier, when time was less precious.

Tuesday 2 May

My final film call is for *Prospero's Books* (1990), Gielgud's last major screen role. It's a *tour de force*: not only does he play Prospero, but for most of the film until Alonso's awakening he speaks everyone else's lines too. I marvel that at 85 he had the courage to play one scene naked in a swimming-pool. He suddenly looks very vulnerable. As with other Peter Greenaway films, it's wilfully obscure but beautiful to look at. After a while I just sat back and enjoy the cloud-capped towers, the gorgeous palaces, and the continuing power and energy of Gielgud's potent art.

Friday 5 May

One of my first interviewees, Nora Swinburne, has died aged 97. She only acted twice with Gielgud, one of the productions being the wartime *Dear Brutus* (1941), when a bomb dropped on the Globe theatre. 'Such a dear, kind man,' she said. 'Nice looking, not very masculine, but very graceful.' It's a fair summary of his appearance.

Saturday 6 May

A brief interview with Coeks Gordon, production manager on the Peter Brook *Oedipus* (1968). He recalls with relish the occasion when he was faced with a difficult request for a prop. 'Peter said he needed an inflatable penis at least six foot, and capable of being inflated on stage. We had it made, and then tested it on stage, with Olivier, Gielgud and everyone all sitting there. We tied a vacuum cleaner to the penis, reversed the flow, and it gradually became upright. There was a stunned silence, and then the damned thing came off the vacuum cleaner, flew all over the stage, and then up into the flies. Everyone sat there, and then Gielgud got up, gave a half-smile, said "What a shame!" and walked out.' Cooks also remembers having to ask the woman running the props department to meet another Brook request, this time for a batch of dildos to be made for use in rehearsal. 'Period or contemporary?' came back the reply.

Tuesday 8 May

I'm thrilled to have reached agreement on my next book, a behind-the-scenes account of the National's production of *Hamlet*, with the excellent Simon Russell Beale playing what I've come to think of as 'Gielgud's part'. I feel I know the play intimately after digging around for his many interpretations. Rehearsals begin later this month, which could hardly be better timing.

Friday 12 May

Yet another theatre death, this time the Motley designer Margaret Harris. She helped me so much, I had hoped she would be around to read the book. Only a few weeks younger than Gielgud, she told me she'd lost touch with him latterly. I imagine he'll be very saddened by the news.

Tuesday 16 May

The revisions are proceeding more smoothly now I've got the final chapters in the right sequence. I realise I've been so careful not to overdose on anecdotes and gaffes that I've gone to the opposite extreme. So I'm enjoying restoring a few that I had reluctantly cut.

Monday 22 May

I spend the morning in a rehearsal room at the National, sitting in on the read-through of *Hamlet*. At lunch I get a message to go to the press office, where someone asks if I've heard the news? What news? That Gielgud is dead. I'm momentarily stunned, then rush to find an evening paper. It says he died yesterday, apparently suddenly and peacefully. I sit dazed and distracted during the next *Hamlet* rehearsal. Certain speeches suddenly have a new resonance: particularly poignant is Simon's delivery of 'Oh that this too too solid flesh would melt'.

The *Evening Standard* diary refers to Morley's 'herculean task of completing his book at speed', which sounds promising. His brief comment is par for the course in errors: he describes Ellen Terry as Irving's wife (oh no she wasn't), and has Gielgud making his professional debut in 1919 (oh no he didn't; he was still at school). In the evening I dash about trying to record various radio and television tributes for later use. I can see they're throwing up extremely useful thoughts from people I missed such as Eyre, Hall and Pinter. I notice that the BBC tribute refers to Gielgud's 'outstanding Richard III'. That would have been one to cherish.

Tuesday 23 May

I buy all the newspapers. I realise I will need several hours to read and absorb all the tributes, especially Julie Kavanagh's lengthy memoir in *The Times*, which continues tomorrow. I play back the radio coverage on *Front Row* and *Night Waves*, which is first class. Peter Hall, speaking from America, is predictably admiring of Gielgud's verse-speaking, his wit and lack of pomposity. Richard Eyre talks of his radicalism and his pioneering work in the 1930s, and suggests you have to have seen him in the theatre to appreciate his greatness, which is very true. On television Pinter talks about his final role, a wordless part in a filmed Beckett play, which he made on his 96th birthday. I'm glad to hear he kept working right up to the end.

I start to think about the practical implications of his death. The first crucial question is, How near is Morley to finishing? I've no way of finding out immediately, so will have to assume the answer is, Possibly quite near. So I need to persuade Methuen to bring my publication date forward to this autumn, which would be the very earliest his book could be ready. I talk to Derek, who agrees, so then I fax Methuen. Suddenly, a response within hours from Max Eilenberg, who agrees we should now aim for the autumn. He suggests we meet.

The timing is not good: I'm still not quite finished, I haven't started to think about the bibliography, notes etc, not to mention selecting photographs. I shall have to work flat out. But I don't see any alternative. Sadly, one matter is settled forever: Gielgud will not see the book.

Wednesday 24 May

It's a weird feeling reading the obituaries, in which writers condense into a single page what I'm struggling to fit into five hundred. In general they've done him proud. Nicholas de Jongh's in the *Guardian* succinctly and stylishly catches his spirit of adventure, his versatility, his mischievous wit. Thomas Sutcliffe in the *Independent* is particularly good on his strengths and limitations, and rightly critical of the more recent view of Gielgud as 'a cherished antique'. On the debit side, Simon Jenkins absurdly links him with Barbara Cartland, who also died this week: 'Like two elderly and splendid queens, they departed the stage on a cloud of velvet and pink chiffon.' He also refers to his 'brief career as a director', a peculiarly inept description of the eighty productions he worked on over a period of 42 years.

Bracing myself for a hail of errors, I turn to Morley's piece in the *Daily Mail*. Ah, Irving and Ellen Terry are still man and wife. (Why was this not reported at the time?) He says Gielgud's first ambition was to be an artist (no, it was to be a stage designer); that he and his brother Val 'virtually invented radio drama' (oh no they didn't); and that he discovered Paul Scofield (oh no he didn't again). Most extraordinary of all, he has Gielgud arrested for 'homosexual soliciting in

Hyde Park', rather than in a public lavatory in Chelsea. All this bodes ill for the Authorised Biography.

Thursday 25 May

A meeting at Methuen with Max Eilenberg and his fellow-editor David Salmo. At my suggestion, and to save time, I hand over the first half of the book for reading. It's in pretty good shape, though not perfect yet. I explain that it may still need minor tinkering, plus any changes resulting from their comments.

Max Eilenberg asks how my book will differ from Morley's, which seems an odd beginning, almost as if I had to justify its existence. During discussions I'm astonished to learn that they're still envisaging a book of 100,000 words. When I explain that it's actually double that length, as agreed with Michael, there's a momentary silence. Max then takes a weighty book from the shelf, the first volume of film director Michael Powell's memoirs. A great book, he says, but we found it very hard to sell at that length. I point out as politely as possible that Powell is hardly a household name as Gielgud is.

Max says they plan to send the book on Monday to an experienced woman editor, who will read and 'recommend cuts'. Gritting my teeth, I point out that I've been working for several months now on the agreed basis of 200,000 words, and that I'm not happy with this assumption that the book is too long. He responds by saying it will be read 'with an open mind'. Somehow this sounds like a threat. I foresee trouble.

We move on to possible images for the cover. I press for the famous 1934 Hamlet photo, which both Michael and I had favoured, or alternatively a matinee idol picture, Gielgud in the 1930s looking debonaire under a trilby. I agree to draft a blurb and put together some celebrity quotes for the back cover. At least they're behaving as if they still intend to publish the book. But in general it's a depressing meeting.

Friday 26 May

I spend the whole morning reading and digesting Julie Kavanagh's two lengthy articles in *The Times*. They're exceedingly well done, a clever weaving in of existing material with what appear to be her own interviews with Gielgud. She's uncovered a lot of personal material, and paints a revealing picture of Gielgud's odd relationship with Martin Hensler. This will no doubt peeve Morley, but it just makes me feel relieved that I was unable to investigate his personal life in any significant way. Among much that is unknown to me, I'm fascinated to read that Gielgud never had a meal alone with Peggy Ashcroft, or talked about anything with her other than their work.

Sunday 28 May

A day spent trawling through the Sunday papers. I'm amazed to see that the *Sunday Times* has run a lengthy piece by Morley on Gielgud's arrest for cottaging, headlining it 'The story John Gielgud didn't want told'. I find the timing, coming even before Gielgud's funeral has taken place, in quite appalling taste, forfeiting any claim Morley might have had to be a responsible Authorised Biographer. I suspect he fears it might be his only chance of getting in first with a detailed account of the incident. His piece as usual is flawed by crazy errors. This time he gets the venue of the cottaging incident right, but the date wrong. He also muddles up the events that occurred on the two opening nights in Liverpool and London of *A Day by the Sea*, which Gielgud was rehearsing when he was arrested. It's a typically shoddy piece of work.

May Progress Report

No time to reflect: everything is now in a state of flux and uncertainty.

Thursday 1 June

Excellent news: Morley's book apparently won't be out until April or May next year, giving me potentially a clear six months. What bliss, and what an incentive to meet my deadline.

Methuen want to use a recent picture of Gielgud on the cover, on the basis that he'll be more recognisable to more people. Max says that in some of the early pictures you wouldn't immediately know it's him. I remind him gently that the word GIELGUD will be blazoned in large type next to his face. But I can see I've lost this argument, since publishers always have the last word on the cover. We've agreed a revised delivery date of 3 July. The first half is going to an editor on Monday, and I'm told 'editorial queries and suggestions' will follow. We seem to have already lost a week, unless Max has been reading it during this time. If so, what does he think of it? Does he still have problems with the length? I think I should be told.

Friday 2 June

A brief paragraph in the paper about Gielgud's funeral, held yesterday 'near his Buckinghamshire home'. Alec Guinness, Richard Attenborough, John Mills, Donald Sinden and Maggie Smith are among the mourners. Later he was cremated at Oxford. It's all very low-key and private, as he would have wanted. I gather he had been due to speak a speech from *The Tempest* at Margaret Harris' funeral, and that news of his death spread through the congregation just before the service. Instead they listened to a recording of him. It must have been a poignant moment.

Sunday 4 June
I listen to a feature on Radio 4, *The Acting Blood*, based on Gielgud's 1995 interview with John Theocharis. It includes all kinds of useful bits and pieces, especially on his parents. There's more detail on his relationship with Olivier, whom he thinks resented his great friendship with Richardson, and also his closeness to Vivien Leigh. 'I became entranced by her,' he says, adding rather unnecessarily, 'I wasn't actually in love with her.' There's a lovely remark about his feelings on 1956 and all that, when *Look Back in Anger* arrived: 'I thought, This is the end for me, I shall have to go to Hollywood like C Aubrey Smith, and play ambassadors and heavy fathers.'

Towards the end he gets very self-critical: 'I'm so aware of my faults, my rashness, my impetuosity, my love of being popular and being liked, ignoring things that I don't want to look at'. He also admits to a fear that he might not be able to face death with any courage. It's a remarkable interview, the bitter irony being that were he still alive I wouldn't have heard it in time to make use of it.

Monday 5 June
It's crunch time on the photographs. I made a preliminary selection at the weekend, but 16 pages seems horribly inadequate for such a rich theatrical life. I note that Holden's book on Olivier has 32 pages, and John Miller's Judi Dench biography 24. I consult Derek, who suggests I float the shared costs idea now. I'm going to have to fork out around £2000 for the existing 16 pages' worth, but I really can't afford to pay for any more. I fax Methuen and press my case for 32 and an equal split. I realise it's not a strong one, as I'm effectively asking them to pay for the extra 16. I notice gloomily that their new edition of Garry O'Connor's biography of Richardson has only *eight* pages.

Wednesday 7 June
Methuen want to see my selection of photographs, plus my suggested layouts of them, before deciding on the number of pages. I'm slightly encouraged.

Thursday 8 June
Publication has been fixed for 12 October, assuming I can deliver a complete script by 3 July. With the final chapter and conclusion to be re-written, and a whole load

of radio, print and television material to check through, not to mention finding the pictures, it's going to be horribly tight. But I'm more than willing to pull out the stops.

Friday 9 June

To Mander and Mitchenson's new premises in the City, where with Richard Mangan's help I'm able to identify and borrow a couple of dozen prints. This is a godsend, as I have no time to nose around other agencies. I ask if the private Gielgud file that he removed on my very first visit is now available. Annoyingly, it's amongst the material not yet unpacked after the collection's move from Beckenham.

Monday 12 June

David Salmo likes my blurb, but thinks it's a bit self-deprecating in parts. It's not easy to praise your own book to the skies, especially when it's still not finished. Still, I manage to force myself to include a few superlatives for the final version.

Tuesday 13 June

I send off photocopies of my layouts for four 8-page sections of photographs. It's been very tricky to get a balance of roles, periods, visual variety, costume, and offstage shots, and still find room for the Terry family, key directors such as Barker, Saint-Denis, Fagan, Komisarjevsky and Brook, and Gielgud heroes such as Ainley and Du Maurier. Even with 32 pages there are many gaps I can't fill.

I read that Gielgud is rumoured to have left £10m in his will. I don't believe it: he enjoyed spending his money too much.

Thursday 15 June

Sadly, because of her filming commitments, Judi Dench is unable to see me between now and my deadline. At John Miller's suggestion I send her a short list of questions in the hope of a written response. It's my last throw.

Friday 16 June

I'm aghast to hear from David Salmo that the first half of the book is now being sent to a different editor, and that she can't start reading it until 22 June – four weeks after I passed the copy to Methuen. How inefficient can you get? He adds: 'As Max mentioned in our first meeting, there will be the necessity for some cuts, but everything will obviously be done with your involvement and approval.' I ring immediately to point out that no one has mentioned or agreed on the *necessity* for cuts, merely that the book would be read 'with an open mind'. Later I get an amended rough for the front of the jacket. The image is a lovely Jane Bown picture, taken in Gielgud's garden. It captures many of his qualities: the shyness, the sensitivity, the roguishness, the elegant dresser. I'm delighted with it, and say so.

Sunday 18 June

I listen to *Centre Stage*, a formidable three-hour Radio 3 programme on Gielgud's achievement as an actor, presented by Michael Billington. Once again there are new bits of information, and a handful of fresh thoughts I can incorporate. Simon Callow is excellent on Gielgud's voice, as is Ralph Fiennes, who has apparently just been to talk to him about playing Richard II. There's a useful account of the aftermath of the arrest from the novelist Paul Bailey, who was there on the famous Haymarket first night. And David Hare contests the view that Gielgud was not a physical actor, arguing that 'he couldn't embody bulk, but he worked by line; nobody could wear a hat better, or have a cigarette at a better angle, or stand better, or wear a suit more beautifully'.

Monday 19 June

Even working all hours, which I shall have to, I can see that two weeks will not give me enough time to complete. I suggest to Methuen that they give me a further week, with all the chronolgy etc to follow a week later. They agree: of course they have no choice. It's nice to have some power for once. All being well, publication can still take place in October.

Wednesday 21 June

John Miller rings with a surprising proposal. He's been asked to chair a celebratory session on Gielgud at the Cheltenham Festival of Literature on 21 October, and wonders if I would take part, alongside Sheridan Morley and Gyles Brandreth. After a moment's hesitation I accept. I'm not keen to meet Morley face to face after his appalling behaviour. On the other hand, it's a golden opportunity to promote the book, while he will have nothing to show.

Friday 23 June

It's a relief to break off from writing and revising for one further interview, even if it's only on the phone. Bill Hays, who directed Gielgud twice for television, now lives in France, but as I know him slightly from way back it's a relaxed interview. He recalls how desperately keen Gielgud was to play Jasper Swift in *Time After*

Time (1986), which also starred Googie Withers, Helen Cherry, Ursuala Howells and Brenda Bruce. The film was based on the novel by his great friend Molly Keane, who came to watch some of the filming in Ireland. Bill also remembers how cooperative he was. 'He was simple and easy to direct, very willing to change things, and very good with the crew. He would never have a stand-in, even for complicated tracking shots that took ages to set up. I think his behaviour shamed a lot of young actors.'

Gielgud evidently took a shine to Bill, whom he called 'Pussy Lamb'. 'He would say, "Let's get away from these monstrous women," and keep giving me little presents. One of them was a biography of Tennessee Williams that he'd bought in Dublin. Unfortunately some of the page sections were printed in the wrong sequence, so he'd done a little guide, marking each section using bits of loo paper. It was weird, but touching.'

He remembers a meal on location when someone at the table asked Gielgud to repeat his Edward Knoblock story. 'John said, "You tell it, Bill, you're better at it than I am." So I did, but then realised I had forgotten the middle part, so I made it up. Afterwards John said: "I don't remember that version. Do you mind if I use it?"' Like everyone else he revelled in Gielgud's schoolboy witticisms, one of which came while they were filming *Quartermaine's Terms* (1987). 'We were filming him standing in front of a fireplace. I looked through the camera, saw a vase on the mantelpiece, and asked if it could be moved six inches to the right. John said: "Ah, those vitally important six inches."'

Monday 26 June
A useful conversation with John Miller. He was at Gielgud's funeral, and tells me a little about it, which is helpful for my final pages. He also clears up the mystery of the conflicting accounts of his death, which took place in his big sitting-room, *not* in the garden, as the *Daily Telegraph* had it ('His last glimpse of tranquil England would have been in his beloved view of the lakeland...'), nor in his bed, as another version suggested. Apparently a reporter and a photographer from the *Telegraph* tried to get into his house the day after he died. What scum they are. John also tells me that Gielgud's wishes not to have a memorial service are being respected. He thinks there should be some kind of celebratory evening in the theatre, and has suggested this to the National, who are thinking about it. It seems to me an excellent idea, especially if it could be held on or about 26 October.

Sunday 2 July
I ring Monica Grey, Val Gielgud's ex-wife, to double-check the dates of her

marriage to Val. She mentions again his part in the crucial meeting the day after Gielgud's arrest. I have the information coming from 'a family source', but she says she doesn't mind if it's attributed to her. I'm pleased: I don't like using anonymous sources unless absolutely necessary, as they always look a little dubious.

Monday 3 July
A brief phone conversation with Kate Griffin, who worked for the Old Vic at the New during the famous 1944-46 Olivier/Richardson seasons, and later read scripts for Olivier during his time at the St James'. 'I was never a pushover for Larry, who was not a generous man,' she says. 'His memoirs were shocking and untrue, he was not himself at the time, but Weidenfeld egged him on. John was very upset by them. He was so different from Larry: his smile, his voice, his responsiveness, you felt all the time that this was someone who looked at you, saw you, and cared, which is more than you can say for some of them.'

Tuesday 4 July
David Salmo tells me in a fax that Methuen's appointed editor is 'working her way happily through your book'. He also has a slightly baffling request, in connection with the first half of the text, to 'leave your disks as they are' so that they correspond to the editor's copy. I'm not clear how can I do this when I've yet to receive the editors' comments.

Thursday 6 July
The disk situation is now clear, and I realise there's a serious problem. Because of the time factor, Methuen have merged the editing and copy-editing process. They now say they want all agreed changes to be made by the editor on her typescript, which she will also mark up for the printer. This is the first time this has been mentioned. It is of course impossible. I've been working on the usual assumption that I would be handing over final disks and hard copy on the delivery date, having had the chance to deal with all editorial comments and suggested cuts in the normal way, and that the mark-up for the printer would be done then. I write to David explaining this. I also point out that I made it clear when I gave them the first half that it would still need fine tuning. And I ask why, when time was so desperately short, a whole four weeks went by without anyone even starting to read the text.

Monday 10 July
I'm working seven days a week, twelve hours a day. It's hideously stressful. I'm

beginning to wish I'd never suggested moving publication forward, especially now that I know that bringing the book out early next year would still have kept it ahead of Morley's. However, I've developed a steady rhythm, and can keep tiredness at bay most of the time. I'm kept going by a sense that the book is really coming together, that I've at last got a decent balance between the personal and the theatrical. Whenever I falter I look again at Morley's painter/polaroid comparison, and the iron returns to my soul.

Tuesday 11 July

A difficult phone conversation with Max Eilenberg about the editing process and the disks. I argue that I can be trusted to look after grammar, style, and consistency of usage, and that all Methuen need do is the technical mark-up for the printer. Eventually he suggests I send him the first chapter so they can set some sample pages, and we'll see what the outcome is. It's a rare victory for common sense.

At a break in *Hamlet* rehearsals at the National I manage a last-minute interview with the theatre's voice coach Patsy Rodenberg. She regrets that speaking the verse beautifully as Gielgud did has become unfashionable. 'If you listen to him compared to other actors of the period, he did it better than anyone, because he was always so truthful. Olivier broke the rules more, which was very exciting, but Gielgud was much more emotionally connected to the text.' I'm intrigued to learn that she uses his recordings with her students at the Guildhall School. 'They think he's going to sound phoney, but once they get past the beautiful voice, they discover a very moving rendition.'

Thursday 13 July

Last night at Sotheby's, at an auction of scores of Spitting Image puppets, the latex Gielgud attracted the top price at £5,300. Alas, poor rubber Johnny, doomed to live out your days in the home of the appalling Michael Winner, Britain's worst film director. Given the real Gielgud's well-known dislike of Winner, this seems a quite undeserved fate.

Friday 14 July

I have won the Battle of the Disks. Methuen have agreed that I should continue as before, and they will arrange for a lightning mark-up of my hard copy the minute they receive the disk. Meanwhile the editor's comments have been flowing in. She makes a myriad suggestions, most of them sensible, for small-scale cuts. They're infinitely more detailed than I expected, but to my surprise focus entirely on tightening up the text within individual pages or paragraphs. I assumed she had also been asked to look at the broader picture, to consider the balance of the material, and so on, but apparently not. This means that, as far I'm aware, no one has looked at my text with any kind of critical eye since Michael Earley left four months ago. I find this astonishing.

Wednesday 19 July
It's taken me a full week to work through the editor's detailed comments, much more than I had anticipated or wanted. I've probably lost 5 or 6,000 words in the process, which I suppose makes it just about worthwhile. But it's put me behind on the revision work.

Monday 24 July
Methuen have rejected the idea of 32 pages of pictures. They argue that it might not be possible to keep to a high standard at that extent. This is nonsense, as a quick glance at Robert Tanitch's illustrated survey of his career shows. What they really mean is that they don't want to spend any extra money. I wish they'd say so. But I don't have time to continue the argument. It means of course that I'll have to do a further set of layouts, dropping half my selection, including many key figures in Gielgud's life. Such a pity.

David tells me the estimated length, based on the first half of the book, is 448 pages. It sounds like a pleasingly substantial volume.

Tuesday 25 July
I receive the sample pages. The typography is fine, clean and classical, like the jacket, but the text type size is obviously too small. I fax David with my response, and he agrees to get it set a size larger. Thank goodness there's no dispute this time. He says there's interest from a major book club, which has asked to see sample chapters.

Wednesday 26 July
I'm finally satisfied with the last six chapters. But the conclusion is proving one of the hardest parts to write. It's not easy to sum up Gielgud's life and achievement in 1200 words, which I've already partly done in the introduction. I suddenly realise I should shift much of that material to the conclusion, and make the introduction a resume of the various challenges I faced in writing the book. But I decide not to make any reference there to Morley, the biggest challenge of them all. And so to the chronology and notes: light relief in comparison.

Monday 31 July
It's done. The feeling of satisfaction is indescribable. I realised at the last minute that it would have taken at least another week to compile proper detailed reference notes. Instead I've indicated the main sources for each chapter. That will have to do, as I'm sure it will for 99 per cent of readers.

Wednesday 2 August
I catch up with the *Hamlet* company, now on tour in Malvern. Between rehearsals I talk to Simon Russell Beale, who was involved recently in a recital at Buckingham Palace in which Gielgud took part. There may just be time to include his eye-witness account.

I ask if he's been influenced by Gielgud. 'I have other, more suitable heroes, such as Charles Laughton,' he says. 'Gielgud has probably had more influence on someone like Ralph Fiennes. But I admired his sheer technique, the way he handled stresses in the verse, and other things we have to work so hard at. I never saw him on stage, but I'd love to achieve that speed of thought and effortlessness he gets in those recordings of *Hamlet*.'

Thursday 3 August
Back from Malvern to a lovely surprise: a letter from Judi Dench answering all my questions. I had finally given her up for lost. She remembers Gielgud's kindness to her when she was being given a hard time by Michel Saint-Denis in *The Cherry Orchard* (1961). She thinks the finest performance she saw of his was the *Ages of Man* recital. In answer to one question she says: 'If we knew what the essence of his talent was, we would all be doing it! On the stage he was one of those people who drew you in. And like Frank Sinatra putting over a song, he didn't dwell on one particular aspect.' She adds a very funny, surreal Gielgud story, and I spend the evening working into the text the best of her and Simon's observations and stories, then faxing them to Methuen in the hope they can be slipped in under the wire.

Tuesday 8 August
Alec Guinness is dead. The obituaries rightly claim that he was more of a household name around the world than Gielgud was, but they also give due credit to Gielgud's influence on his early career. I'm pleased that the quotes on the back of my book's jacket begin with his comment that 'John Gielgud did more to liberate the English theatre from the fustian attitudes of the twenties and early thirties than any other man'. Selfishly, I feel relieved that I talked to him in good

time, but sad that he won't be around to read the book.

Friday 11 August
The proofs have arrived. At first glance it looks like a job well done. I have three working days before travelling to Elsinore with the *Hamlet* company. I shall need every moment to read the 558 pages. But I wonder where those extra 110 came from?

Saturday 12 August
A belated reply from the poet Elizabeth Jennings. She describes Gielgud as 'the great pin-up and inspiration of my life'. They corresponded for many years, sent each other their own books, and in recent years he sent her champagne at Christmas. Unfortunately the 'witty, charming, graceful letters' he wrote have been lost in one of her many moves.

Thursday 17 August
My second day at Elsinore. I can now put flesh on those pictures of Gielgud playing Hamlet here, outlined against the castle courtyard walls, and his accounts of his struggles against the elements to make himself heard on the open-air stage. There's no doubt there's a special magic in hearing the famous words spoken under the 'brave o'erhanging firmament'.

Over breakfast Simon Day, who's playing Horatio, remembers a brief correspondence he had with Gielgud. 'I was trying to raise money to go to the Bristol Old Vic drama school. I was skint and desperate, so I wrote to some of the theatrical nobs, and Gielgud sent me £100 by return of post. Eight years later I was setting up a theatre company with Lucy Briers. I wrote to him again, and he sent another £100, again by return of post. He was the most generous of men to young actors.'

Thursday 24 August
Back from Elsinore, to find the copy for the index waiting for me. It's a disaster, a chaotic mess, full of irrelevancies, and at no less than 69 pages ridiculously long. I tell David it's unacceptable, and he agrees. How on earth could a professional indexer get it so wrong? Where did they find her? No time for a new one to be compiled from scratch if the schedule is to be maintained, so I agree *very* reluctantly to undertake a rescue job myself.

Monday 28 August
Re-creating the index has taken up four solid days of my life. The only minor compensation is that I no longer have to cover half the cost. Methuen, who chose the indexer, now get it free.

Wednesday 30 August
The proofs of the pictures have arrived. Allowing for the limited number, they look good. I'm glad we've got in Jane Bown's fine picture of Gielgud with Richardson, especially as she's generously waived any fee. I hastily correct a 'Morleyism', which has him playing Richard III rather than Richard II at the Queen's in 1937.

Friday 1 September
I finish checking the revised pages and index proofs. Publication is confirmed for 26 October. Tomorrow I'm off to Greece for a much-needed break. I'm exhausted, but elated.

Monday 11 September
Back from a relaxing week on the island of Andros to a pleasing item in the *Times* Diary, concerning 'an unseemly literary scramble'. Headed 'Missed cue', it reveals that Morley received a £50,000 advance from Hodder, but is 'alarmed by the arrival of three upstarts', meaning me, Gyles Brandreth (a reissue of his pictorial biography) and John Miller (ditto the Gielgud memoirs).

If we three are upstarts, Morley is clearly a latestart. His book is described as 'work in progress', which sounds gratifyingly unfinished. It even makes me wonder whether a May publication date is a reality. He's reported to be 'philosophical, if a little twitchy, about the sudden rush' of Gielgud books, which I imagine is an understatement. I enjoy his plaintive and none-too-subtle attempt to reduce his rivals' sales: 'I am the authorised biographer, so I hope people will think my book is well worth the wait.'

In the evening I bump into Michael Earley at the National. He tells me Morley made a further attempt through Methuen to stop my book, just after Gielgud's death. He wouldn't go into detail, but I assume this was along the lines of his comment in the notorious painter/polaroid letter, in which he said he felt betrayed by both Michael and me. Nothing in his appalling behaviour any longer surprises me.

Saturday 16 September
In the new wing of the National Portrait Gallery I come across a room full of computers, offering the very latest in information retrieval. I can't resist scrolling

through the Gielgud entry, where I find several photos I've not seen before, including a stunning 1936 portrait taken in America by the critic Carl Van Vechten. It's one of the most character-revealing pictures of him off stage. I curse again the fact that my selection had to be assembled in such a frantic rush.

Monday 18 September
A useful session with Margot Wheale, Methuen's publicity manager. We discuss reviewers, serial rights possibilities (I suspect there aren't any, as the book is not sensational enough), and I raise the question of a launch, preferably at the Gielgud theatre, with maybe a celebrity speaker. She says they'll think about it. Apparently I'm to speak at the Birmingham Writers and Readers Festival, and there's a possibility of an event at Waterstone's in Manchester. With dates also fixed at Cheltenham and my local festival in Richmond, it's beginning to cook.

Afterwards I catch a moment with Methuen's managing director Peter Tummons. He thinks the book-club sale unlikely, since there is so much competition, but is sure they can sell the American rights. He raises the possibility, depending on sales, of bringing out the paperback a little sooner than usual, to coincide with publication of Morley's book, and ride on the back of his publicity. Now that *would* be fun.

Tuesday 19 September
I ring Derek Granger to find out if he's a candidate for reviewing the book. He's not, which is a pity; he writes so well. He mentions Gielgud's funeral, which he says was 'a weird occasion', and gives me a more roguish and colourful account of it than I have had from other sources.

Wednesday 20 September
Margot rings to tell me the *Literary Review* has asked for their review copy to be sent direct to their reviewer, one Sheridan Morley. Although it's widespread here, I dislike this practice of a book being reviewed by an obvious rival. Even in normal circumstances it seems to me impossible for the review to be objective; in this instance, God knows what he'll write. I'm only relieved that it's to appear in a specialist magazine rather than one of the dailies or Sundays.

Tuesday 26 September
John Miller rings to talk about the Cheltenham Festival event. We're to be in the main room in the town hall: a thousand seats, which are apparently already selling well. He wants each of us to start with one pre-arranged topic, and offers me first

option. I suggest Gielgud's work as a director, which I think often gets overlooked. He says the National are still thinking about the idea of a celebratory gala evening. If it comes off it's likely to be around Easter time, linked either to his birthday or the anniversary of his death. I hope it works out, and not just for selfish reasons.

Friday 29 September
I ring Methuen to find out about finished copies, due yesterday. Annoyed to discover they have been delayed. The printer is apparently citing the fuel crisis. Now I've heard everything.

Monday 2 October
The delay at the printer is serious. They now say they can't deliver copies until tomorrow week. So publication will have to move on a week, to allow reviewers time to read it. It's unbelievably frustrating, but there's no alternative. The launch, now moved to 1 November, is agreed in principle, which is some compensation. Margot is to try to get the Gielgud theatre for lunchtime that day.

Tuesday 3 October
John Miller rings again about Cheltenham. Gyles Brandreth wants to talk about whether Gielgud was the greatest actor of his generation. Apparently he told John: 'You'll be hard-pressed to stop me and Sheri.' John is all too aware of this, and says he's determined to rein them in, and not allow them to dominate proceedings with endless anecdotes. He says Gyles' book is now out, with a new introduction and conclusion amounting to around 6,000 new words. I had better get a copy.

Wednesday 4 October
A further talk with Margot. At 4,300 copies the bookshop advance orders are looking very healthy. The *Daily Mail* has said No to serialisation, which I expected. Actually it's a relief: could I ever live down appearing in such an appalling paper?

Saturday 7 October
I scour the three bookshops in Richmond for a copy of the Brandreth book, and am surprised to find that none of them have any. It's not even on the Waterstone's database, which is heartening. Perhaps the fuel crisis has been even-handed? In the evening I listen to some gentle chat about Gielgud on Radio 4's *Loose Ends*, with John Miller and playwright Peter Nichols among the participants. In introducing them, Ned Sherrin mentions the three current books, then mischievously refers to 'rather a long period of gestation from Mr

Morley', which won't please the Authorised Biographer.

Monday 9 October
The Gielgud theatre is booked, for lunch time in the circle bar. On the question of a suitable celebrity speaker, I suggest Simon Russell Beale, as one Hamlet to reflect on another. I talk in the evening to John Miller, who was not very happy with the *Loose Ends* programme. He says that afterwards Ned Sherrin suggested Morley had behaved appallingly in publishing the article on Gielgud's arrest immediately after Gielgud's death. Very true.

Tuesday 10 October
The book has arrived. It's a wonderful moment. It looks exceedingly handsome, and I'm thrilled. At 580 pages it seems good value for £20 – I had expected it to be £25. *Gielgud: A Theatrical Life* sits solidly on my desk, its subject looking beadily up at me from under his panama hat. I could swear there's an extra twinkle in his right eye since I last saw the picture.

Later, as I examine the book more closely, I'm brought down to earth. The frontispiece, Gielgud as Hamlet, has been printed on text paper rather than the glossy type used for the other photos, and it looks annoyingly cheap. In fact this is the first time I have known of its existence. I realise I was never shown a proof, and curse Methuen yet again for not consulting me. I also notice that a small section of pages in the middle of the book has not been trimmed properly. It only protrudes slightly, but the defect is noticeable. I ring David, who promises to check if other copies are similarly affected.

Thursday 12 October
Frustratingly, the poor trim is on all the copies. David says it's not considered serious enough to return them for reprinting. I suppose they're right, especially this near to publication. But it's distressing to have such a flaw appear at the last gasp, after everyone, and me in particular, has worked so hard to make it perfect. I just hope the booksellers don't see it as a problem.

Friday 13 October
Simon Russell Beale is unable to be at the launch because of a radio commitment. Happily another fine Hamlet, Michael Pennington, has agreed to step into his shoes. I hope this will encourage the press to attend.

Monday 16 October

A final call from John Miller about Cheltenham. He's spoken to Morley, who predictably wants to talk about his book, the letters and diaries he has, and the scandal. John is keen not to dwell on the private life, and has told him he must keep it brief, and avoid long anecdotes. John wants to air a good range of topics, including Gielgud's stage partnerships with Richardson and Peggy Ashcroft, the influence of Barker, Komisarjevsky and others, and the influence Gielgud himself has had on the younger generation of actors. I suspect, as he does, that we'll be hard-pressed to cover the ground.

Tuesday 17 October

Old habits die hard. The 1977 television version of *Heartbreak House* is being shown at the National Film Theatre, with Gielgud as Captain Shotover. This being one I missed, I'm unable to keep away. I recall that Shotover was one of the rare Shaw parts he had actually wanted to play. After seeing it, I can't think why. He's a confused and fantastical character, and Gielgud, encased in a vast white beard, seems uncomfortable with him, unsure whether to play it for comedy or seriousness. But his long philosophical speech in his intimate scene with Lesley-Ann Down, playing Ellie, is beautifully spoken.

Afterwards I buy a copy of Gyles Brandreth's reissued memoir in the National bookshop. Oddly, the jacket has the same typeface as mine has. I notice the photos are no longer integrated, but grouped in two conventional sections, which makes it less classy looking. Five out of his 23 pictures duplicate mine, which is not serious. The new introduction and conclusion are mostly the familiar anecdotes, and material that's emerged since his death. But there are new shards of information about Gielgud's last years that I can usefully slip into the paperback of my edition. I'm astonished to read that his rate for a day's filming in his final years was £50,000, though the second day was free. No wonder he did all those cameos.

Friday 20 October

I get a call from Richard Brooks, the *Sunday Times* media editor, who's doing a piece for Sunday. He's been speaking to Morley, so focuses initially on the familiar official/unofficial issue. I eventually steer him on to the book itself, and we talk at some length. In the afternoon I travel to Cheltenham, for tomorrow's clash of the biographers. Though I suspect Morley will behave himself in public, I am very nervous.

Saturday 21 October
John Miller, Gyles Brandreth and I meet in the Writers' Room an hour early. No sign of Morley. Gyles is chumminess incarnate, doing a witty and convincing impression of himself. On stage we do a sound-check, and watch the Gielgud clips which will begin and end the event. Though I've seen *Swan Song* before, Gielgud's delivery of Othello's 'Farewell the tranquil mind' speech brings tears to my eyes.

Morley sweeps in at the last minute ('The story of his life,' Gyles whispers to me). He seems harassed, looks slightly unkempt, and sounds too loud. He graciously fills us all in on how far he has got with reading our various books. He mutters about 'a certain amount of lost sales', and says defensively that his hands were tied, as he had agreed not to publish the book until a year after Gielgud's death. (This is news to me.) When we're introduced he is full of fake bonhomie: 'How nice to meet you after all his time, Jonathan.'

On the platform it becomes clear that his aim is to play the entertainer, and stuff in as many anecdotes as possible. His first contribution is a lengthy, exaggerated and irrelevant story about 'my grandmother Gladys Cooper'. He plays up his links with the stars: 'It was very hard to love Larry, though some of us occasionally tried.' He repeats some of his earlier claims in print, such as the absurd idea that 'John really invented radio Shakespeare'. There is no open sparring between us, although I notice that when I quote a remark about Gielgud made to me by Dirk Bogarde, he brings in 'my book about Dirk' at the earliest opportunity. His mind is quick, but his mouth can't always keep up, as he rushes helter-skelter through the stories, guffawing like a pirate after each punch-line. Gyles is more subtle, mixing his anecdotes with more considered remarks. But while Morley wisely avoids imitating The Voice, Gyles can't resist it. Unfortunately he sounds more like Coward.

Morley promotes his book heavily, claiming that Gielgud chose him because he thought 'I was a safe pair of hands'. He stresses that his book is 'not just the last of the line, but somewhat separate', and hopes that people will buy it in the spring. ('Don't worry, we will,' Gyles mutters mischievously.) I realise at that moment that I should have brought a copy of mine on stage, as Gyles the seasoned performer has done.

As promised, Morley brings up the scandal. He gets embarrassingly carried away, and starts to make all kinds of wild claims. He says the greatest thing Gielgud did aside from his acting and directing career was to change the law governing homosexuality. (Gyles convincingly refutes this absurd claim.) He refers to Gielgud's court appearance as the 'most famous gay trial since Oscar Wilde's' (it wasn't a trial, he just appeared briefly before a magistrate), and says that 'Because of John, the laws of this land were changed. We're not talking here about rape, or minors, or boy scouts.' He burbles on about his own interviews with policemen ('It was a frame-up'), and with the judiciary. Then, perhaps sensing he's become too excited, he adds bizarrely: 'All this is not because I'm some prurient gay rights campaigner: I have children, grandchildren and a huge family.' So that's all right then.

All this material, he says, is central to his case for having a book that is different 'from the many admirable ones we have here today'. He argues that 'this is the one new area, because I have the letters', and mentions ones Gielgud wrote to Lillian Gish after the scandal broke. For me the one new piece of information amongst all this nonsense is Alec Clunes' reaction to the move by a handful of actors to have Gielgud drummed out of Equity. Clunes, who was running the Arts theatre, told the cast of the current production that they were at liberty to sign the petition displayed on the noticeboard in the green room, but if they did so they should leave the theatre before the next performance.

I'm intrigued by Morley's body language. When he's not speaking, he's looking at the floor most of the time. I almost begin to feel sorry for him; all this bluster makes him seem very insecure as well as completely ridiculous. I notice that the errors tend to fly more frequently when he's worked up. During the course of the session he gets several facts wrong, and when he substitutes King Lear for Othello in an anecdote about Orson Welles that appears in Gielgud's memoirs, I only just manage to bite back a correction, and notice John doing the same.

At one stage the anecdotes get out of hand, and although John manages occasionally to bring the discussion under control, we have to abandon most of the serious topics, which is extremely frustrating, not to say unprofessional. As we troop offstage at the end Morley buttonholes me, and asks me where I got the letters I used in my book. I explain that a lot of them were already published, and others were in the Mander and Michenson collection. Then he says: 'I must have you on my radio show at some point, but there's been so much Gielgudiana recently....'

I'd been wondering how he would cope with the signing session in the book tent – or, in his case, the non-signing. In fact it descends into farce: while Gyles, John and I satisfy the demand for signed copies, not only does he have no Gielgud volume to offer, but all his other books have been left in another venue by the festival staff. Exit Authorised Biographer, pursued by nobody.

Sunday 22 October
The *Sunday Times* piece ('Gay Gielgud was barred from US work') inevitably

focuses on the scandal and its consequences, but is generally accurate. My book is described as 'unoffical', but that's all right, as it's given just about equal prominence with Morley's. His publication date is now said to be March, i.e. two months before the anniversary of Gielgud's death. A journalist's error? Or is Morley preparing to break the conditions of the deal he allegedly struck with Gielgud? We shall see.

Monday 23 October

I drop in on the launch of another Methuen book, Nicholas de Jongh's account of stage censorship, *Politics, Prudery and Perversions*. It's held in a chic Kensington art gallery, the entertainment is a male stripper, which seems nicely ironic. I talk briefly with Nicholas, who enthuses about Gielgud the man. I bump into Max Eilenberg, who tells me there was great interest in my book from two American publishers at the recent Frankfurt Book Fair.

I manage to catch a word with Keith Baxter, and apologise for not having contacted him. He says he's seeing Morley tomorrow, which presumably means his book is still not complete. I also talk briefly to Siân Phillips, mainly about *Heartbreak House*. She confirms that Gielgud didn't enjoy the experience. She also remembers his chaotic directing on his last production, *The Gay Lord Quex* (1975), then recalls a gaffe involving her ex-husband Peter O'Toole. Seeing Gielgud walking along the street on the day of Binkie Beaumont's funeral, he offered him a lift. After declining politely, Gielgud said to O'Toole: 'You know you're not nearly as awful as people say you are.'

Tuesday 24 October

A wonderfully encouraging letter from Christopher Fry, my first independent reaction, and a rave: 'It's a great work – really so – which exists in its own right, not simply as a biography; though as that, too, it's a good, clear, beautifully proportioned mirror.' Being a kind man I suspect he's a kind critic, but I'm still a bit overwhelmed by such praise. I fax the quote through to Margot, for use on all future press releases.

Wednesday 25 October

Gielgud has left £1.5m in his will. I'm not sure if that includes the proceeds from the sale of his house. Much of it is to go to theatrical charities and friends, but the bulk to charitable causes selected by his executors according to his known wishes. The press report implies the gay-rights group Stonewall might benefit, since he was donating money to it up to his death. His portrait of Ellen Terry goes to the

National Portrait Gallery, and some personal items to the Theatre Museum. But there's no mention of his papers, cuttings books, and photographs. *Please*, not the Theatre Museum....

Saturday 28 October

My first review in the national press. Robert Gore-Langton in the *Daily Express* praises me for dealing with the scandal in 'commendably unsensational detail', and for 'wisely resisting recycling the tired anecdotes'. Good, he noticed. But although he calls the book 'industrious' and 'an honourable effort', he takes me to task for not saying enough about the nature of Gielgud's acting. This depresses me a little, because I think he probably has a point. I feel this was one of the consequences of the last-minute rush, which prevented a final reflective read-through, both from me and Methuen.

Meanwhile extracts have started to appear in the *Guardian* from the diary kept by Richard Eyre while making his *Changing Stages* series for the BBC. Before filming began he interviewed Gielgud, 'in case I drop off the twig', as Gielgud put it. I look forward to seeing the result next weekend: his posthumous appearance will be nicely timed for my publication day.

Monday 30 October

Encouraging news from Danny Parnes, Methuen's sales manager. He tells me the book is on display in the windows of six key London booksellers, including lovely old Hatchards in Piccadilly, Gielgud's own favourite. Happily, the Gielgud theatre has also agreed to sell copies. Whether people coming to watch Jerry Hall take her clothes off in *The Graduate* are prime targets for the book remains to be seen.

Tuesday 31 October

The new issue of the *Radio Times* has a large picture of Gielgud as Mercutio on its opening page, and another smaller one further on in a feature spread on British theatre. Not of course to mark publication of my book, but as a trailer for Richard Eyre's series. But the timing could hardly be better.

In the afternoon I do an interview with Julia Somerville on LBC. It's an enjoyable quarter of an hour, during which she plies me with intelligent questions, giving me time to get in most of the points I'd planned to cover. Afterwards, removing her headphones, she says: 'I could go on talking about Gielgud until four in the morning.' I think she means it: she's clearly a Johnite. Or does she say this to all her guests?

Wednesday 1 November

The book is launched. The Gielgud theatre proves the perfect spot: Clive Francis' wicked caricatures of Gielgud fill the walls of the circle bar, and posters for his productions of *The Lady's Not for Burning* and *The Importance of Being Earnest* hang in the corridor. There's a good turnout from the profession, despite the continuing storms, floods and rail chaos. Michael Pennington is very complimentary about the book; I kick myself (and Methuen) for not having a tape recorder to hand. He also makes a beautifully crafted and eloquent speech about Gielgud's talent, and what his personality and presence meant to other actors.

I decide to abandon my own prepared speech, which suddenly feels too formal and plodding. Instead I simply thank everyone who helped me with the book, and express my regret (not entirely truthfully) that Gielgud wasn't able to read it. Afterwards I sign copies, do interviews with journalists from the *Evening Standard* and *Daily Telegraph*, and fend off some persistent questions about my correspondence with Gielgud from a man from the *Daily Express*. It's altogether a deeply satisfying occasion – and not a single mention of the Authorised Biographer.

Thursday 2 November

Publication day, and two useful diary items about the launch in the *Daily Express* and the *Evening Standard*. At lunchtime I do an interview at Broadcasting House, down the line to BBC Radio Birmingham. The focus is on Gielgud and Shakespeare, the rivalry with Olivier, and his films. With Julia Somerville I had prepared some notes, but now I feel confident enough to wing it, which is pleasing.

Afterwards, like all nervous authors on publication day, I tour the bookshops. Disappointingly, less than half of the dozen I visit in the West End have copies in stock. In a couple they call up the details on the computer, which to my horror says that publication was last September, and the book is no longer available. To make matters worse, I discover that Hodder have reissued two of Gielgud's autobiographical books in one volume, calling it *Gielgud on Gielgud*. There it sits, cheek by jowl with mine, looking very competitive. My mood improves a little at Hatchards, where I sign their entire stock of 36 copies. But overall it's a dispiriting experience. I fax Danny Parnes with the details, hoping he can retrieve the situation fast.

Later I talk on the phone to one of the guests at the launch, who passes on a nice *bon mot* straight from a playwright's mouth. At a party he heard Alan Bennett remark of the Authorised Biographer: 'He's not very Sheridan and he's not very Morley.'

Friday 3 November

A handful of annoying misprints and misspellings have come to light from various sources. I suppose this was inevitable given the speed with which the book was produced, but it's still extremely irritating to see them there. I hope no one picks up the absence from the index of Mrs Patrick Campbell. I'm relieved she's not around to berate me personally.

Saturday 4 November

A glutton for punishment, I go round my local bookshops, again with mixed results. Waterstone's have three branches in Kingston, but not a copy between them; but in Richmond they're well stocked, and I again sign copies. These visits serve to remind me of the sheer number of new biographies being published, all jostling for precious space. In the evening I sign the National bookshop's remaining half-dozen copies: the book's selling well, faster apparently than Gyles' book, and they're already re-ordering, which is an encouraging sign. But if it doesn't sell well here there would be no hope at all.

Sunday 5 November

Friends and family come round to my house for a lunch party to celebrate publication. I play Gielgud's rendering of Hamlet's soliloquy 'Oh what a rogue and peasant slave am I'. Once more he holds an audience spellbound.

There's a positive and nicely timed review by Charles Osborne in the *Sunday Telegraph*. Yet though he praises my 'many splendid stories and interesting new information', the review is intellectually disappointing, more a re-cycling of material from the book than an attempt to analyse its merits or defects. He also reviews Gyles' memoir, which he delights in especially for 'its collection of Gielgudian faux pas'. My fear is that this rather buffoonish aspect of Gielgud is going to figure much too largely in the reviews.

In the evening I watch the first programme in Richard Eyre's series on theatre, *Changing Stages*. Gielgud, in grey-green corduroy suit, figures prominently. Interviewed well before his *Newsnight* appearance, he's twinkling and rubicund, and full of mischief, notably about Lilian Baylis ('I don't think she knew her arse from her elbow'). He remembers his days as a matinee idol among the Bright Young Things, when he led 'a sort of semi-Francis Bacon existence', and reflects on his stimulating talk on *Hamlet* with Barker at the Ritz hotel ('I managed to keep Mrs Barker out of the room for two hours while he gave me notes').

Self-deprecating to the end, he suggests Olivier was right to criticise him for showing off when they both played Romeo in 1935. When Richard suggests that perhaps Olivier was doing the same, he says: 'Yes, but his showing off was so dazzling. My showing off was more technical, more soft, and...' glancing sideways at his interviewer, 'oh, effeminate, I suppose.'

Thursday 9 November
A celebratory lunch with Derek. I broach the idea of Sybil Thorndike as my next subject, but he's sceptical about sales. 'It would have to be a labour of love,' he says. I mention Michael Redgrave as an alternative. This time he's more optimistic. I promise to think seriously about the idea.

Saturday 11 November
I enjoyed Methuen's ad in today's *Daily Telegraph*. It linked the book with Arthur Miller's new collection of essays under the heading 'Books of a Lifetime', calling it 'the definitive biography of the actor of the century'. Here's looking at you, Sheri.

Monday 13 November
This evening I gave a talk on Gielgud at the Richmond Festival. As usual I was over-prepared, and only able to cover half the topics I had intended to speak about. I was very nervous at first, but in the Q and A session afterwards I relaxed, and even cracked a joke or two. I signed a dozen or so books at the end, not all of them for friends. I've never quite understood the magic aura of the signed copy, but I'm not complaining right now.

Wednesday 14 November
According to Christopher Gray in the *Oxford Times*, Gielgud's career is 'charted lucidly and most amusingly in Mr Croall's well-written book'. However, he blots his copybook by suggesting that 'for an appraisal of the man' readers must wait for the Morley volume. How does he know?

Wednesday 15 November
A generous letter from Bill Gaskill: 'I read your book with great pleasure. It is wonderfully clear and unfolds that amazing career with great honesty and affection. Not too many anecdotes, just enough to keep the image of the old blunderer – gaffeur perhaps – alive.' He adds that he likes my description of Gielgud's directing methods, faults and all. Coming from a skilled director and knowledgeable man of the theatre, all this is welcome praise indeed.

Thursday 16 November

The first review worthy of that name, from Joyce McMillan in the *Scotsman*. It's not just that she finds the book elegant, brilliant, hugely enjoyable, intelligent, generous in spirit, richly detailed, though this naturally helps. No, it's the fact that she reviews the book rather than the life, while still giving you a lot of information about Gielgud. She has criticisms, but given the quality of the review I take them seriously – for example, her view that I sometimes neglect the world outside the theatre, or that my concluding chapter is not substantial enough, both of which I feel are fair comments. I'm amused to see that she calls it 'an authorised biography'.

Friday 17 November

After the Lord Mayor's Show comes the muck cart. The *Evening Standard* reviewer Nick Curtis seems determined to be abusive about the book. He castigates me for 'itemising and analysing' every one of Gielgud's productions and performances, which I thought was one of the biographer's tasks. He then says I do the same for 'virtually every costume', which is not the case; indeed, one of my worries is that there is not enough description of costumes and sets. He calls the book 'a laborious and startlingly arid portrait', and accuses me of throwing in a familiar anecdote when I sense 'things are getting a bit dry' – and there was I trying desperately to keep most of them out.

Even more annoyingly, he accuses me of always being on Gielgud's side: 'Croall is always there in his defence, digging out the one good review to counter the bad ones, or pointing out how the biggest theatrical disaster actually, somehow, marked a step forward.' This is totally untrue, and makes me furious, as does his absurd remark that my conclusion 'reads like a proud headmaster's pat on the head to a favoured pupil'. I know reviewers can come to totally opposite conclusions about the same book, but I can't help thinking there's a hidden agenda here. Would it be paranoid to guess at a Morley connection? I can understand now why writers and actors sometimes want to hit a critic.

Thursday 23 November

After seeing a gentle Athol Fugard play *The Captain's Tiger* at the Orange Tree I talk to Sam Walters. He tells me Morley told him with some glee a few days ago that he'd finally delivered his completed text. This suggests to me that Hodder will be hard pushed to get it out before May. If so, that gives me at least a six-month clear run. Excellent.

Tuesday 28 November

A good detailed review in the *Hampstead and Highgate Express* by James Roose-Evans, who directed Gielgud in his last stage appearance in *The Best of Friends* (1988). He was someone I never got round to interviewing, partly because he'd already written a good account of his production that I could draw on. From his sympathetic review I learn who Gielgud was dining with on the night of his arrest: James Barnard (?who) and Paul Denn (misprint for the critic Paul Dehn?). He describes the book as 'superbly researched', which is pleasing after my bruising from Curtis.

Sunday 3 December

In its 'Twenty Books for Christmas' slot the *Sunday Express* sums up my three and a half years' work in two words: 'Friends' reminiscences.' Well, yes and no. In the *Sunday Times*, in a page gloriously headed 'Santa's show-stoppers', Christopher Bray goes overboard with 85 words. The first seventy are about Olivier and *Brideshead Revisited* and Gielgud's performance as Edward Ryder. The next 15 are mine alone: 'Croall is similarly attentive to nuance in this monument to our classiest classical actor.' I have yet to decide whether 'monument' is a term of praise or abuse.

Tuesday 5 December

Max Eilenberg confirms the sale of US rights to Continuum, which he describes as 'a very respectable independent publisher with a foot in both trade and academic markets'. The advance is $15,000, which is also very respectable. At this rate Methuen might even get their money back before the paperback comes out.

Thursday 7 December

Peter Tummons rings to say Methuen need to put an urgent reprint in hand so that the bookshops don't run out in the critical pre-Christmas fortnight. Including a thousand copies sent to Australia, they've already sold the entire 5,500 print-run. This is wonderful news. The down side is that they want to reprint without making any corrections, since this would add an extra two or three days to the schedule at a critical moment. Since it's a modest reprint of just a thousand copies I agree to the plan, though it pains me to let even one copy go out with those minor mistakes still in there.

Friday 8 December

An excellent review in the *Times Literary Supplement* by the actor Jonathan Cecil, who thinks the book 'a worthy tribute to a loveable man and a dedicated artist'. He likes my 'light touch' and, more surprisingly, 'my love of anecdotes'. He reckons 'practically all Gielgud's famous gaffes are here'; he should see the rejection file. Cecil was directed by him in Peter Ustinov's *Halfway up the Tree*, and describes him as not a great director but 'a superb, fastidious teacher', which is neatly put.

Saturday 9 December

In his round-up of theatre books in the *Independent*, Aleks Sierz calls mine 'a model of research and readability', which is pleasing. So too is his brief comparison with Gyles' memoir: while his book is 'brisk and full of quotations from Gielgud', mine is 'more leisurely and more satisfying'.

Sunday 10 December

I'm invited by Gyles to come on his LBC chat show. Annoyingly, by the time historian Roy Porter has given a brilliant summary of the Enlightenment, Judy Campbell has gossiped at length about the Pinter/Proust production at the National and her daughter Jane Birkin, Rohan Pelling has spilt the beans about editing the *Erotic Review*, and Gyles has flirted and flattered and jested for all he's worth, ninety minutes have passed and there's no time left for Gielgud. So I have to return an hour later, and gear myself up all over again. In the end it's worth it: Gyles calms down and we chat about Gielgud, most of the time seriously, for a very fair ten minutes.

Tuesday 12 December

To Kensington Town Hall for a talk on Gielgud – not by me, but by Frances Hughes, who is secretary of the Shakespeare Reading Society. Gielgud was its president for forty-two years, and not long ago sent it £100. Tonight, on the society's 125th birthday, they're blowing his gift on wine and mince pies for the hundred or so members (including two of the Terry family) who have turned up to celebrate his life.

It's a peculiar sensation, hearing someone lecture on a subject you know intimately. Frances is both lively and informative, and could well have done the book herself. She's especially good on Gielgud's love and appreciation of painting, and comes up with snippets of information that are new to me. I've been generously allowed to sell copies of my book afterwards, and manage to shift another dozen to the somewhat elderly audience.

Wednesday 13 December

Gyles gets the notice in *The Times*, where theatre critic Benedict Nightingale commends his 'lovely tales' and the 'sense of delight' that permeates his book. Mine is described merely as 'a bigger and more solid account', which in the context feels like criticism. Annoyingly, mention is also made of Morley's 'definitive biography' coming next year.

Friday 15 December
Another review from one of Morley's fellow national critics, Michael Coveney in the *Daily Mail*, who sums up the book in the phrase 'dogged, but thoroughly readable', which I suppose is better than nothing, though not *much* better.

Tuesday 19 December
The longest review yet, in the *Western Mail*: two whole pages and five photographs. The first half re-cycles the entire blurb, adjectives and all. Since I wrote it, I have now effectively reviewed my own book, which is a very peculiar experience.

Friday 29 December
A lovely postcard from Moira Lister, who says she's enjoyed the book enormously: 'It's beautifully and wittily written and very easy to read, and you have captured John superbly.' It's this kind of insider reaction, from people who knew Gielgud well, that I value more than the comments of the critics, even those who have bothered to read the book properly. Their opinions are what make all the work worthwhile.

Saturday 30 December
A good positive review in the *Daily Telegraph* from Paul Bailey, who feels I catch Gielgud's essence, and that the book 'honours what was best in him – his modesty, his dedication to his craft, and his generosity to his fellow-actors'. This seems to contradict his initial description of the book as 'worthy', unless he's using the word in its positive sense.

More annoying is his reference to three 'irritating omissions and mistakes'. My substituting of Emlyn Williams for Eric Portman as the original Crocker-Harris in *The Browning Version* certainly comes under that heading, and I'm still kicking myself for this careless slip. But Bailey also claims that I write of the death of the actor Frank Vosper 'as if it had no significance – but he was probably murdered'. Vosper went overboard after a party on an Atlantic liner, and may have simply been drunk. But the *cause* of his death, never resolved, had no significance for Gielgud. Bailey's third point, that I failed to mention a peer's threat to horsewhip Gielgud after the cottaging incident, is just plain wrong: it's there in black and white. Ironically, the source for this piece of information was Bailey himself, in a radio broadcast shortly after Gielgud's death.

Sunday 31 December

To Wotton Underwood, at last. While Gielgud was alive I felt unable to take a look at his grand house there. I felt it would be like spying, as if the place were out of bounds to me, given his later attitude to my book. But now he's not there, the book is out, the year is ending, and my curiosity wins the day.

I'm intrigued to find the village is in a cul-de-sac, and really no more than a hamlet. No pub, no shop, just a church and a handful of large houses dotted around a rough meadow. A disappointment: the house itself is not visible unless you walk up a private drive, which I decide not to do. But I get a view of the large walled garden, of which Gielgud was excessively proud. And it's satisfying even now to get a general sense of the place in which he spent the last third of his life.

I walk the short distance to the tiny All Saints' church, where his funeral took place. The inside is simple and unadorned, with a fine wooden roof and bare pews, like many another English village church. In the visitors' book I look up the day of his funeral, and find that one of his relatives has written the words 'Beautiful atmosphere'. It's a simple setting in which he chose to make his final exit. Now that I've seen it, I feel my work is finally done.

– Epilogue –
The Battle Continues

In the aftermath of my book's publication there were several more skirmishes in the Battle of the Biographers. The most intensive took place when Morley's biography was finally published in May 2001. It was called *John G* and, so that there should be absolutely no misunderstanding, the words 'The Authorised Biography' were printed not just on the front and back of the jacket, but at the top of every page. The reviews were extremely mixed. One of the more positive ones appeared in the *Sunday Times*, where Humphrey Carpenter called the book 'masterly and moving'. Morley's fellow-critic Benedict Nightingale also praised it, writing in *The Times* that the book 'combines thoroughness and authority' (though his reference to Gielgud directing Coward's *Cavalcade* at Covent Garden under Georg Solti, when it was actually Mozart's *Don Giovanni*, slightly undermined his own authority).

Other reviewers voiced fundamental criticisms. Alastair Macaulay declared in the *Financial Times*: 'Morley has trashed Gielgud's authorisation. Gielgud himself valued accuracy: Morley is scandalously slapdash.' He concluded: 'Its main distinction is that it wades into Gielgud's homosexuality with hobnailed boots, and gratuitously "outs" others such as Alec Guinness and Dirk Bogarde in a prurient manner'. He added, to my quiet delight, that 'Croall's book feels much more like an authorised biography than Morley's'.

In similar vein, Peter Conrad argued in the *Observer* that Morley had 'wasted his access to the great man, whose character and significance elude him'. He chided him for the 'meretricious haste' in which he had written the book following Gielgud's death, suggesting he had 'merely collaged clippings and anthologised the usual clangers; no psychological perceptions are on offer here'. He ended witheringly: 'A great life calls for a great biographer, not an all-purpose scribbler on the fringes of luvviedom.'

Understandably provoked, Morley wrote a letter of complaint to the *Observer*, stating: 'I have never claimed to be a psychologist.' In an attempt to refute Conrad's description of him, he cited his thirty years as a drama critic, his previous 15 biographies, and added: 'I come from three generations of actors and directors.'

But it was a highly critical review in the *Sunday Telegraph* by Helen Osborne, widow of the playwright John, which really stung him. Dripping with personal animosity, her review began: 'For what seems like an eternity, Sheridan Morley has been a blob on the theatrical landscape.' She went on to accuse him of 'shamelessly exploiting his theatrical connections (grandmother Gladys Cooper, actor-father Robert)' and of 'ungallantly waiting on Gielgud's death' before completing his book. 'He promises a time bomb, but what we get is a damp squib,' she wrote. She criticised his 'obsession with Gielgud as a homosexual actor', and derided both his accuracy and his style: 'John G has been untimely ripped from his database. Quotations and attributions are unacknowledged. Penmanship is all over the slate.' Worst of all for her victim, she ended by describing my book as 'certainly more authoritative' than Morley's. 'It is amusing, informed, modest. In comparison Morley is a muff.'

Morley's reply the following week was remarkably inept. To her accusation that he exploited his family connections, he criticised her for changing her professional name to Osborne when she 'became the last of John's many wives'. On the matter of unacknowledged attributions, he accused her of 'lifting' more than half a dozen quotes from his book, when she had perfectly properly quoted, with clear attribution, a number of passages for the purpose of criticism. Meanwhile he argued that my book 'could scarcely be called authoritative': it had, he explained apparently seriously, 'never appeared in any bestseller lists'. Calling her review 'impertinent', he ended: 'Gielgud and Osborne were never exactly devoted to each other, but I am sad to see John's widow pursuing the vendetta beyond their graves.'

With this wide spectrum of reviews whirring around in my head, I sat down to read the book for myself in a state of great curiosity, which quickly turned to one of amazement. It was not just the sloppy writing, which was to be expected, or the persistent self-regard of its author. There was also the astonishing number of errors, many of them crass or ridiculous, some almost unbelievable. I decided to keep a note of them, and by the end had found a grand total of 240: no less than 188 in the text, and a further 52 in the Chronology, which was a complete mess.

The initial mistakes about Gielgud's family were remarkable enough. Within the first few pages Morley claimed that on her marriage his mother Kate had to give up a promising theatrical career (she never had one), that his father Frank's great-grandparents were eminent Polish actors (they were actually his grandparents), that his paternal background was 'partly Russian' (it was Polish/Lithuanian), that his aunt's stage name was Mabel Terry (it was Mabel Terry-Lewis), that his brother Val was 'the founding father of BBC radio drama' (this was Cecil Lewis) and that the designer Edward Gordon Craig was 'part of the Gielgud clan' (he was a Terry, son of Ellen).

But worse was to follow. There were scores of wrong dates, incorrect play titles and theatres, misquotations, muddles in chronology, and mistaken attributions. Many of them concerned Gielgud's work in Shakespeare. Morley said that he had once played Brutus in *Julius Caesar* (he hadn't), and that he was *Othello* in an early radio production of Shakespeare's play (he was Iago, Henry Ainley was Othello). Remarkably, he even had Gielgud travelling to Stratford in 1949 to direct *Love's Labour's Lost,* 'a play he had neither seen nor read' (he had seen it, had probably read it, but he never directed it). On the film front Morley again showed supreme imagination. Gielgud was said to have played the title-role in the Jules Verne silent *Michael Strogoff* (the film was never made), to have been cast as the Inquisitor in the film of *Saint Joan* (he played Warwick), to have played Caesar in a film of Shaw's *Caesar and Cleopatra* (he declined the role) and in *Caligula* to have been seen 'in a pool with very small boys and buxom blondes' (this was Peter O'Toole).

There were other careless errors about his fellow-actors and directors, most of them trivial in isolation, but cumulatively devastating. It was, for instance, Peggy Ashcroft and Gwen Ffrangcon-Davies, not Angela Baddeley and Joyce Carey, who co-starred with him in a certain revival of *The Importance of Being Earnest.* Lilian Baylis' first director at the Old Vic was Ben Greet, not Robert Atkins. Orson Welles was playing Othello in London, not Lear. Komisarjevsky did not direct Gielgud in *Medea,* but in *Crime and Punishment.* Michael Redgrave did not live with Edith Evans; they just had an affair. It was Frith Banbury, not Alec Guinness, whom Gielgud told not to fidget during *Hamlet* rehearsals. The conductor for the premiere of Gielgud's production of *The Trojans* was Rafael Kubelik, not Georg Solti. Lee Strasberg was director of the Actors' Studio, not the 'Method School'. And so it went on, relentlessly. The infection even spread to the photographs, in one of which Gielgud was said to be playing the title-role in Gordon Daviot's play *Richard of Bordeaux,* when he was actually playing Shakespeare's *Richard II.*

I soon noticed another major flaw. Having access myself to much of the printed material that Morley used, I was appalled to find how fast and loose he had played with the normal rules about quoting the views or memories of others. At times he shamelessly edited the words of critics and others without acknowledging this, omitting or adding words, changing tenses, or running together sentences which were not adjacent in the original, so distorting the meaning. Also, though I could not prove it, I had a strong suspicion that some of the matters Gielgud allegedly 'told me' were actually Morley's stitching together of existing printed material. The lengthy extracts from these alleged personal interviews just didn't sound or feel like Gielgud's voice.

There was also the matter of balance, especially in relation to Gielgud's arrest.

He gave the incident inordinate prominence, devoting 26 pages in a chapter headed 'Annus Horribilis' to the history of attitudes to homosexuality, and exploring in detail several of the more notorious cases before getting on to the arrest itself. Even here, where you might expect him to take extra care, he committed two fundamental errors. He described Gielgud's 10-minute appearance before a magistrate as 'a gay trial', and stated that he was 'prosecuted for buggery and gross indecency', a potential libel, when in reality he was charged with the minor offence of 'importuning male persons', and fined £10. Morley also mentioned the support Gielgud was given by Sybil Thorndike, who was, he said, 'no stranger to police courts, where she had frequently made personal appearances as a leading suffragette'. Now although Sybil, whose biography I later wrote, was a supporter of the Votes for Women movement and went on marches, she was never actually a suffragette.

On matters of style, he seemed unable to make up his mind whether to call his subject John, thus casting him as an old friend, or the more formal Gielgud; sometimes he used both labels in the same paragraph. All too often his writing descended into cliché ('the audience were rolling in the aisles') or inappropriate usage ('he chickened out'). He crassly described the wonderful TV version of *Brideshead Revisited* as 'a heritage movie'. The most tasteless of his many vulgarities was his description in his last months of Ralph Richardson (whose date of death he managed to get wrong by a full eight years). Richardson was appearing with Gielgud in the film of *Wagner*, and was, according to Morley's charming description, 'as usual by now appearing to be several slices short of a Sacher Torte'.

As I reeled from all these horrors, a passing remark in a newspaper gossip column, which accurately quoted me saying that Morley had made my book 'difficult', began a further series of letters from him. After running through his well-rehearsed grievances about my treacherous and deceitful conduct, he described my book as merely an adequate clippings job containing no new unpublished material whatsoever. This was palpably nonsense. He also claimed that Michael Earley had behaved treacherously, telling him that my book would never see the light of day. Naturally I sent a copy of the letter to Michael, who replied that the claim was false, that the letter was 'inflammatory and even slanderous', adding drily that he would hardly have made such a promise 'after we had contracted the book and agreed a rather high advance!'

The long-running dispute now entered the letters pages of the *Daily Telegraph*, after a piece in the Peterborough diary column which noted that Morley, described as 'that blustery expert on all things thespian', had become involved in 'a nasty spat'. Mention was made of Morley's heart-rending confession in relation to my appearance on his territory: 'I feel like a portrait painter who suddenly finds a bloke with a Polaroid trying to snatch his work.' Morley rose to the bait, accusing me of 'biographical carpet-bagging', and ending loftily: 'If there were such a thing as a biographer's union, I would now be applying to have Croall's membership withdrawn.'

In one letter Morley had told me that his amazement at my disgraceful behaviour was shared by two other respected biographers, Michael Holroyd and Hugo Vickers, both of whom, he claimed, had never heard of such conduct. I sent copies of the relevant correspondence to both of them. In reply Vickers told me: 'I have never had the conversation with him to which he alludes...my name has been taken in vain on this occasion'. In passing he recalled 'the "Get off my patch" review Sheridan gave to my 1988 Vivien Leigh book in the *Sunday Times*, for which he was ticked off by elderly thespians in his family!'

Michael Holroyd's reaction was to use our dispute as a peg for an interesting article in the *Sunday Times*, in which he described in some detail several clashes on the biographical battlefield through the ages, and various attempts that had been made to prevent them. He mentioned a scheme for a list of contracted non-fiction titles to be held at Book House, for the benefit of authors and publishers contemplating a new biography. But publishers vetoed it, fearing 'it would be raided, brilliant ideas stolen, and quick-fire writers encouraged to run off with them'. This made me wonder whether, if such a scheme had been in place, and I had been made aware of Morley's contract, I would have ever written to Gielgud.

Holroyd wrote even-handedly about our dispute, explaining: 'Morley quotes letters from Gielgud granting him sole authority. He stands amazed at his own good nature and his rival's audacity. But Croall, also indignantly quoting letters, contends that he too had copyright permission from Gielgud.' He suggested that our dispute was 'now reaching boiling point', and that we were due 'to meet for a pitched battle' at an event later that year. 'I am glad I am not chairing it,' he confessed. 'It might be more peaceful to referee a Mike Tyson fight.'

This was by no means the end of the story. I wrote to Hodder, Morley's publishers, offering to send them my catalogue of errors, and suggesting they paid me a modest fee for the many hours I had spent compiling it. They declined to receive it, their publishing director Roland Philipps stating blithely that 'there is a lot of contrary information about Gielgud's career, but we have caught some errors in time for the paperback publication next year'. Meanwhile in one letter Morley let slip the fact that his book had been read by many theatre specialists. Who, I wondered, were these alleged specialist readers? Were they awake when they undertook this gruelling task?

Our private correspondence dragged on for weeks, with Morley's accusations becoming increasingly strident, and his references to his book's significant sales figures increasingly frequent. That autumn there was a Platform evening at the National, where Gielgud was the subject of a discussion between me, John Miller and Gyles Brandreth, with Ronald Pickup, Denis Quilley and Gillian Barge representing the profession. Morley chaired the event, so obviously felt compelled to avoid mention of our dispute. Afterwards he told me he hoped never to see or hear from me again. The feeling was of course mutual.

In early 2002 Peterborough in the *Daily Telegraph* returned to the subject, announcing: 'Seconds out, round two: the ongoing spat between Morley and Croall has gone one step further down the road to total war.' They focussed on the Morley errors, but made one of their own, then published my letter correcting it. Morley responded, stating that I had now gone into print 'largely, I suspect, because on current figures my authorised biography is easily outselling Croall's, and he needs any publicity he can get'. He then explained that the multiple errors I had found in his book 'have been in no way validated, or indeed caught, by any other of nearly 50 reviewers'. He was right: when the paperback eventually appeared, only 12 of the errors on my list had been corrected.

That autumn Morley published his memoirs, prophetically titled 'Asking for Trouble'. Earlier in a letter to me he had threatened to devote a whole chapter to our dispute. In the finished article this had dwindled to less than a page, in which in characteristic error-mode he stated that our books 'appeared more or less simultaneously in the spring of 2001', when he knew very well that mine had appeared six months earlier.

More substantially, he continued to assert that I initially wrote to Gielgud suggesting that I write a book merely about his career, whereas I of course had used the word biography from the beginning. He also insisted that Gielgud had written to me withdrawing his permission to continue, when I had received no such letter. However it was pleasing to read that 'the whole unhappy affair somehow put me off the idea of another massive biographical project', and that I had played some part in this welcome career move. 'If Croall and the barbarians were at the gates,' he concluded melodramatically, 'maybe I'd be better off spending my sixties and, hopefully, my seventies elsewhere.'

This sounded like an excellent plan. But it was annoying to see such distortions in print in a book rather than a newspaper, and I wrote to Morley about them, expressing also my surprise at the omission of the promised chapter on our dispute. In reply he said he had decided to cut it down since no one would have heard of me and my book, so it would all just be too boring and irrelevant. Meanwhile he suggested that I should be banned from all reputable publishing houses – and went on to reveal that I already had been black-listed. This was news to me, as I'm sure it was all those reputable publishers.

His paranoia seemed to know no bounds. In passing he had lambasted me for a letter recently printed in the *Stage*, in which I asked for memories from theatre folk of my next subject, Sybil Thorndike. I had mentioned that the book had been authorised by the family, including Sybil's daughter Mary Casson. I was surprised, though I suppose I shouldn't have been, to read a letter from Morley the following week, in which his self-absorption was once again exposed: 'I should like to point out that my 1977 biography, the first to appear after her death, was indeed authorised and approved by her elder son John Casson as head of the family. What Croall is writing, and good luck to him, is "the second authorised biography of Sybil Thorndike". Why not say so?'

I wrote to him by return as follows:

'Your letter of 6 November is ridiculous. Of course I knew of your 1977 "biography" of Sybil Thorndike. I have it on my shelves. With its 150 heavily illustrated pages it is, as you yourself say in the acknowledgements, 'not a fourth Thorndike biography, but the first complete Thorndike chronicle'. You make clear that it had John Casson's blessing, but nowhere is it described as 'the authorised' biography, with all that this implies for original research, wide-ranging interviews with friends and colleagues etc. This is the kind of book I intend to produce: hence, with Mary Casson's agreement, the label 'authorised biography'. To call my letter in the *Stage* 'a pathetic advertisement' is just – well, pathetic, as is your ludicrous suggestion that I have been 'banned from all decent publishing houses'. Meanwhile, the easiest way of not hearing from me again is to get your facts right the first time round, stop writing me these absurd, pompous letter, and learn a little humility.'

For once there was no reply.

But in April 2004, during the planning of a gala to celebrate Gielgud's centenary, Morley's fury was aroused once more, this time not just by me. A small committee that included Gielgud's main trustee had decided that, given Morley's well-deserved reputation for journalistic inaccuracy and excessive self-promotion, and his obsession with Gielgud's private life, he would be a liability as host of the occasion. Meanwhile, as one part of the celebrations, I was to give a talk on Gielgud at the National Portrait Gallery.

When Morley got wind of these happenings he fired off what can only be described as a four-page rant to John Miller, copied to me. Having offered his services, he was angry, hurt, humiliated etc to have been passed over as host in favour of Ned Sherrin, whose connection with Gielgud he was at a loss to understand. What, he wondered plaintively, had he done to make enemies of John and Richard Mangan (who as editor of *Gielgud's Letters* had also been involved with the planning). He was, in short, dumbfounded at this decision, and ended up pleading to be allowed to act as co-host of the gala, or at the very least to introduce one of the actors.

Inevitably my name also cropped up, with the same old accusations. Why on earth, he asked, was I being allowed to pass myself off as Gielgud's 'biographer' at the National Portrait Gallery? My book was nothing but a scissors-and-paste hack work. And so on. There was however one new piece of 'information'. He claimed he had received an apology from Michael Earley's successor at Methuen, Peter Tummons, who allegedly stated (though of course not in writing) that I had indulged in sharp practice and deliberately misled people. This, I suspected, like his conversations with other biographers about my behaviour, was yet another of his fantasies, as I believe was his latest claim, to have raised the matter of our dispute with both the Society of Authors and the Biographers' Club. However, as a member of the Society I thought it prudent to write to them, setting out just for the record my version of events. I didn't bother to contact the Biographers' Club, having told them earlier, in response to an invitation to join, that *pace* Groucho Marx, I couldn't face belonging to a club of which Morley was a member.

I had been wondering whether, following his memoirs, Morley would ever undertake another theatre book. Given his embarrassing and prurient obsession with Gielgud's homosexuality, it didn't entirely surprise me to discover that his plan was to write a book about the effect down the years on gay actors of Britain's repressive laws. Fortunately, the proposed book, which he called *It Was Never So Gay*, was turned down in June 2004, apparently on commercial grounds, by Roland Philipps, who was now at John Murray.

Once the dispute became public I began to get wind of other incidents that underlined Morley's appalling insensitivity, and provoked the disgust of many of his fellow-critics. In the 1980s he had tried to get Michael Coveney sacked as drama critic of the *Financial Times*. On the very day the popular *Daily Mail* drama critic Jack Tinker died of a heart attack, and his colleagues in the office were in tears, he rang the paper to ask for the vacant job. Subsequently, he persuaded the *Daily Express* to take him on in place of Robert Gore-Langton, a family man with four children, one of them terminally ill.

In February 2007 Morley died suddenly in his sleep. The following year, having completed my biography of Sybil Thorndike, and with the full authority of the Gielgud estate, I began work on a new edition of my biography, this time with full access to all his private papers, and to members of his family. *John Gielgud: Matinee Idol to Movie Star* was published by Methuen Drama in May 2011, and was agreeably well received. It went into paperback the following year, which also saw the publication of my compilation of *Gielgoodies! The Wit and Wisdom (and Gaffes) of John Gielgud.* All this marked a richly satisfying end to my lengthy but ultimately rewarding association with this fascinating man.

– INDEX –

People
Gielgud and Shakespeare are not included, as they appear throughout the text. Interviewees and their interviews are in bold type.

Lightning Source UK Ltd.
Milton Keynes UK
UKOW07f0133241114

242061UK00001B/24/P